THE COMPLETE FUNDRAISING HANDBOOK

THE COMPLETE FUNDRAISING HANDBOOK

by

Sam Clarke

Published by

DIRECTORY OF SOCIAL CHANGE

in association with the

Institute of Charity Fundraising Managers

THE COMPLETE FUNDRAISING HANDBOOK
by Sam Clarke
Published by the Directory of Social Change
in association with the
Institute of Charity Fundraising Managers
First published January 1992. Fully revised second edition published March 1993.

The Directory of Social Change, Radius Works, Back Lane, London NW3 1HL
ISBN 1–873860–21–8
Printed and bound in Great Britain by the Bath Press.

To my father

Contents

5. Skills

6. Sources of information

Index

The first edition of The Complete Fundraising Handbook was published in January 1992. This second edition, first published in March 1993, has been completely revised to take into account the provisions of the 1992 Charities Act, most of which came into force into 1993. The precise requirements of the Act are set out in the Act and in the regulations attached to it. The Act covers public fundraising collections, the use of professional fundraisers and commercial promotions. Detailed guidance on the legal requirements is available in a number of specialist publications and general advice can be obtained from the Institute of Charity Fundraising Managers.

FOREWORD

Sam Clarke succeeded me as the Central Fundraising Director for OXFAM – a very demanding job by any standards– and early on proved that he had the skill, imagination and good administration to maintain the upward growth of OXFAM's income at the acceptable level of costs set by the Trustees. I do not think that there could be a better apprenticeship for writing this admirable 'no-nonsense' handbook for fundraisers both new and experienced. It is a practical book and as a journalist friend of mine used to say "a very good read". And so I have no difficulty in recommending it to the reader.

If fundraisers want a patron saint, I can think of no better choice than the Good Samaritan who demonstrated all the qualities that are needed in their profession for success: *compassion*, when he crossed the road to pick up a badly battered man lying in a pool of blood in a ditch; *courage* in getting off his horse in a particularly dangerous part of the road where the thieves might still be hiding; *action and skill* in knowing how to bind up the wounds with the use of a soothing oil; and finally *funds* so that he paid the Inn Keeper to look after the wounded man and promised that, if it was not enough, he would provide.

The parable illustrates that fundraising is not primarily about *money*: it is about *need*, about a human need that cries out for help, and about the response to put that need right or to make it easier for the victim to bear that your organisation can offer. So whenever you write or talk about your cause, always start with the need and explain it clearly and simply in human terms and then describe how your organisation can make some relief towards it. And never exaggerate what you are capable of doing.

And do not forget that when you accept money from a donor, you accept at the same time a responsibility to that donor to ensure that his generous gift is used wisely and with experience and economy. This means that you as a fundraiser must be constantly inquiring from your colleagues involved in the work of the organisation as to how the programmes are going and ensuring that they are well run. So play your part as a truthful friend to your donor, telling of successes and also of disappointments. Everyone knows how difficult it is to bring about change for the better in human affairs, and you will find that the informed donor will support you through thick and thin – the first Director of OXFAM, Sir Lesley Kirkley, used to call it "the educated pound".

The fundraising profession demands from its practitioners long hours, hard work, skills and the proper understanding of techniques, all supported by effective and well-managed administration.

But at the same time it offers you a hidden agenda as it is now called – a chance to be the agent of change for the betterment of the human condition. A chance to stand up effectively for human rights which are the key to human happiness, to justice and to the welfare of the human race. It offers you the unique chance to play a tiny part in a vision of a new society in which all of us may dwell in peace and harmony.

Guy Stringer CBE FRSA
Lately the Director of OXFAM

Acknowledgements

I would like to acknowledge the enormous help and encouragement given to me during the preparation of this book by a large number of fundraisers who gave freely of their time and experience. In particular to Andrew Thomas, Nick Lowe, Janet South and Sally Miller who supported and advised me, as well as making invaluable suggestions.

1. INTRODUCTION

1.1 The contemporary scene

In today's competitive fundraising world, the fundraiser is faced with an unprecedentedly difficult environment in which to raise funds. This will put huge extra demands on all levels of voluntary organisations, their trustees, staff and volunteers.

There are six major factors which serve to trouble the waters for fundraisers. These are:

- The economic climate prevailing in the country and how both donors and beneficiaries in all sectors (local authorities, companies, trusts) will react to this.

- The dawn of the European Single Market on 1st January 1993, when harmonisation with Europe was taken one step closer.

- The development of policies to move many of the old and sick from institutions back into the community, which will provide new roles and make further demands on voluntary organisations.

- The reorganisation of the health service and the entry of hospitals as serious players in the fundraising market.

- The introduction of Local Management into schools and again the growing demand for charitable funds from bodies which up until recently were wholly funded from statutory sources.

- The resultant rise in the number of charities competing for funds. A typical year will see over four thousand new charities being registered. Though the new entrants do not necessarily make any significant demands on the public's generosity, most are potential fundraising organisations. In time each will develop its appeal and launch one more cry for help. It is not that this is necessarily bad; just that it makes life harder for the fundraiser.

The next few years are obviously going to be hard ones in which to raise funds efficiently. Professionalism must continue to rise to meet this challenge; and if the causes are good, at least for the foreseeable future, the money will be found.

1.2 How to use this book

The book is written as a reference book. It can be dipped into or it can be read all the way through. There are a wide variety of organisations, and people with differing roles within them and with wide differences in their experience of fundraising. The book has been written with all this in mind and has something to offer everyone.

1.2.1 The structure of the book

Section 2: This section is especially appropriate to those seeking a new fundraiser, those who are themselves new fundraisers or anyone who needs to produce a fundraising strategy. It sets out:

- The principles of fundraising – offering ten important principles for all fundraisers and fundraising (Section 2.1).
- The fundraiser – what makes a good fundraiser; are you one? Can you spot them when you need them (Section 2.2)?
- The fundraising office – what you need to set up an efficient and effective office (Section 2.3).
- The fundraising strategy – a look at those elements that go into making a successful strategy (Section 2.4).
- The donor – a brief introduction to your all important partner, the donor. This is expanded further in Section 3 (Section 2.5).

Section 3: This part of the book talks in more depth about the main sources of income, what their characteristics are, how much they give and everything else you need to know. This section should be essential reading for anyone either about to raise money or who is already doing so. It includes:

- Statutory funding – including European, central and local government and how you should approach them (Section 3.1).
- Trusts and foundations – how you can best get help from these important sources (Section 3.2).
- Companies – what you can expect from them and how to ask (Section 3.3).
- Individuals – how individual giving differs, how they give and what turns them on (Section 3.4).
- Other institutions – dealing with a number of other types of donors (Section 3.5).

Section 4: This section lists the major fundraising techniques commonly used. This is the part of the book which includes the most ideas and suggestions together with checklists, how to get started sections and examples of many fundraising materials. It includes:

- Local fundraising – this all important mixture of methods, seen both from the centre and from the point of view of the individual (Section 4.1).

- Direct mail – how to appeal to your donors and how to acquire more (Section 4.2).

- Sponsorship – ways of attracting support for particular parts of your work (Section 4.3).

- Capital and big gift campaigns – looking at how to raise a single large sum (for a building perhaps) and how to generate big gifts (Section 4.4).

- Legacies – how to build up that flow of major legacy gifts (Section 4.5).

- Events – looking at the essential ingredients of running events and how to reduce any risk (Section 4.6).

- Committed giving – how to build up a flow of regular giving without having to ask! (Section 4.7).

- Membership – the role of membership in fundraising and its advantages (Section 4.8).

- Schools – how to approach schools and young people (Section 4.9).

- Gambling – games of skill or chance can add to your income substantially: here's how (Section 4.10).

- TV and radio appeals – the really major sums raised all involve TV: how to tap this essential medium (Section 4.11).

- Giving at work – a lot has been written about this scheme. Read what's in it for you (Section 4.12).

- Advertising – to advertise or not? Learn from the mistakes of others (Section 4.13).

- Commercial promotions – how you can link your charity with another body and benefit both (Section 4.14).

- Credit cards and financial products – if you have a substantial list of supporters consider this section carefully (Section 4.15).

- Trading – slugging it out on the high street will not necessarily help, but there are other ways to successfully trade (Section 4.16).

- Personal solicitation – read how fundraisers are getting really close to their donors (Section 4.17).

Section 5: This section backs up the sources and the techniques with a set of skills, some of which are necessary in order to raise money effectively. These have been selected as the most useful ones from the very large number that are used by fundraisers. They are:

- Getting help with your fundraising – essential reading for everyone wanting to raise money (Section 5.1).

- Working with volunteers – perhaps the main resource to call upon (Section 5.2).

- Writing a fundraising proposal – vital advice for anyone approaching an institution for help (Section 5.3).

- Producing effective materials – read this if you propose to print multiple copies of any materials, for example annual reports (Section 5.4).

- Working with patrons, celebrities and trustees – how you can benefit by involving the famous (Section 5.5).

- Saying thanks – how this often overlooked courtesy can pay (Section 5.6).

- Use of the phone – how to boost your fundraising efforts simply (Section 5.7).

- Involvement – how to improve both your fundraising and your donors' involvement in your work (Section 5.8).

- Recruitment, training and secondment – how you attract and retain good staff, including secondment (Section 5.9).

- Targeting and profiling – how to pinpoint supporters using computers (Section 5.10).

- Testing, evaluation and control – showing how you can monitor and improve your fundraising operations (Section 5.11).

- Tax-effective giving – showing the important opportunities for reclaiming tax on gifts (Section 5.12).

- Market research – how to find out about your supporters (Section 5.13).

- Marketing – linking marketing to fundraising (Section 5.14).

- Public relations – showing how PR is vital for good fundraising and what it can do (Section 5.15).

- Using computers – spelling out the essentials of how computers can help in your fundraising (Section 5.16).

Section 6 – The appendices. Here you will find details that would not lie well in the body of the text. In particular:

- Useful addresses (Section 6.1).

- Bibliography – listing many fundraising publications found to be useful (Section 6.2).

- Community trusts (Section 6.3).

- ICFM codes of practice – listing in detail some of the most important pieces of guidance on some difficult fundraising issues (Section 6.4).

- Sample forms – showing the standard forms of words for covenants, deposit covenants, loans, payroll giving, legacy and codicils and Gift Aid (Section 6.5).

1.2.2 Who should read this book

The simple answer is that everyone who has any sort of fundraising responsibility should have a copy:

- Trustees will want to know what to expect of fundraisers, how to employ them and what they might need.

- Senior managers will want to know when it's time to have a specialist fundraiser and how to manage them.
- Fundraisers of course will need a copy as a reference and background guide to the many techniques that are available.
- Fundraising groups should have a copy to give them good ideas for their own fundraising.

So the book has been written from as many points of view as is possible. It takes in the interests of both large and small charities, and non-charitable voluntary organisations.

The book should be useful to school governors; to managers in the health service; to campaigning organisations; to charities undertaking research; and to those providing services both at home or overseas. Indeed, to almost any body that is needing to raise funds at all.

1.2.3 Improving this book

SUGGESTIONS FORM

It is the intention for this book to be revised and improved when it comes to producing further editions. In order to do this, it is important to get some feedback from readers. We are offering a small prize of a free copy of the next edition to the ten best suggestions or ideas for the next edition that are received from readers. Help us keep the book relevant. Photocopy and return:

I would like to suggest these improvements _____

_____

_____

I would like to see more on the following subjects _____

_____

_____

I am enclosing fundraising ideas/examples/case studies _____

_____

Name _____

Organisation _____

Address _____

_____

Please return to Sam Clarke at the Directory of Social Change, Radius Works, Back Lane, London NW3 1HL.

---

2. GETTING STARTED

The purpose of this section is to cover some of the key aspects of successful fundraising. These need to be understood by the trustees and directors who are responsible for seeing that the income needs of the charity are met and by the fundraisers who have to do the actual work. They will help identify the people, the attitudes, the equipment and the approaches needed to get a fundraising programme under way.

2.1 The principles of fundraising

Over the years fundraisers have developed sets of principles to help guide their activities and successfully develop new approaches. From an

---

MYTH: THE EDUCATED POUND

We owe this one to ourselves. We truly did believe that we had a large liberal constituency which we could expand via education, that we could assume on the growing awareness of social affairs and anticipate a generation where a more analytical and thoughtful kind of fundraising would provoke a more thoughtful and analytical response. Hence the Third World charity would talk about debt charges, the environmental charity would talk of Antarctica, the child care charity would talk of deprivation.

Again, there are small truths here. A small number of our supporters are indeed motivated by instincts other than emotion. But, in the main, I have to report that this keen eyed generation of more thoughtful donors has yet to emerge and is now unlikely to do so. The compelling image remains that of the famine camps in Africa, the battered child in Liverpool and I hope Greenpeace won't mind me telling you that their successful fundraising hooks this year have not been Antarctica or acid rain, but whales and seals. Indeed, it can be argued that things have got worse, that donors today are more emotional, less informed. What can a donor know about a telethon appeal which is classified 'Children in Need'? What does Sport Aid actually do? We should salute the promoters of the new generation of mass concerts for Band Aid or Amnesty, but we have to worry about those hundreds of millions of people simply seeing it all as a Good Thing, unaware that Nelson Mandela is a different product from most.

There was a chilling story from the last Amnesty concert in Britain, that the young audience hissed the final message from the stage about prisoners of conscience because they were impatient for Bruce Springsteen. We can make no assumptions whatsoever that our public has become more sophisticated and thoughtful.

From a talk given by **George Smith** at the International Fundraising Workshop

---

understanding of these principles and by carefully applying them, a fundraiser will quickly be able to identify and distinguish probable success from likely failure.

2.1.1 Fundraising is a people business

This is a most important but obvious principle: *people* give to *people* who ask on behalf of *other people* who need help: people do not give to organisations.

In practice this means that fundraisers will constantly need to bear in mind that they are communicating with *real people* – even though they will not necessarily be in personal contact with them all the time – about *real human issues* about which the potential donor may also have first-hand experience and very clear views. Equally, the fundraiser, whether a volunteer or a professional, is only human: they will have their own personal views about the cause they are raising money for; they will need to be committed to it and to understand it. And finally, the beneficiary may see the fundraising material and even be represented on the boards of organisations. The need to present a sensitive but truthful case, whilst making it powerful enough to persuade donors to give, can cause conflicts within the organisation. All this demands sensitivity and understanding from the fundraiser.

One commonly practised way of ensuring that gulfs do not open up, especially where the fundraiser is not in close touch with the beneficiary or the donor, is to build up a programme of visiting. This could involve staff visiting projects, office-based fundraisers meeting donors in their own homes or invitations to open days or meetings.

2.1.2 Commitment

Possibly the first thing a donor can detect in a fundraiser is their level of commitment. Commitment is one of the most important attributes that a fundraiser can bring to the job. For it soon becomes evident in the many communications that fundraisers have to make whether or not they are really committed to the cause they are espousing. The new fundraiser should be given every opportunity to develop real commitment: the old fundraiser who is becoming complacent and whose belief is now somewhat frayed at the edges, should find a way of becoming re-motivated or consider a job move.

2.1.3 Truthfulness

To build a firm and lasting relationship between the organisation and the donor, the fundraiser has to be truthful. By its very nature, fundraising requires the ability to sell an idea. This creates a pressure to tell only partial truths. The very complex socio-economic factors that go into poverty today are a good example: if we are to raise funds by writing a short letter to a potential supporter, how can you hope to describe what lies behind the poverty? And yet how can you give a proper explanation without straying into the politics of the situation, however unattractive that may be to the donor?

You also need to be truthful about the value of your work. If a cherished part of a charity's programme or one of its projects fails for some reason, can this be withheld from donors? Although there is not always an opportunity to convey this sort of information to all your supporters, you should try to keep your most committed supporters fully in touch. If you grasp the nettle in this way, you will find that a full explanation can help create a deeper respect for the organisation and a better understanding of its work.

2.1.4 Selling the benefit

Some charities and causes are so well-known that if you mention the name – Barnardos, Comic Relief, or Cancer Research – people have an immediate (if often incorrect) impression of what the charity does and what the money will be used for. However, most organisations do not have that level of public awareness; thus it is important when fundraising to assume ignorance on behalf of the donor. For example, when describing the plight of a political prisoner, it will be helpful to describe what it is like to be held, possibly tortured, and to have to live as a refugee thereafter. If raising funds for homelessness in the UK, you should not presume that a largely middle class audience will know what it is actually like to be homeless, so this might have to be described. Specific benefits to beneficiaries might be illustrated by reference to individually named people (or in a suitably disguised composite if anonymity is required), in as graphic and pictorial a way as possible.

While a charitable gift can offer only limited benefit to the donor, the question of benefit to the donor is still very important. In reaching donors effectively the fundraiser will have to be able to combine a proposition which is almost totally altruistic with one which identifies the interest of potential donors. This is dealt with in more detail later in the book.

2.1.5 Volunteers

The fundraising work can be undertaken entirely by paid staff. Some organisations have taken this route for its clarity and controllability. However, this is not necessarily the only nor even the best approach. The success of any fundraising venture can depend on the number and type of people who are doing the asking. For this reason, many of today's most successful voluntary organisations have built their fundraising on the efforts of hundreds or thousands of men, women and children all doing their bit for the charity. So if you plan to involve volunteers in your fundraising, including your volunteer trustees or management committee members, there is an obvious logistic reason why you will need to develop mechanisms for deploying and managing this resource effectively.

There is a further reason for using a volunteer to ask for support: how much more convincing it is for someone who is themselves committed to giving either their time or their money to the organisation to ask for help. The only question is whether they can present the case as clearly as a paid professional – and this is the challenge for any fundraiser wanting to exploit the potential of volunteers.

2.1.6 Professionalism

The professional body for charitable fundraising is the Institute of Charity Fundraising Managers (ICFM). Fundraising often gets a bad press. These days there is little excuse for fundraisers not to be entirely professional in their approach. Using the media, contacting important business leaders and communicating with government all demand the highest standards of practice. At the same time the opportunities for any mistakes to be magnified are very great. The role of the fundraiser is to act as a channel between donor and beneficiary, to remain committed to the cause of the beneficiary, and to be responsible for ensuring that the money is spent on the purposes for which it was given and that it achieves results. The Institute is there to set standards in fundraising, to help promote good practice, and to ensure that relevant training is available.

ICFM CODE OF CONDUCT

1. Professional conduct
2. Injury to others
3. Honesty
4. Professional competence
5. Conflict of interests
6. Confidentiality

These are the headings of the **Institute of Charity Fundraising Managers** code of conduct which all members are bound by.

2.1.7 Making the ask

A piece of research commissioned by a major charity asked non-supporters what was the main reason why they had not supported the charity. The idea behind this was to identify any possible blockage to giving. The answer was altogether more simple: the main reason for not giving was that the people approached (there were over a thousand of them) had *not been asked* to support the charity.

Some charities do not exploit the opportunities that exist to raise money. Others ask, but do not do so effectively. The whole purpose of fundraising is to raise money, and it is often forgotten that the call to action, the punch-line, is the essential piece of the message. It is somehow assumed that the potential donor will understand the message by virtue of simply having received the piece of paper it is written on. Good fundraising requires the donor to receive the message, to understand it and to respond to it.

The good fundraiser must ask clearly and directly for exactly what they want. They may also need to repeat the message and to ask more than once. And they must make it as easy as possible for the donor to respond.

2.1.8 Saying thank you

The act of giving includes elements of faith, hope and charity. Faith that the fundraiser truly represents the cause and will act as an efficient conduit for the money. Hope that the gift, however small, may make some difference. Charity as an act of altruism, a gift without the expectation of any material return. In making a decision to give, a whole range of feelings and thoughts may be aroused in the donor. It is important for the fundraiser to be aware of and to understand this process.

Saying thank you can do two things. It can be an act of enlightened self-interest on the fundraiser's behalf and it can be the completion of the process of stimulation you have started.

The process of giving also requires that the donor is reassured that the right decision has been made. It is for this reason that some car manufacturers spend significant sums advertising the benefits of their vehicles to those who have already purchased one. In the case of a voluntary organisation, saying thank you and reassuring the donor that the gift has made or will make an important contribution to a needy cause encourages the donor to spread the word to others (see Section 2.1.4).

Many organisations in the 1980s followed the policy of saying thank you to supporters only when they had to. Those who say thank you on every appropriate pretext will see this investment repay itself handsomely in donor loyalty and may well be surprised at the level of repeat giving that can be stimulated by this process. Apart from anything else, many donors probably consider failing to say thanks to be an act of considerable discourtesy which will be remembered long after the reason for giving has been forgotten.

2.1.9 Opportunism

Opportunism is the great friend of the alert fundraiser. It is more than just a question of taking opportunities when they arise: sometimes there are things going on in the world which can give you a useful peg to bring your charity to prominence. Often this relates to events that will receive public attention. If you can find a way of associating yourself with such an event then you will gain more attention than you would otherwise receive.

On other occasions it is a matter of attitude. You will need to grasp every opportunity that presents itself. When a well-known supporter is awarded libel damages, should your letter not be in their in-tray the next morning?

The clearest examples of opportunistic fundraising are to be found in newspaper coverage. If, for example, there is a feature in the paper focusing on your cause, then the results of any advertising placed in the paper on the same day will be substantially greater provided that the editorial coverage is generally supportive of what you are doing.

The annual calendar provides opportunities at different times of the year. For example, St. Valentine's Day provides an opportunity for the ingenious fundraiser to devise a successful fundraising event. Christmas is an even better fundraising opportunity.

2.1.10 Persistence

Don't give up. Don't give up . . . If you feel your cause is important, and if you feel that you can share this view with a potential supporter, then persist in asking. A good reason why people fail, is that they take no for an answer and give up too soon. There may be a better way of presenting your case or another opportunity to invite people to give their support.

2.2 The fundraiser

Employing a professional fundraiser may be the right way to create a properly resourced organisation. The right approach to this can turn a difficult transition into a success story. This section discusses when a professional fundraiser is needed, how to recruit a fundraiser and how to get the most out of this appointment, considering the very considerable expenditure that is involved.

2.2.1 When you need a fundraiser

It is not essential for every voluntary organisation to appoint a member of staff as a fundraiser. Many grant-aided bodies will neither need nor want the expense of fundraising staff. They can leave the task to the senior executive or to trustees and board members. For others, volunteers will be able to raise all the funds they need. For yet others, their growth and the pattern of their funding will lead to a time when a decision is needed on whether to recruit a professional fundraiser.

For voluntary supporters to take at least some responsibility for the fundraising remains a desirable option whether or not there is any staff time devoted to this function. For organisations with more than a handful of staff, the overall responsibility for seeing that the money is raised will need to be concentrated in the hands of a senior executive.

A combination of executive responsibilities and volunteers doing most of the work allows the organisation to develop without undue emphasis on fundraising, and staff can concentrate on the development of the organisation's programme. While the funding still comes from a small number of large donors, this structure remains possible. However, as soon as it is decided that support from a wider section of the public is needed, then staff will almost certainly be needed to undertake or organise some or most of the fundraising work.

The main consideration when deciding the right time to employ a fundraiser is a financial one. Can you afford to, and what effect will it have on the administrative costs of the organisation? Not many organisations are lucky enough to obtain sponsorship for their fundraiser, so you will have to consider the costs involved. On the other hand, can you afford not to? As a rough rule of thumb, to employ a junior fundraiser on a full-time basis will cost at least £15,000 plus a further £7,000 in overheads. To

The advertisement for a small organisation's first paid fundraiser.

justify such an expenditure, you will need to generate at least £100,000 a year in extra revenue as a result of this appointment – although it can take some time to achieve results on this scale.

In the early days it may appear that much of what a fundraiser is doing is to raise the costs of their own salary. This is a difficult psychological task at the best of times, and it is far better if the fundraiser's salary can be paid out of general funds. In any case, those appointing a fundraiser for the first time should take a long-term view. It will take several years to develop the full potential of the fundraising effort put in. Any appointment of a fundraiser should be seen as part of the organisation's longer term strategy, and the fundraiser should be set targets for the money to be raised in each of the first few years of the appointment.

2.2.2 Recruitment

The practical details of how to set about recruiting fundraising staff are covered elsewhere in this book. There are a number of particular responsibilities and implications that stem from the recruitment of a fundraiser. The first factor is the effect on the organisation's budget. The costs of employing a fundraiser will go well beyond those of paying a salary. Is a car needed and, if not, will there be travel expenses? How much should be set aside for the production of brochures, the mailing of appeals and the costs of other activities? Precisely what will be required will depend on the nature of the fundraising opportunities available. What is certain is that the organisation will need to budget and plan very carefully for the inevitable costs of fundraising in addition to the costs of paying the fundraiser.

The person with the management responsibility for the fundraiser will need to consider two further points. Firstly, the objectives appropriate for this new venture, which should be set at a realistic level recognising the opportunities but not set too high to present an insurmountable obstacle to success. Secondly, the induction process and the training that will be needed. It is important to consider how exactly to evaluate the effectiveness of the first few years of the post. You will have to take into account the learning and induction periods when nothing much happens, the development phase when contacts are made but are not yet brought to fruition, the benefits of any increased coverage in the media and other PR generated by the fundraising work, and the importance of the committed support that is generated, such as covenant giving that creates a steady stream of income over a number of years.

With the arrival of the organisation's first paid fundraiser, it will be important to discuss and agree what the organisation stands for and how it should be projected. There will be a natural and healthy tendency to project only the most attractive aspects of the charity's work, and to do this in a way that may not entirely reflect reality. This can create problems later on. It will skew the organisation towards the interests of the donors. A good example of this phenomenon is child sponsorship which, from a fundraising point of view, is a perfect idea; however from the beneficiary's point of view this sort of relationship has not always been the best way of receiving the help, and the relationship can be seen as unduly patronising. Over time, and to the credit of some sponsorship agencies, they have moved away from this 'perfect product' to one that better meets the requirements of all concerned. The onus is on the organisation, its senior staff and the trustees to lay some simple ground rules for the fundraiser. Normally this will be done through a clear and universally agreed mission statement which can then be associated with a set of communication guidelines.

2.2.3 Motivation of fundraisers

Finding what motivates a fundraiser is important. Fundraising can be a rewarding and exciting business if the activity is well organised and supported. Yet it can be a lonely, exhausting and frustrating experience. An understanding of the motivation of fundraisers is important.

Not every organisation has a dedicated fundraiser just waiting in the wings to be discovered. Usually they will have to be recruited, and although they may bring skills to the job of raising money, they may initially have no great commitment to the aims of the charity. Sometimes they may be committed to your general cause but ignorant of the particular charity's role. This can be an ideal position from which to recruit them. More often their motivation will be a general sense of contributing to the welfare of society; a wish to give their working life or part of it to doing useful and beneficial work. Though this may appear woolly, it is an often encountered motive of successful fundraisers. Loyalty can be effectively built up over a relatively short time, especially with plenty of exposure to the organisation's programme. For this reason it is important not to look for total commitment or understanding at the outset. Indeed the outside perspective can provide valuable insights for most organisations.

Fundraisers work better with some recognition of the part they are playing. It may be recognition from their friends and relatives or it may be recognition from their peers. In larger organisations fundraisers can be treated extremely poorly by other staff and by the trustees; their work may be taken for granted, and they often have a myriad of obstacles thrown across their paths. In such situations, these problems will need to be addressed. Some organisations attempt to motivate their fundraisers by giving incentives in the form of a commission on money raised. This is the worst possible motive that a fundraiser can have, and one that will inevitably lead to conflict. The Charity Commission, the ICFM and most independent consultants frown on this as a form of remuneration, and there are good reasons why fundraising managers should too. The problem with this form of remuneration is that the fundraiser begins to have divided loyalties. Their responsibilities are no longer to the welfare of the charity and thus to its donors, but to themselves and their own interests. Donors too would become extremely uncomfortable if they believed that this was a significant factor in fundraising or that a percentage of what they were giving was being syphoned off in a commission payment. The acceptable alternative is a merit award. This is not a commission but does recognise that there is value in fundraisers, as with others who are recognised for meeting their targets. Typically a fundraiser might receive an extra 10% on top of the basic salary if all agreed targets (financial and non-financial) were met in a specified period.

2.2.4 Nature of the fundraiser's job

An understanding of the role of the fundraiser helps to clarify what sort of person is likely to be suitable.

First of all fundraising has never been a sinecure. It is a tough and demanding job, often requiring long and unsocial hours – the greater the commitment generated, the longer the hours that will need to be put in. It is not an occupation that is generally friendly to family life.

Because it is a job that is usually tightly targeted, there is the constant anxiety akin to that of a sales representative for missed targets and how to claw them back.

Front line fundraising requires those involved to be both prepared and able to articulate a direct appeal for help; this is usually, but not always, for funds. British reserve makes many people uncomfortable with the notion of actually **asking** for money. Anyone who has this difficulty will not be a natural fundraiser – whether the task in hand is to write a four-page appeal letter, to organise a committee to run a ball, or to personally visit a major donor.

A good fundraiser needs confidence, patience and tact. Confidence, because a confident appeal is harder to refuse. Patience, to deal with the particular concerns of donors, for example, when they ask for the third time to hear about the income ratios of the organisation. Tact and sincerity, to ask a supporter face to face for a legacy, or to suggest a variation in a Will.

There is also the problem of rejection. Many approaches will be unsuccessful, simply because of the enormous competition for funds, or just through bad luck. A good fundraiser has to be able to cope with rejection, starting each fresh approach as if it were the first, and to be prepared to learn from each approach to do the next one better.

Since fundraising often involves keeping in touch with thousands of supporters all of whom imagine that they are special, good organisation is essential. Fundraisers have to keep voluminous files of correspondence and information on donation history. All this must be organised so that no past event or piece of generosity is forgotten. A good memory for faces helps too.

Fundraisers who come afresh to an organisation will find that imagination is an invaluable asset. The task may be to dream up new activities that will inspire existing supporters and to create events that the public is going to be enthused by. Circumstances are always changing and new opportunities emerging, so new fundraisers need to identify new approaches and not simply rely on what was done in the past.

Finally, the fundraiser who already has a number of existing contacts in an area or sector will be at an enormous advantage. In no way is this a prerequisite. Having contacts does not necessarily mean that they will be right for the organisation. A good alternative is to have the confidence to ask anybody for what is needed, and the ability to make new contacts.

2.3 The fundraising office

In order to succeed as a fundraiser there are some essential items of equipment which are needed. Some other items may also be useful. All of them can be acquired from a range of sources.

2.3.1 The essentials

The most important single piece of equipment for the fundraiser is the telephone. Without it you are at a serious disadvantage. It should not be a telephone shared with others, because of the volume and length of both outgoing and incoming calls. It is an advantage if the fundraiser's telephone is in a quiet place, where discreet calls can be made in privacy.

The next essential is your own desk. Again not shared, nor in such a noisy environment that any rational thought becomes difficult. The third essential is a diary and a year planner.

2.3.2 Other aids to fundraising

To communicate effectively with people it is not always appropriate to do this by telephone. For example, to make a submission to a company or trust, a typewritten application is essential.

For this and for a number of other purposes a word processor will be very useful. You will also need a printer that will produce a high quality of printed output. The price of these machines is falling daily to the point that they are now nearly as cheap as typewriters. Perfectly satisfactory equipment can be bought in the High Street for under £750.

Busy and effective fundraisers are constantly on the move and likely to be out of their offices for a significant proportion of the time. To catch all of those incoming calls that might otherwise go unanswered requires some form of answering service. The best idea is undoubtedly to arrange for someone to answer your calls. Failing that, an answering machine will cost around £100, and incoming calls can be checked from afar.

A later and invaluable aid is a facsimile machine. Small ones cost less than £300, and again the prices are falling.

Sooner or later your fundraising programme will turn to companies and trusts as a source of funds. In this event, the guides to companies and trusts listed in Section 3 are invaluable, and you will want to have copies readily to hand.

2.3.3 Resourcing your office

The first instinct of a fundraiser should always be to scrounge: it conveys the right attitude of scrupulous parsimony, and it can be a very effective way of getting the equipment you need. Try first your own trustees and supporters. Next try local companies. The banks are especially useful for getting desks and filing cabinets. If not there are a number of dealers from whom second-hand office equipment can be obtained cheaply. Computers are difficult to buy second-hand unless you already know the equipment and its software well.

2.3.4 Staff needed

For the first time fundraiser the employment of support staff will be an undreamed of luxury. They have to do everything, or find volunteers to help them get it done. However, as time goes by and as public interest is aroused, there may come a time when further help is needed.

If you are paying for staff, the cost has to be justified by the income being raised. As a rough rule of thumb, the fundraising office should be generating at least 5 times its annual costs in funds raised, and ideally 10 times this amount.

An important part of your fundraising work is to ensure that communication systems between the fundraiser and those giving support (even in cash or in time) are maintained. As the fundraising develops, an early requirement will be a personal or secretarial assistant to deal with the telephones, the word processing and any personal callers. Good assistance with these tasks can represent a real liberation to a harassed fundraiser, enabling them to get on with more important jobs. A later requirement could well be administrative help to keep lists of supporters up-to-date and in a state fit for regular mailings. This task can encompass the responsibility for preparing thank you letters and for carrying out any simple computer housekeeping.

2.3.5 Integration of fundraising

In some organisations the fundraisers are outsiders, the latecomers and the interlopers in the real work of the organisation. Any lack of integration into the staff team reflects this attitude and can seriously affect their ability to do a good job. Integration of the fundraising function is thus an issue that needs to be confronted at both an organisational and a geographical level.

The fundraiser cannot be hived off as if they did not exist and must be trusted and valued as much as any other functional part of the organisation. They need clear links with the service delivery part of the charity so that an accurate and up-to-date message is projected about the work of the organisation. What is more, this link is vital in order to provide the fundraiser with a good supply of story material that can be built in to appeals. But this is not the only reason for close working. Financial information about the needs of the organisation is vital too. Imagine meeting a major donor and being asked how badly the organisation needs help. To answer this question properly requires constant access to the facts.

In organisational terms therefore, fundraising should appear as a main activity and not be made subservient to service delivery, finance or administration. This simply recognises the fact that there will be nothing to administer and no services to deliver if the money is not raised.

2.4 The fundraising strategy

Your fundraising strategy is the backbone of your fundraising. Getting it right demands a good deal of attention at an early stage. Not thinking through what you are doing can waste your time and efforts.

2.4.1 Outlining the needs

The starting point for any strategy is to define the needs of the organisation. This can be done at three levels.

First, the level of the organisation's own financial requirements if it is to undertake its programme of work. This will usually take the form of annual and rolling budgets based on your plans for the short and medium term.

The next requirement is to establish what human or societal needs are being addressed by the organisation. What exactly is the need? What are the consequences or implications of this need? And what will happen if nothing is done about it? How are the needs changing and what do you foresee happening over the next few years? Who is doing what to meet the need? How does what you plan to do fit in with what others are doing? Is what you propose to do an effective way of meeting the need? If the need is not important and your role not clear, developing a good fundraising 'case' becomes very difficult.

Finally you should consider how the need can be expressed in human terms. It is well known that donors tend to respond best to the needs of individuals whether they be human or animal. Statistics and generalities will never provide a sufficient case on their own.

2.4.2 Identifying the sources

In constructing a fundraising strategy a useful starting point is to identify your likely funding sources and what is on offer. These include:
• A grant from a central government department,
• A grant from a non-governmental agency (such as the Arts Council),
• A grant from a local authority (county or district) or local health authority,

- A contract with one of the above to deliver a specified service,
- A contract with another body (perhaps a commercial organisation or another voluntary agency) to deliver a service,
- Support from individuals through membership or donations, and eventually... legacy income,
- Support from individuals raised through collections, fundraising and entertainment events and activities,
- Grants from trusts and other grant-making bodies,
- Support from companies (cash, kind, sponsorship, facilities, skills, secondments),
- Support from individuals in the form of their time (as volunteers).

These are the main types of funding available to you. What is most appropriate for your organisation will depend on many different factors. You will have to think through which ones you should aim to develop. Some of the factors to take into account are:

Past experience: The results of your fundraising so far provide a good indication of both what to do and what not to do. Things that have gone well can be developed to do even better. Donors that have supported you can be encouraged to continue their support, perhaps at a higher level. New donors can be brought in to match the support you have got from existing donors. Effort and resources can be invested in the development of those areas of fundraising that appear to work.

Scale of need: Large needs may require large funds. These can be raised in large grants from a few sources, or in multiples of smaller gifts from a large number of donors. You will need to develop fundraising sources that have the capacity to make a realistic contribution to your overall need.

The attractiveness of the cause: Some causes seem able to sell themselves. People working with cuddly animals or starving babies have causes that are extremely compelling. If you are lucky enough to be associated with such a cause, then all types of fundraising become much easier. If not, then you have to work hard to make your cause seem important, to present it effectively to donors and make it seem compelling as something to support.

The style of your work: Are you radical or conservative? Young or old? Innovative and at the leading edge, or steady? Every organisation will be able to identify institutions and individuals that share its vision and outlook. Equally there will be those that don't, and these will be much less likely to give their support.

The resources and skills available to you: Do you have the collectors to mount a collection, the contacts to develop a big gift campaign, or the organisational ability to run a major event? It will always be best to do what you are good at doing.

Your natural constituency of support: Is this government? Trusts? Individuals? Who has a stake in the problem or need you are addressing?

Can you get them to share in its solution by becoming an investor in your work?

The type of organisation you want to be: A membership organisation is very different from an organisation that is funded by government, and a fundraising organisation very different from one that relies from earnings from the sale of its services. Your fundraising enables you to do what you want to do. Your fundraising strategy will help you become the sort of organisation you want to be.

Short term and long term: Some sources are essentially short term, whilst some can develop into long-term relationships and partnerships. If you are there for the long term, you will need long term sources of income. You will want to get as much as you can committed on a long-term basis. You will want to turn supporters into regular supporters. You will want to organise a successful fundraising event even more successfully next year.

2.4.3 Clarifying the constraints

In fundraising, action will be limited by a range of constraints, some which stem from the nature of the organisation, some which are internally generated, and others which are externally imposed.

Geography: An important constraint is the geographical remit of the organisation. Is it a national or local organisation? Or is it local, but with national significance? Some sources only give to organisations with a national remit, others only give locally. Central government is national; local government is local; companies may give nationally through head office, but make smaller local grants through local plants or branches; local people are concerned about their own local communities, but are also concerned about wider issues in society. This precludes some sources, but opens up opportunities for others. And if what you are doing locally is particularly innovative or interesting, it may catch the interest of national funders, both because they like being associated with excellence and because the project may provide the answers to similar problems in other areas.

Appropriateness: Some sources are completely inappropriate because what the donor stands for is the complete opposite of what the charity stands for. The British Heart Foundation will take sponsorship from margarine producers but not butter producers; the cancer charities will not accept support from tobacco companies. If they did so, they would create bad PR for themselves and problems with their donors. They could not be seen to be endorsing a product which causes the problem. There may be other reasons for refusing a grant. For example, a campaigning organisation might not wish to be seen in the pocket of a vested interest or the government. It is often quite difficult to draw up an all-embracing set of rules on where you can and where you can't fundraise. But it is important to discuss and try to agree the constraints before you set about asking, rather than creating problems for yourself afterwards.

Resources: The resources available to you determine what you can and what you can't do. If you are planning to organise a public collection, do

FUNDRAISING CONSTRAINTS: AN EXAMPLE

The following is an excerpt from a national charity's policy on fundraising from companies. It went on to consider the area of joint promotions and sponsorship.

1. POLICY ON FUNDRAISING FROM COMPANIES

This policy is based on the premise that the principle of seeking and accepting support from companies is acceptable provided that:

a. The terms of the charity's relationship with a company are clearly defined.

b. By its association or linking with a company, the charity is satisfied that its aims, work and reputation will not be jeopardised directly or indirectly.

c. The charity does not become excessively dependent on a particular company or the commercial sector.

2. UNSOLICITED DONATIONS

The charity should accept all unsolicited donations from companies unless:

a. Conditions are attached which the charity finds unacceptable.

b. A single corporate donation is of an amount which would need consideration under criteria 1c. above.

3. SOLICITED DONATIONS

The charity should not solicit donations from companies whose policies and activities adversely affect those we seek to help – ie, children and families with children, or those with whom we work to achieve the same aims.

The Director/Deputy Director are responsible for deciding whether to approach a company for a donation, having first consulted staff and the Directory of Social Change reference books on company giving. In case of doubt about whether a company falls into one of the above categories, the Director/Deputy Director will make further enquiries, and may refer the matter to the Executive Committee for a decision.

you have sufficient people to rattle the collecting tins? If you don't, and you can't find them, you will find it difficult to make a success of the venture. Money is another important resource. Much fundraising involves investing resources now to achieve a result later. And some fundraising, such as a direct mail or advertising campaign or even a large building appeal, can require a substantial immediate expenditure. Anyone soliciting legacies is unlikely to see their efforts rewarded for several years. You need to know **how much** it is going to cost and **when** the results will come in to see if you can afford to do it. Although lack of resources can be a constraint, to some fundraisers this is a challenge. They will find the people or the money they need to mount a campaign somehow.

Legal constraints: The law is there to protect people. It can affect you in several ways. There are specific rules for collecting money from the public or raising money through lotteries and raffles set out in the Charities Act and the Lotteries Act. There is an overriding requirement to spend the money you raise on the purposes for which you have solicited it. And there are strict rules concerning when tax can be reclaimed on covenant and Gift Aid donations. Breaking the rules can bring your charity into disrepute or land you in gaol. Knowing the rules is important, and keeping within them is even more important.

What other organisations are doing: What others are doing effects what you do. Not many organisations can expect to get away with being 'me too' imitations of others. In some way they must distinguish themselves. Two ways of doing this are by differentiation and by focus. Take, as example, charities in the overseas development sector – Oxfam, Action Aid and WaterAid. Action Aid has a strategy of differentiation and WaterAid a strategy of focus. All three support remarkably similar work. Action Aid target support directly towards children and make much of it in promotional material; WaterAid focuses both fundraising and assistance in the water sectors; on the other hand, Oxfam succeeds as the market leader doing neither.

2.4.4 Determining the strategy: some techniques

There are a number of simple techniques in strategic planning. A fundraiser's version of the Ansoff Matrix can help you identify the possibilities. With Audiences along the vertical axis and Fundraising Techniques along the horizontal, the possibilities divide themselves into:

- Withdrawing, consolidating or doing nothing.

- Using existing methods with your current audiences (for example by assuming to get better response rates on existing appeals).

- Developing new audiences using current techniques (for example, by moving 'down market'), or extending the geographical coverage.

- Fundraising or 'product' development by researching new ways of raising money from the existing audience (such as payroll giving).

- Diversification – possibly the greatest risk – by applying new ideas to new audiences (starting a new programme of events, for example).

WAYS TO DEVELOP YOUR FUNDRAISING

Fundraising techniques >> Target Audience ⌄	NEW	EXISTING
		SAFETY AREA:
EXISTING	try out new techniques with existing supporters	expand existing schemes
	DANGER AREA:	
NEW	try out new ideas with new target audiences	extend known techniques to new audience

This matrix developed by **Ansoff** illustrates the most dangerous and safest ways of developing the fundraising work of a voluntary organisation.

A particularly useful technique for helping existing organisations to determine the most suitable strategy in a systematic approach, is to use the SWOT analysis beloved of marketers around the world. This Strength-Weakness-Opportunity-Threat matrix is simply a way of identifying the current position of the organisation and fitting the strategy to the organisational needs.

SWOT ANALYSIS

STRENGTHS	WEAKNESSES	A SWOT analysis identifies
long history	woolly image	strengths, weaknesses, opportunities and threats.
high reputation	outdated practices	This example was carried out
international links	unfocused fundraising	on an organisation that had just split into two parts and lost a
committed staff		major government grant.
strong membership		Though their problem is an immediate one, this sort of
		analysis can help map out
OPPORTUNITIES	**THREATS**	possible directions for the future.
volunteers	lack of short term funding	
increasing membership	poor image undermines fundraising	

2.4.5 Resources

No strategy can be complete without reference to resources. This represents the link between theory and practice. The resources needed may include training, equipment, literature to explain the cause and facilitate giving, and the money and systems needed to handle the donations.

Good record keeping and an effective mailing list are essential if you are getting money from supporters. This may require a good computer and the software and the additional equipment needed to enable it to do its job.

Equally important is the need for good fundraising literature: explanatory brochures to send out with your correspondence, fuller reports detailing the work you do, your annual accounts setting out your financial position, and display material – everything from posters to exhibition stands and a promotional video. You will need to decide what you require to be effective, and make sure you have it.

2.4.6 Other strategic principles

Be cost conscious: Everything possible should be done to **save money** both in the organisation and in its fundraising. For two good reasons. First there is a moral imperative upon the fundraiser to ask supporters for only what is strictly necessary, and to use as much of the sums given as possible on the work of the organisation. Many donors really do give of the widow's mite, and good stewardship is owed to them. There is a pressing practical reason too. If fundraisers are striving for a return ratio of say 5:1 of income to expenditure, then to maintain this ratio requires either extra income from the fundraising effort or lower costs.

COST EFFECTIVENESS

Income

From Local Authority	35,000	35%	The budget for this small charity illustrates the importance of keeping costs under control. If it is decided important to keep fundraising costs below 10% (currently at 10.4%), then there are two options, both of which should be explored. The first is to raise another £5000; the other is to reduce expenditure by a mere £500. This shows the need for a careful scrutiny of costs.
From covenants	7,218	7%	
Christmas appeal	35,893	36%	
Sundry income	22,514	22%	
Total Income	**100,625**	**100%**	

Expenditure

Programme costs	87,625	87%	
Fundraising costs	10,500	10.5%	
Administration costs	2,500	2.5%	
Total Expenditure	**100,625**	**100%**	

All fundraising activities should adhere to some **cost effectiveness ratios**. For mature fundraising schemes these may be as high as 10:1; other types of fundraising will never be able to do much better than 2 or 3:1. It is not sensible to expect new ventures or recently recruited fundraisers to produce these returns. Thus sliding scales of cost effectiveness are often used such that in year one a ratio of 2:1 is required; in year two, 3:1 and so on. Only with very clear planning and standards are fundraising targets going to be met. Donors and trustees would

PROBABLE START UP COSTS FOR SUCCESSFUL FUNDRAISING

1-5%	5-15%	15-40%	This table illustrates how much you can expect to pay for a range of fundraising techniques. For example, for every pound raised on appeals to companies you might expect to spend between 1 and 5 pence. This is a rough and ready guide and one that may not fully take into account the management costs of undertaking it.
Donor mailings	House to house	Temporary shops	
Appeals to trusts and companies	Lotteries	Some events	
Give As You Earn	Collecting boxes	Radio & TV appeals	
40-70%	**70-100%**	**100%+**	
Permanent shops	Advertising	Cold mail	Adapted from **Kroner**.

undoubtedly prefer not to spend anything to raise the money. The reality is that an expenditure of 20% (representing a 5:1 ratio) is often the norm and is acceptable to most donors.

Someone has to pay: An important decision is whether to charge for any services being provided. Many charities exist to provide a service to beneficiaries, and it is a part of the purpose of the organisation to do that on a free or highly subsidised basis. This then means that the amount raised determines the volume of work that can be undertaken. You will have to decide for yourselves how appropriate it is to charge and the levels of subsidy that can be offered. This must be reviewed frequently as the services provided are often the principal drain on the charity's resources. It is important however, to cost what you do carefully and accurately. Someone has to pay for it. Your funders, your sponsors, your donors... or the users.

Avoid risks: The cash used for fundraising purposes is intended ultimately to benefit the beneficiaries of the charity. Naturally they would be pleased to hear that this money had been invested wisely to generate lots of funds for the charity; they would not be at all pleased to hear that their money had been lost on a high risk venture. It is important that fundraisers do everything to reduce risk. This might involve piloting or testing new fundraising ideas where this can be done; it demands that you identify the worst possible thing that can happen in an event and insure against it; and that you scrap the activity when it looks set to fail. For example, an event like a concert in the Albert Hall will depend for its success on the sale of tickets. If very few tickets are sold, the losses will be very large. In this case, the best insurance would be to get a sponsor to underwrite all the costs. You can then give the tickets away if you can't sell them to ensure a full house.

Don't be dependent: It is a problem to be over-dependent on only one source of funding. If this fails, then the organisation can go into a financial crisis from which it may prove difficult to emerge. One approach to this problem is to diversify your fundraising activities and sources. This is one reason why so many charities were especially interested in the prospects of payroll giving by employees when it was introduced, as it seemed to promise a secure source of continuing income.

The long-term approach: Most organisations are not just interested in the results this year but also in the income which can be secured for the future. Fundraisers have a choice: they can concentrate on getting cash now or they can devote some of their resources to ensuring a continuing flow of funds for the future. Among the areas of fundraising where this is necessary is the development of retail chains, appeals for legacies and the use of covenants. There are inevitable costs in the short-term but the experience of most fundraisers is that the value of **long-term giving** soon outweighs that of casual giving.

The multiplier approach: A good way to multiply fundraising results is to **cascade**. For example, many charities over the last twenty years have operated regular collection schemes. In these, householders are visited monthly by a local collector and give their 50 pence or so. These are collected by an area representative and in turn sent in to the charity HQ. In this way one person at the centre is able to mobilise literally thousands of people and raise what in some cases has been millions of pounds. The cascade effect can multiply the number of people supporting you and the amount you can raise.

2.5 The donor

Knowing your donors and how they are likely to respond to you is a key to successful fundraising. This should also determine how you organise yourselves and present your appeal.

2.5.1 Who are the donors?

There is a wide range of potential donors to your cause. The main categories are discussed in Section 3. Each has different characteristics, a different motivation, and a different way of giving. It is therefore important for the fundraiser to have a clear idea of who they are communicating with.

Donors will range from the institutional to the individual, from the rich to the poor, from the involved to the disinterested, and from the concerned to the mildly interested – and most types in between.

Central government gives through its many departments and by making funds available to a number of intermediary organisations such as the Arts Council. Local government is a major contributor to local organisations meeting local needs through grants and payments for services. The European Commission supports voluntary organisations in the UK through a number of grant programmes, particularly for training and retraining for employment. Foundations and charitable trusts are major sources of funding as are companies, and both are easy to contact. There are a whole range of other organisations that can give, ranging from health authorities through to the voluntary grant-giving groups such as the Rotary Club. Finally the individual – from the rich industrialist to the widow giving her mite or a large legacy.

2.5.2 The ways of giving

Not everyone chooses to give by making a donation, and even when they do, it can be made in any number of quite different ways. The first and most important distinction is between contributions of money, contributions of goods or services, and contributions of time.

Literally millions of people in this country give freely and generously of their time as their contribution to charitable causes. The Charities Aid Foundation surveys on volunteers suggest that 55% of all adults have volunteered for something in the last 3 months. The average time given was around 5 hours per month. This represents a truly huge reservoir of active support, clearly some of which will be of help in fundraising, though of course not everybody wants to be involved in this type of activity. Much volunteer time is spent on fundraising. The National Volunteer Survey conducted by the Volunteer Centre UK suggests that over 60% of voluntary effort goes on fundraising.

Giving in kind can also be important. For the most part the growth and continuing success of charity shops depends on gifts of surplus goods. It is interesting to note that most of the advertising done by retailing charities appeals for both volunteers and goods, but rarely for customers who seem to follow the supply of goods. Charities can often be successful in attracting goods from manufacturers or other suppliers, that they badly need themselves (such as vehicles, facilities, furnishings or equipment), or which they can turn into cash by offering them as prizes in raffles or competitions. The attraction of this is that the cost of the gift is likely to be only marginal to the donor while its value to the recipient can be considerable. And where it is impossible to secure an outright gift, a hefty discount can often be negotiated. Services are valuable gifts too; one frequently requested service is that of free design and printing. Another way of helping is for a supporter to identify and even approach other potential donors from amongst their friends and contacts.

Gifts of money can come in all shapes and sizes. The two important aspects are the timescale over which it is given and the tax implications of the gift. Legacies and covenants are good examples of gifts where the benefit will be either wholly or partially in the future: in evaluating these forms of giving, account must be made of the timescales involved. It is usually true that developing long-term giving will be more cost effective in the long run than simply trying to raise money on a one-off basis.

The tax implications of giving is a technical area that any fundraiser must understand well. It has implications for how the appeal is promoted, the administration of the donation and the communication with donors. Company giving, covenants, deposit covenants, Gift Aid and legacies all need to be handled in particular ways. In soliciting and handling donations made in these ways, professionalism must be to the fore.

2.5.3 Why people give

It is difficult to generalise about why people give. Different causes and organisations no doubt benefit from the different motivations of the people who support them. This is perhaps best exemplified by a number of examples. A large corporation will give in the belief that the welfare of the company and its shareholders is best served by ensuring the well being of the communities in which it operates: self-interest in other words. Governments and local authorities will have a whole set of agendas motivating their giving patterns, which relate to their statutory duties and responsibilities, current areas of interest and priorities, and political and public pressures.

It is perhaps most interesting to look at the middle ground of those altruistic individuals who make up by far the largest volume of giving: many reasons are given and the results of research will show motives that overlap to a great extent.

Concern is probably the single greatest reason for people to give. This will embrace the older person who loses a pet and makes a gift to an animal cause as a surrogate. It will cover the parent who is horrified at the sexual harassment of children and wants to make some kind of response. And it will describe the individual who sees the pitiful faces of starving refugee children or a vanishing environment on the television news and telephones in to make a donation. Giving provides someone with the opportunity to do something significant for a cause they believe in.

Guilt probably comes a strong second as a motive for giving. The idea that we are rich and they are poor. Or the feeling that life has been good to the donor, provided a house, a job and so on. People develop strong feelings of guilt at their own position and may desire to salve these feelings with some charitable act. Many religions teach that charity or an equitable share of resources is to be striven for. Some even recommend that members allocate a certain share of their income to charity.

Another motive and one which seems to touch an increasing number of people, is **personal experience**. Those people who themselves or whose families have been hit by cancer, heart disease or some other illness are likely to be especially motivated to give. Likewise, those who have children at a school or playgroup. All research indicates that this is one of the most powerful motivators for giving.

The final motivator is that **they are asked**, and in being asked they become interested in the cause. The reason for most people NOT giving is that they are never asked.

"Money is just piling up; it's disgusting. We must get rid of it. But it's not easy to do."

DM: Let me explain my feelings about giving: To me money is work, present or past. So giving it away is a question of what you are prepared to work for; what justifies your effort. So I choose projects to support in terms of whether I would be prepared to work for them.

The real appeal for me is when something just won't get done unless I give a donation. So my preference is to give where my personal contribution is useful.

SC: *Will you give anything other than money?*

DM: In successful relationships, yes. For example when I gave money to help with improved cancer screening. There I was involved with the technical people and helped pull together various technical skills. In another case dealing with natural medicines, the charity wanted to get natural medicines approved. After much discussion they were persuaded that it was really a political issue and changed their approach. I was happy to contribute.

That's the ideal when it's possible. In Ethiopian famine relief, for example, that's not possible and it gives me less satisfaction.

SC: *What sort of things do you give to?*

DM: In one health project, they needed a laser printer. We bought it. I could see the gift would make a difference. It was a worthwhile project and I supported the idea. I want my gifts to help do things that would otherwise not happen or when quick action is needed. I'm all in favour of risk too. That's the advantage of private giving. Money for a building appeal would be low on my list and as for running costs, I'd have to support the idea concerned.

SC: *How do you respond to direct mail appeals?*

DM: 99% of what we get sent goes straight into the bin. Occasionally when we are conscious of a special need we may respond. Then it's just a convenient medium. If someone comes to the door they get £1 or so.

SC: *How do you get to hear of needs then?*

DM: Usually we seem to bump into people who need money. I've never been approached by a fundraiser. I do buy Christmas cards but I know that's peanuts. We would go to a charity concert but only if we were interested in the concert itself.

SC: *Do you give regular gifts?*

DM: The money is in a trust so there's no point in covenanting. As for regular giving, there has to be a very good reason.

SC: *How do you decide how much to give?*

DM: There is no scale for us. We would give anything. But we would think twice if a donation depleted the trust completely.

SC: *Do you give to the larger charities?*

DM: Basically my feeling is that charity people get full marks for devotion but they do sometimes go at their work like a bull at a gate; they don't always research the alternatives properly. Larger organisations get it wrong as often as they get it right. Smaller ones get closer to their beneficiaries. They know what they are about.

SC: *What do you think about campaigning?*

DM: I feel strongly that charity ought to be covered by the state and that our taxes should be used for this. I am quite happy for my money to be used to pressure the state. That's totally legitimate.

SC: *If you give to a charity do you expect to hear from them again?*

DM: I expect them to keep me informed on what has happened. It's also interesting to see what has been achieved. The most surprising thing though is that we have never been asked to give again. I'd like it if people did come back.

SC: *And what happens if the project does not succeed?*

DM: That's life. You try hard and take the risk. But I want to be told the truth if a project fails. People who have made money remember situations when things might easily have turned out differently, without attaching blame.

This interview was conducted by the author with DM, a London businessman running his own company. He still works full-time and has set up a trust fund containing some £300,000. His wife is also involved with giving this and other income away. The views of this donor are not necessarily those of other donors.

3. THE SOURCES

This chapter sketches out the main sources of funding – statutory, charitable trusts, companies, individuals and organisations – describes their characteristics and identifies the main opportunities and skills that are likely to be applicable.

SOURCES OF PUBLIC SECTOR SUPPORT FOR VOLUNTARY ORGANISATIONS 1988/89

Grants to Housing Associations	£1,075m
Quangos	£76m
Tax Concessions	£639m
Local Authorities	£614m
Central Government	£382m
Health Authorities	£27m

This chart shows where the total of all statutory funding of £3,498m in 1988/9 came from.

3.1 Statutory funding

A grant from one of the arms of government can add major funding to your organisation. This is a difficult area which may require time and a good deal of effort, but can be worth the wait.

3.1.1 The overview

Statutory funding covered here includes:

- The European Commission;
- Nationally by Central Government;
- Locally by Local Authorities, and Health Authorities;
- Quangos, which are government supported official bodies often with some grant-making function (such as the Arts Council).

For many organisations statutory funding is the mainstay of their work. For others it is marginal or just another of many sources. The scale of the funds available from statutory sources is vast and is likely to increase steadily as government moves away from direct provision to the purchase of services under contract. The table below illustrates the size of government funding.

The size of the funding available should not lure you into the belief that you can easily turn on this particular tap. If it is possible to generalise about so many quite different sources of funding, it would be to say that the process of getting a statutory grant is slow and tortuous. The outcome will depend on a whole range of factors which will be outside your control such as the time of year, the political climate and the state of the economy.

3.1.2 European Community

The European Commission's key community interests are: unemployment; poverty; women; ethnic minorities; people with disabilities; education and culture; Eastern Europe; the third world; environment and energy; and consumer interests.

There are a number of small grant programmes (see Grants from Europe, the annual publication produced by NCVO), but the main source of funding for voluntary organisations is the European Social Fund which is concerned with training and employment, particularly for the young and long-term unemployed. Normally at least half of any project's funding must come from a UK public source (including government, local authority or a trust) to match the EC contribution. A total of £21 million was available to voluntary organisations through the voluntary sector allocation in 1991.

Full details and information on how to apply are available from the National Council for Voluntary Organisations which has a specialist department on the European Social Fund.

3.1.3 UK Government

As the table indicates, the UK government departments give large sums of money each year to the voluntary sector.

Each government department has a different set of criteria and programme for giving to the voluntary sector. The major programmes are through the DTI's training division and the Department of the Environment's Urban Programme for inner cities.

Several forces are at work which affect the availability of money. The first is the general state of the economy. The second is the importance given to the role of the voluntary sector by government in meeting social and community needs. To this must be added the strong interest in effectiveness and accountability heralded by the recent Efficiency Scrutiny on government grant-making and by the emergence of the 'contract culture'.

In practical terms when making grant aid available, the government is distinctly interested in promoting government policy through the medium of the voluntary sector, and this can have important consequences for the traditional and cherished freedom of action of the sector. Increasing scrutiny and having to negotiate contracts means that considerable effort has to be put into winning government funds.

CENTRAL GOVERNMENT GRANTS TO VOLUNTARY ORGANISATIONS

Department	1988/89 £000s
Agriculture Fisheries and Food	151
Defence	6,696
Education and Science	5,023
Employment	47,325
Energy	896
Environment	115,486
Foreign and Commonwealth	1,197
Health	38,050
Home Office	24,422
Lord Chancellor	745
Northern Ireland	13,643
Overseas Development Administration	63,024
Scottish Office	42,501
Social Security	3,783
Trade and Industry	9,576
Transport	608
Welsh Office	9,347
Total	**382,473**

3.1.4 Local Authorities

Local Authorities consist of counties (47 in England and Wales) and Districts (333 in England and Wales) – although the current structure is under review. They contribute over £400 million to voluntary bodies annually, and despite the current squeeze on funding represent a major source of funds. The main functions for which they are responsible include education, social services, recreation and leisure services, and transport and housing; it is in these areas that they are most likely to make grants. At the lowest level of the local administration are the parish councils who have powers over a limited range of local issues and in a few cases are able to give grants.

Grant-giving can be done in a number of ways; it can include the giving of services or support in kind, the offer of premises, subsidy towards rent or rates or straightforward grants. An alternative form of funding is by way of fees through your charity fulfilling the local authority's statutory

PAYMENTS BY LOCAL AUTHORITIES TO VOLUNTARY ORGANISATIONS

Area	1988/89 £000s	1988/89 %
Housing	21,796	5
Education	115,902	24
Social services	159,733	34
Leisure/recreation/arts	75,062	16
Local economy/planning	31,608	7
Policy and resources	60,329	13
Amenities and countryside	2,761	1
Law and Order	1,546	-
Total	**475,309**	**100**

This gives an estimate of the breakdown of how local authority giving and fees are directed.

obligations. This relationship is more likely now to be carried out on a formal contract basis for example for the provision of transport for the elderly, or housing and care for people with disabilities. Such income comes in the form of fees for defined services rather than as a grant, and will normally be considered taxable for VAT purposes.

Local authorities have a wide range of mechanisms for coordinating their giving. Joint Finance is an example of central government money being made available for new initiatives and administered jointly by council and health authorities. Senior staff are usually designated as link people to liaise with voluntary organisations seeking financial assistance. The application will be decided by committee, and some councils have set up special grants committees for this purpose. On occasions, council officers have their own discretion on grant giving, a point you should check. There is usually a rigid timetable for the submission of applications.

Of all the government arms, local authorities are open to personal and political pressure in a way that others are not; lobbying is thus an important part of your approach.

3.1.5 Quangos and Health Authorities

Quangos are organisations set up by parliament to carry out a particular brief but outside the direct control of a ministry. In many respects their attitudes and approaches to grant-making will be similar to those of government departments, but they may exhibit a greater degree of flexibility. These bodies give in their own specific fields mostly in the form of cash grants. Most produce guidelines for applicants which set out the priority areas for grants and the application procedures.

Health authorities also make grants to voluntary organisations for health care, health prevention and health promotion projects. The scale of grant-making varies from authority to authority as do the procedures for securing a grant. In addition to grants, the purchaser-provider system in the NHS now provides opportunities to negotiate contracts for delivering services.

GRANTS FROM QUANGOS TO VOLUNTARY ORGANISATIONS

Body	1988/89 £000s
Training agency schemes	
Voluntary projects programme	7,620
Youth Training Scheme	92,000
Community programme	345,000
Employment Training	65,100
Action for Community Employment	45,100
Community Volunteering Programme	798
Youth Community Projects	786
Community Projects	17,152
Youth Help	753
Arts Council	162,692
Sports Council	19,169
Commission for Racial Equality	1,808
Countryside Commission	2,596
Nature Conservancy Council	2,100
Health Education Authority	596
Highlands and Islands Development Board	878
Equal Opportunities Commission	40
Total	**760,588**

3.1.6 Getting started

1. Find out what, if any, links you have had previously with any statutory authorities, and whether any of your trustees or members have good links with any likely funding sources.

2. Do your research to identify and match possible funders with various aspects of your organisation's work.

3. Approach possible funders to discuss their requirements and how best you should present your application.

4. Prepare a full application or proposal to be submitted in due course. This may need to be submitted on an application form. Check first.

3.1.7 Getting in touch

Before getting in touch with any arm of government it is worth using the reference books available to identify which department or committee is likely to be relevant and who the key people are. If in doubt a phone call to the department concerned will identify who the right person to contact is. If at all possible, try to arrange a meeting to establish contact and identify the important factors you will need to take account of.

Especially at local government level, it is worth recruiting potential allies. Either people whose name or reputation speaks for your organisation or, better still, people who sit on the council or particular committee who can help vote your application through. You should also try to develop good relationships with council staff, both in the grants unit and in the relevant council department.

Where an application is needed, you will have to conform to the required format and provide all the information that is requested. Once you have received a grant, you will need to note the grant conditions and the requirements for monitoring, evaluating and reporting back.

To find out who to contact at the European Commission you can contact the Commission's UK press and information office. To contact central government read the Central Government Grants Guide, or you can contact the Voluntary Service Unit at the Home Office. To get in touch with your local district or county council consult your local Council for Voluntary Service or the chief executive's department at the relevant council.

3.1.8 Three good ideas for statutory funding

1. Don't be shy about making friends and chatting up the people who may be making the decision on your project's application. If you have any qualms about this just think about all the less valuable projects that may be approved because no one speaks up for yours.

2. Consider whether it is a useful ploy to ask for funding on a matched basis. That is, your request is only granted if another named funder provides funding as well. The matcher could even be your own organisation! This is attractive to funding bodies as they are then seen to be making their money work even harder than normal.

3. Time your applications so that you give them a relevance that will encourage funders. This can be done by arranging publicity yourselves, by linking applications to themes of current interest and concern to the funder, or by using national and local media coverage of issues as integral parts of your application. But beware of appearing to put undue pressure on funding bodies through the media, as they may well react against it.

3.1.9 Techniques and skills

To be successful in raising money from statutory sources you will need persistence, persuasion and personal contacts. In addition you will certainly need a depth of knowledge about your organisation and be able to speak and answer questions with authority.

You may have to make a personal presentation of your case and you will need to be able to compose a clear and persuasive written proposal.

3.1.10 Reference

In this book see also:
4.3   Sponsorship
5.3   Writing a proposal
5.15 Public relations
5.5   Involving patrons

Useful sources of information (see Bibliography 6.2 for full details):
Charity Trends, CAF
The Central Government Grants Guide, DSC
Grants from Europe, NCVO

Useful sources of advice:
UK Press and Information Dept, European Commission
Voluntary Services Unit, the Home Office
Department of Education and Science
Department of Employment.

3.2 Trusts and foundations

One of the most important sources of funding for small or newly established charities is the charitable trust or foundation. These give very large sums collectively across a wide range of needs and are much more flexible than government sources.

3.2.1 An overview

This section covers those bodies whose main purpose is to give grants to other voluntary sector bodies. Mostly these will be charitable trusts, themselves constituted as charities. Almost all have charitable status and can only make grants to other charitable bodies or for a charitable purpose. Some carry the name Foundation. For the purposes of this book they all have similar characteristics and will be dealt with together under the title of trusts. Also covered in this section is the growing sector of Community Trusts.

Trusts are a very important area for fundraisers as they are set up with the express intention of giving money away. The skills needed and the approach required is similar to that required in the case of corporate and statutory fundraising (though arguably the wide range of opportunities in companies demands wider skills). More than for most other grant sources, trusts are affected by the relationship that you can build with them and by your reputation. One role that some trusts adopt is the promotion of innovation and new ideas. Many emerging organisations

DO'S AND DON'TS IN APPLYING TO TRUSTS

DO....
- plan a strategy
- plan ahead
- select a good project
- believe in what you are doing
- select a target
- write an application tailored to the needs of the trust
- use a personal contact
- prepare a realistic and accurate budget
- be concise
- be specific
- establish your credibility
- keep records of everything you do
- send reports and keep trusts informed
- try to develop a partnership or long term relationship
- say thank you

DON'T....
- send a duplicated mailshot
- ask for unrealistic amounts
- assume trusts will instantly understand the needs you are meeting
- make general appeals for running costs
- use jargon
- beg

A checklist prepared by **Hugh Frazer**, formerly of the Northern Ireland Voluntary Trust, offering sound advice on what to do and not do when approaching trusts.

WHAT CHARITABLE TRUSTS GIVE TO

Area supported	£'000s	%
Medicine and health	20,047	12.00
Poverty	1,418	0.85
Assistance to special classes	12,529	7.50
Housing	1,910	1.14
Children and youth	4,071	2.44
Aged	1,443	0.86
Social welfare	9,422	5.64
Moral welfare	720	0.43
Education	11,008	6.59
Sciences	1,131	0.68
Humanities	76,246	45.63
Religion	3,730	2.23
Environment	24,351	1.46
International	20,992	12.56
Totals	**167,094**	**100**

Source: **Directory of Grant-making Trusts 1991**, Charities Aid Foundation. Figures are for the top 200 grant-making trusts. The Humanities category includes donations by the Arts Council and Regional Arts Associations.

owe their existence to the support from the outset of clear sighted and progressive trusts who were prepared to shoulder whatever risk there may have been at that stage of the organisation's development.

From statistics provided by the Directory of Social Change the current level of giving by trusts is nearly £600 million a year (from the top 300 trusts). This means that trust giving is substantially larger than company giving but much less important than governmental and individual giving. This rate of giving is tied directly to the income earned on the underlying assets of the trusts which are in turn linked to the growth or decline in the economy.

Of the 160,000 registered charities, it is not known precisely how many are grant-giving nor how many are fundraising; some are both. It is certain that there are a very large number of smaller trusts which have money to give. There is a great deal of published information on the larger trusts. The challenge for the fundraiser is how to find out about smaller and newer trusts where no information is available.

Applying to trusts remains one of the lowest cost areas for fundraising. Though no funding source can be taken for granted, raising money from trusts remains an easier task for the fundraiser than many.

3.2.2 Background of trusts

Many of today's larger charitable trusts and foundations are of relatively recent provenance. Many of the biggest date back to foundations endowed by great Victorians – the Rowntree Trusts for example. Others are of much more recent creation. The Gulbenkian was created in 1956, Wellcome in 1936, BBC Children in Need in 1927 and Telethon Trust more recently in 1988. Few of the major trusts are of the antiquity of the Royal Society (1660). In many cases the trusts are still controlled or have representation from the family of the founders.

THE PRINCE'S YOUTH BUSINESS TRUST

The **Prince's Youth Business Trust** was started without an endowment. The trustees had to go out and raise the money through an appeal to trusts, companies and individuals matched by a special government donation. They expected their money to come from:

Special donations	£17m
Corporate appeals	£12m
Regional appeals	£8.5m
Grants	£2m
Gifts under £10,000	£1m
Total targeted to end 1989	**£40.5m**

3.2.3 Larger trusts

The structure of the larger trusts is highly professional`. At the top end of the income scale there is likely to be a secretary or director (the title varies from trust to trust) who is in executive charge of the trust. They will report to the trustees and will in turn have a small administrative staff reporting to them. The trustees will be responsible for deciding where the grants go, basing their decisions on the recommendations of the professional staff. The trustees may be supported by local advisers or experts in the specialist areas which are central to their interests. This often ensures that trust staff have a panoramic view of the field in which the fundraiser works and can wield a good deal of incisive questioning.

At the smaller end of the trust scale are those who share administrative facilities or even have the administration carried out by a firm of solicitors or accountants. It is this which often makes it very difficult to build any relationship with smaller trusts unless you have some personal contact with a trustee.

3.2.4 Community trusts

The last few years has seen the emergence of Community Trusts. These are an alliance of local donors often coordinated by a local Council for Voluntary Service designed to channel local giving into local projects. At the time of writing nearly 40 have been formally established and new ones are being developed. A few Community Trusts have already raised around £1 million (within a period of 5 years, or so), and this is invested as capital to develop a stream of income from which to make grants. One reason for this development is to create an alternative source of local grants to those available from the local authority. This source of funding is clearly one to watch. The current list of Community Trusts is given in Section 6.3.

3.2.5 International foundations

At the other end of the geographic scale are international foundations. Most of the larger ones are situated in the US, but there are many in Europe and a few in Japan. These are less likely to be interested in domestic issues in the UK and Ireland and will be looking for a wider significance in the projects they fund. Two Directory of Social Change grant guides cover these: Peace and Security (out of print) covers UK and overseas trusts with an interest in peace, security and international relations, and US Foundation Support in Europe details US foundations with significant grant programmes in the UK and Europe. The European Foundation Centre in Brussels keeps information on European foundations and can provide informal advice.

3.2.6 Trust giving

Trusts are constrained by their founding trust deed and by the requirement to support charitable work. This does not mean that they have to give to organisations that are charities, but that the work they support must be **per se** charitable. Some are constrained by their constitution to supporting charitable bodies. So if your organisation is not or is not yet a charity, but the work you are applying for is charitable, you will need to find an intermediary body to receive the grant. You can get advice on this from your local Council of Voluntary Service.

Many trusts are little more than a vehicle for the giving of an individual. In this case personal contact with that individual is essential if you are to stand any chance of a grant. Some are vehicles for company giving. Here the motivation is likely to be identical to that of the company itself and the officers of the trusts will probably be senior staff of the company. Such trusts are best approached in the context of company giving (see Section 3.3).

Most trusts simply make cash donations. These can be one-off grants or for a number of years (usually up to three). Even if a one-off grant is secured, it is possible that the same trust may be willing to support another aspect of your work in future years. It is important for the fundraiser to be clear about the long-term goals and funding strategy of the organisation and to show how the grant proposal fits into this. Where the proposal is for a building or to purchase a piece of equipment, the application should try to show how the facility will be used and how the running costs will be met. Where it is towards running costs, the application should try to show what will happen when the grant runs out. Besides grants, some trusts are prepared to make interest-free or low-interest loans, but this is unusual, unless there is some return expected from the project. However there is one very important consideration. Each trust is different and has a different approach to grant-making. Some prefer giving start up money; some preclude money for capital projects, while others will only provide support for these. The most popular area of support is medical research, whilst the least popular is salaries and overhead costs in any area. All this can be ascertained from the trust itself or from its literature (if it publishes anything) or from one of the grant guides (see below for details). It is imperative that you use all available intelligence to ensure that you send only appropriately targeted literature to trusts.

3.2.7 Getting started

1. First of all, find out what if any links you have had with trusts previously and what happened.

2. Then find out whether any of your trustees or members have good links to any likely trust funding sources.

3. Do your research to identify and match possible funders with various parts of your organisation and its work.

4. Approach possible funders to discuss what their requirements are and how best you should present applications.

5. Prepare a full application or proposal to be submitted in due course.

The main sources of information are (a) the literature produced by trusts themselves, but only the largest publish reports or guidelines for applicants and (b) a number of published grant directories, which include:

Directory of Grant Making Trusts (brief information on around 2,500 trusts)

Guide to the Major Trusts (detailed information on the top 300 trusts) – Volume 1

Guide to the Major Trusts (information on the next 700) – Volume 2

Regional grants guides (DSC publishes the London Grants Guide and the West Midlands Grants Guide; the local Council of Voluntary Service usually publish a grant guide for its area or provide a list of trusts).

Guide to Grants for Individuals in Need and the Educational Grants Directory (both list trusts providing charitable grants to individual, from DSC).

3.2.8 Getting in touch

Where possible getting in touch with trusts should be a several stage process. It might include the following elements:

1. General PR to make people aware of your organisation and its work, so that when you approach trusts, they may have heard of you.

2. A phone call to establish contact. This can determine whether there is a best time in the trust's year, whether a trust can give to your cause and how you should go about it.

3. A letter can then follow to lay out the plan in detail. Paper is the medium in which most trustees deal and from which your request will initially be judged. You should not expect to be able to avoid this.

4. You might try to arrange to meet a representative of the trust. This could be either at your premises, if there are people or things to see, or on neutral ground. It is this encounter which can seal the fate of so

many applications. You should therefore try very hard to meet your potential funders face to face.

5. If you have contact with a trustee or the chair of the trustees, then you can try to discuss your proposal and enlist their support.

3.2.9 Six good ideas for trust fundraising

1. Thoroughly research your application from the available information and by making contact with the trust concerned.

2. Present a concise but complete written document setting out your needs, including an introductory letter, the background, your organisation's needs, a budget and references.

3. Particularly if the project is new or unpublicised, use as much reference material and names of people as possible. This should include the names of several well-known sponsors who can vouch for its validity and the organisers' integrity.

4. Arrange for members of the trust, whether they be staff or trustees, to visit you. Remember one picture is worth a thousand words. It is quite unusual for someone who has visited a project not in some way to support it later. Very often trusts will back the ideas and energy of a key individual in your organisation.

5. Invite trusts to consider giving which is matched to the gift of another organisation or individual. Many donors find this an attractive form of leverage and warm to the idea of their gift effectively being worth double its face value. There is of course a risk that the second donor will not respond and you lose the first donation: this is unusual.

6. If you find you have raised more money than you need as a result of approaches to several trusts, be truthful and go back to them with alternative suggestions. Offer to extend the project or improve it and only then offer to repay it.

3.2.10 Techniques and skills

The techniques and skills required for raising money from trusts are equally necessary for raising money from other sources. Essentially these are persistence, persuasion and personal contacts. Knowing about your organisation is also essential as well as the ability to personally present your case in whatever form is required.

3.2.11 References

In this book see also:

And from elsewhere:
  Charity Trends, CAF annually
  Directory of Grant Making Trusts, CAF
  Guide to the Major Trusts, DSC
  Rural Community Councils
  Charity Information Bureaux
  Councils for Voluntary Service
  Northern Ireland Council for Voluntary Action
  Wales Council for Voluntary Action
  Scottish Council for Voluntary Organisations
  The European Foundation Centre

3.3 Giving by companies

Increasing interest is being shown by companies in how they can help their communities and help themselves. There are many good opportunities to build partnerships with companies.

3.3.1 Overview

Companies, like so many other bodies, use a wide range of approaches for their charitable and community support. Most now allocate an annual budget for this purpose. Some use their own charitable trust to disburse their funds, others use the services of the Charities Aid Foundation. They do this to obtain the tax reliefs available on charitable giving. But however the money is distributed the policy making and grant decisions remain with the company.

CAF estimates that total corporate giving is currently standing at £142 million annually. In real terms giving has been increasing substantially – at least from the top 400 donors. The lowest of the top 400 largest companies gives an annual sum of £40,000 while the largest givers such as British Telecom are giving in excess of £10 million annually.

A further huge fund of potential donors was revealed by CAF in their surveys of the small company sector. Here from a small sample they projected annual giving of at least a further £474 million.

Alongside the charitable giving by companies is business sponsorship (see Section 4.3), commercial promotions (see Section 4.14), and corporate giving and fundraising (see Section 4.12).

3.3.2 Background to giving

Giving from companies has developed rather similarly to that of charitable trusts. However the climate changed considerably in the 1980s. This period saw a growing acceptance by companies of their responsibility to the community, the development of the Per Cent Club, Business in the Community, the practice of secondment, and much more professional management of this aspect of their affairs. The 1990s have seen a continuation of these trends, but in a climate of economic downturn, companies are increasingly looking for good investment opportunities for their funds where grants will make a significant impact or generate recognition.

3.3.3 Structure of giving

The main areas of interest to companies are the promotion of enterprise, education and training both in schools and for employment, the arts, the environment and charities. Some divide their budgets into these categories. Most are interested in relating their community support to their business interests and needs. They give support in a number of ways, including cash giving, sponsorship, advertising in brochures, joint promotions, secondments and gifts in kind; staff giving is an increasingly important area. Sponsorship is divided into corporate sponsorship, which is often considered alongside charitable and community involvement, and brand sponsorship (and also joint promotions) which is the responsibility of the marketing department and where the support comes from a different budget.

The giving by major companies is often handled by a Community Relations or Corporate Affairs section. These are run by the people within the company who are charged with ensuring that the company is seen favourably by those communities that it perceives as being important to its own business interests. Though each company is structured differently, much of what used to be considered as charitable giving is now subsumed into this area of corporate life.

Advertising in brochures, which has been estimated to run at £20 million each year, can be a useful addition to the revenue of an event. This form of giving may come out of the marketing budget. But this does not mean that the company will be looking for a very direct payback as most of this support is seen as 'goodwill' rather than commercial advertising.

Gifts in kind are one of the more difficult sort of donations to manage. Three sorts are common. The first where a company offers some of its excess (or often unsaleable) stock can be extremely difficult. It is relatively unusual that a charity is able to sell something that the company has not been able to; the risk is that a great deal of effort is put into being seen to accept and value the gift and then it is found that any value it has is unrealisable. The second is the offer of redundant furniture, furnishings and equipment. This can be of surprisingly good quality and is a useful form of support. The third is what is requested by the charity itself. For example the loan of a vehicle for an event or fixed period can be very valuable and can offer good PR for the donor. Equally the offer of office space, technical advice, office services or other commonly used services can be invaluable. Companies often find it easier to give in kind rather than in cash. And the best approach will normally be by telephone talking directly to the person able to make a decision. The large retail chains will have rules on what their local branches can and cannot offer in response to requests from local charities.

An important and growing area of giving to charities is that of secondment. Especially at a time of recession, companies may be planning to lay off middle and senior management alongside the normal process of retirement. This has been used as an opportunity to encourage

Sponsorship: "Heineken's sponsorship of the British Trust for Conservation Volunteers project to refresh the Cerne giant in Dorset produced outstanding press and TV coverage and reinforced our advertising bye-line," reported one of Heineken's executives. This is a good example of how your project might be attractive to a corporate sponsor.

some of these people to work in the voluntary sector. The usual method is for the employer to pay the wage costs for a given period. Secondment is both carried out as direct support and through clearing houses. High fliers in any company are rarely available for secondment as are people with a specific desire to be involved directly in fundraising. An increasingly common form of secondment is task-based and of limited term, say 100 hours to undertake a marketing survey.

Staff giving is a growth area. However the two keys to it are in having access to staff in their place of work, and having the people available to canvass their support. Either way the company can help by supporting your efforts to reach its staff. Some companies have schemes to match any funds given or raised for charity by their staff.

3.3.4 Motivations

There is no particular obligation for companies to give their money to charities. Indeed altruism is not a word that is always appropriate to describe their giving. Enlightened self-interest is a better term. Some giving is overtly in support of company objectives, while other parts are clearly geared towards their community affairs policy. One objective of their policy will be to project the company favourably to the public and in the local community where the company operates. Most large donors talk openly of the need to gear their giving to those activities that will generate a high public profile. However, some giving by companies does remain purely altruistic. It is important to differentiate sponsorship from giving and brand or product sponsorship from corporate sponsorship. Sponsorship will normally be paid for out of corporate PR budgets or marketing budgets, and is undertaken to obtain overt and specific benefits for the company. With the giving programmes the benefits are often less tangible and to the fore. Different people will be responsible for the different budgets and the approach may be completely different when seeking support from the various sources.

In some cases where you have access to the most senior staff, personal preference plays an important part. For example, the reason that those charities that actively use royal patrons are so successful, must in part relate to the preference by senior business people to be seen well in that quarter. Equally, the old syndrome of appealing to the chairman's wife indicates that there are other ways of succeeding than the strictly rational or commercial!

Companies will generally be able to give to almost anything. Surveys of what they say conclude that most companies will not give to:

• Local appeals outside their plant area.

• Purely denominational appeals; this does not preclude support for social projects run by denominational bodies.

• Circular appeals.

• Overseas appeals, although some do support emergency and aid appeals on the basis that this is of interest to staff.

OUR PHILOSOPHY . . .

The nature and purpose of corporate sponsorship is frequently misunderstood. NatWest is one of Britain's largest corporate sponsors and we want our customers, our shareholders – and those who seek our help – to understand the reasoning behind our involvement.

Is it pure altruism? Not really.

NatWest has grown from roots stretching back hundreds of years to become Britain's leading bank – and thus one of Britain's largest public companies.

Our day to day business finances the economic activity on which the nation's prosperity depends. In doing this we touch the lives of millions of people but, equally, our own success ultimately depends upon the prosperity and stability of the communities we serve. We have realised that what is beneficial for society is usually good for us too.

As a founder member of the Per Cent Club, NatWest has for some years committed itself to re-investing a fixed percentage of its annual pre-tax profits for the benefit of the community. At present this amounts to over £10 million per annum.

How do we spend this considerable sum?

Our business brings us into daily contact with the community at all levels and in a wide variety of places. Often we see projects where commitment, initiative and enthusiasm are plentiful, but an extra 'something' is needed to make worthwhile plans a lasting reality.

Frequently we can supply that lasting ingredient – be it money, expertise or equipment – to get a scheme off the ground and to keep it going.

Society benefits – and so, in turn, do we, as a healthy society is good for business.

NatWest's commitment to caring for society starts at the top. Directing NatWest's community programme is one of the functions of the bank's Social Policy Committee whose members include both NatWest's Chair and myself as Group Chief Executive.

But the commitment spreads throughout NatWest.

Many organisations benefit from the voluntary, part-time involvement of our staff (a commitment which the Bank is often pleased to bolster with cash sponsorship under the NatWest cash sponsorship scheme), whilst the NatWest Staff Samaritan Fund (financed entirely by the generosity of our employees) makes around 200 donations a year, particularly in the field of health care.

*This is the introduction to a leaflet describing **NatWest**'s attitude to its corporate giving which they call sponsorship.*

To find out what a company gives to is not always easy. Large companies tend to have community affairs offices and are usually willing to meet fundraisers or to discuss their policies over the phone.

A useful first step is to study the company directories which give some details of company giving and preferences. Two published by the Directory of Social Change focus on company charitable support: A Guide to Company Giving, which covers the top 1,300 companies and The Major Companies Guide, which gives much more detail on the top 400.

For further information, the best way is to identify a supporter or volunteer who is employed by the company. Insiders can usually find a great deal if they put their minds to it and may well be the best person to present the application.

Keep in touch with company news and events. This can often generate interesting ideas and opportunities. For example a plant close down or a new branch opening. All companies have a community of stakeholders on which they depend: these include staff, customers, suppliers, government, shareholders and lastly, but importantly, senior management: anything that enhances the position of the company with one of these groups is likely to be interesting. Read the papers: the business press, the national press, the local press. Get hold of the company's annual report which will help you understand their business and identify their interests.

3.3.5 Getting started

1. First of all find out what, if any, links you have had with any companies previously and what happened.
2. Then find out whether any of your trustees or members (or even your volunteers) have good links with any likely companies either because they are employees or directors or simply through their contacts.
3. Do your research to identify and match possible funders with various aspects of your work. In particular identify whether there are any local companies that are known for their generosity or have an interest in supporting your cause – maybe to be seen in a better light locally. Good research at an early stage is rarely wasted.
4. Approach possible funders to discuss what their requirements are and how best you should present applications.
5. Prepare a full application or proposal to be submitted in due course.
6. Check your ideas with another fundraiser.

3.3.6 Getting in touch

The personal approach is best, but often the most difficult to achieve. In smaller companies there is usually no staff member responsible for giving and therefore approaches have to be at board level. Visits are useful when discussing bigger donations with the bigger companies, but difficult to get for anything small. It is quite unusual to be able to coax company staff to visit projects needing funds.

Circular letters suffer the fate of most of the thousands of appeals a company receives each month. They are put in the bin. Letters should therefore be directed to an individual and personalised. Because companies receive too many appeals, their first instinct is to say no. Many fundraisers have even suffered the experience of writing a non-appeal letter and receiving a proforma rejection!

Where possible getting in touch should be done in several stages. It might include the following elements:

1. A phone call to establish contact. This can determine whether there is a best time to apply, whether a company gives to your cause and how you should go about it.

2. A letter can then follow setting out your proposal in brief detail. Paper is the medium through which most companies will judge your request.

3. Finally you might try to arrange to meet a representative of the company. This could be either at your premises, if there are people or things to see, or at their offices. It is this encounter which seals the fate of so many applications. You should therefore try very hard to meet your potential funders face to face. Being well prepared and appropriately dressed is important.

3.3.7 Six ideas for good company fundraising

1. Put yourself in the position of the company. Why should they give their shareholders' funds to you? Why should they choose yours rather than any of the other appeals? Think of the benefits that they may get out of it. And mention these when you make your appeal. For sponsorship, these benefits will be at the centre of your proposal.

2. Use all the contacts you can muster in the company to help get your appeal supported. If you know the spouse of a board member get them to put in a good word. If you only get acquainted with the executive's secretary, invite their co-operation by making sure that your application gets to the top of the pile with a good word accompanying it.

3. Think laterally of the ways the company could help. Might it be more useful for them to offer staff time; a vehicle; access to company staff for a payroll canvass or promotion? It is likely that everyone else will be asking for cash. And the company may find it easier to give in kind.

4. Consider whether there is a senior executive who might become a trustee or serve on a fundraising or development committee and bring new ideas, discipline and contacts to your cause that are worth many times what a donation might be worth. The invitation, even if not accepted, may be seen as flattering. If this level of involvement is turned down, a request for advice may not be.

5. Don't assume that every company will give. Be prepared with parallel approaches to a number of different companies.

6. Consider who might be the best person to make the approach or sign the letter. It may not be you.

7. Every time you go into a company, for any reason, say for example if you want to buy a new computer, use that opportunity to talk to the company about your work and invite their support. It is often a useful way of getting them to release an extra discount long after the lowest price has been agreed.

3.3.8 Techniques and skills

To be successful in raising money from companies you will need a wide range of skills and appropriate attitudes including persistence, persuasion and personal contacts as for trust and government funding. In addition you will certainly need a depth of knowledge about your organisation and to be able to speak and answer questions with authority.

You will have to make a personal presentation of your case and to be able to provide a clear and persuasive written proposal.

Especially useful in the company area is the ability to be imaginative and to come up with ideas for joint activity that are likely to be beneficial to the company concerned.

3.3.9 References

In this book see also:

And from elsewhere:

Charity Trends, CAF annually

Major Companies Guide, DSC

A Guide to Company Giving, DSC

Raising Money from Industry, DSC

Finding Sponsors for Community Projects, DSC

Rural Community Councils

Councils for Voluntary Service, and Charity Information Bureaux

Northern Ireland Council for Voluntary Action

Wales Council for Voluntary Action

Scottish Council for Voluntary Organisations

Action Resource Centre

REACH: The Retired Executives Action Clearing House

Business in the Community

The Per Cent Club

Association for Business Sponsorship of the Arts.

3.4 Giving by individuals

The majority of charitable giving in the UK is from individuals. This is therefore the key area for fundraisers. Most organisations need to develop the support of individuals in their community, or those who share a concern for their cause.

3.4.1 Overview

Clearly decisions on giving by governments, trusts and companies are made by individuals but this is not out of their own pockets and is subject to the rules and procedures of the institution. In this section we cover the giving that is unconstrained by any institutional considerations, even though some of the money you get may appear through trusts, companies or other bodies.

Giving by individuals represents a huge and growing opportunity to every fundraiser – probably the only source of giving that is universally applicable to any voluntary organisation – and certainly the largest source of income to charities currently. CAF estimate that between £3,000 and £4,500 million is given each year by individuals to charities in Britain. Linked to this is the estimate that 80% of the adult population gives something – some 25 million people – and 65% give time through volunteering. This pool is certainly large enough to provide something for everyone, even at times of recession. Most people only give when asked. So the challenge of the fundraiser is to find people to ask, and to then get them to give generously and to continue to give over a period of years.

Not only are the public the most easily accessible group of prospective donors, they will generally give an almost instant response to an appeal.

3.4.2 Structure of giving

Fundraisers should be aware of the myriad of ways in which individuals make their contribution to the causes of their choice. From the donor's point of view any one of these might be how they do 'their bit' for the charity. From the fundraiser's standpoint however, there is likely to be a clear hierarchy of preferred ways of giving: for example, a catalogue purchase (carrying with it a low profit element for the charity) is likely to be very much less valuable than a covenant.

Research by the Charities Aid Foundation suggests that donors support charities as follows:

Door-to-door gifts	35%
Buying raffle tickets	31%
Sponsoring people	30%
Street collection gifts	30%
Church gifts	16%
Buying in jumble sale	15%
Buying in charity shop	12%
Attending charity events	10%
Buying by catalogue	9%
Giving by covenant	7%
Giving through advert	3%
Giving to appeal letter	2%
Giving via payroll	2%

3.4.3 Motivation

Each individual donor may have a number of reasons for giving which are personal to themselves. It is possible however to identify a number of common themes.

Direct personal experience is a significant reason behind many gifts. This may involve experiencing living with a member of the family suffering from cancer or with a handicapped child, or some other personal experience relevant to the cause.

This does not explain the interest in overseas charities where most people do not have any direct contact with the cause. Here, the motive will range from a religious or moral belief that the distribution of resources is simply unjust, through to those who respond to the image of a pitiful malnourished child on their television set. For some, especially those who sponsor overseas children, the motivation may be more to do with surrogate children either because they do not have their own family or because they have flown the nest.

Though it is said that there is a general preference for wide-eyed children and cuddly animals, the facts about where the money actually goes suggest other preferences. These are broadly:

Medicine and health	34%
General welfare	26%
International	18%
Preservation & environment	7%
Religious causes	6%
Animal welfare	5%
Youth	4%

Rather than be led by global figures for giving, every effort should be made to find out as much as possible about a potential donor's real interests where they are to be personally canvassed.

The attitudes of individuals to the role of charities are important too. A large majority believe in the importance of the welfare state, and so may have reservations about how much of the work being done by the voluntary sector is to plug the gaps in social and welfare provision. They do however believe that they have a personal responsibility to give to charity. There is also a strong feeling that there are too many charities all doing the same thing. There may also be a feeling that too much is spent on administration (often this is unjust) or that the money will simply not reach the charity (after reading the latest charity scandal to hit the headlines).

3.4.4 Getting started

It is not enough to decide you are going to raise money from individuals. You will have to do a great deal more thinking first. Read Section 2 in this book which sets out the general principles of fundraising, and then Section 4 which discusses many of the techniques for raising money.

Then decide which opportunities are most appropriate, what resources you have and how you can best deploy them.

3.4.5 Getting in touch

Creating the right message and directing it to the right person should elicit the desired response. So who then are the right people and what is the right message? The right people are those who fit the identikit picture you have constructed of a potential supporter for your charity, and whose motives indicate a propensity to give to your cause. Research will help identify such people and their characteristics. The right message is the one (there may be several) that builds on the motivation of the potential donor; starts from their understanding of the cause; takes account of their natural reservations; and comes in the right medium. Once the right people have been identified, their behaviour and habits will suggest what sorts of ways of talking to them are appropriate. For example, if senior business people are the targets, then local fundraising events or press advertising are unlikely to succeed; what is needed perhaps is to make personal presentations and to organise small receptions. This is discussed in greater detail in Section 5.14 on Marketing.

3.4.6 Four good ideas when fundraising from individuals

1. In approaching individuals, always try to identify clearly and precisely how much money is needed, and how their contribution can be an important part of this. It should not be an unattainable figure, and for your ongoing work it may be necessary to set an arbitrary target.

2. In couching the appeal, the need that you are addressing should be expressed in human terms with graphic images of the problem and how your work helps individuals. Try to avoid leading with abstract statistics describing the global importance of the problem unless it is to back up examples of individual need. It is said that:

    One hungry person **next door** to you **is equivalent to**
    One hundred hungry people in a **nearby** town is **equivalent to**
    Ten million hungry people in **Bangladesh!**

3. Be direct and ask for exactly what you want. Prospective donors will not know the size nor the nature of the contribution expected of them. You must tell them. And as with all good communication:

    • Tell them what you are going to tell them. Then...

    • Tell them. Then...

    • Tell them what you have told them.

4. Target your appeal as carefully as you can, by making your message as personal and relevant to the prospective donors as possible, and by excluding those people to whom this approach will not be relevant.

HOW DONORS RATE YOUR CAUSE

Helping children	3.7
Physical handicap	3.7
Sensory handicap	3.6
Elderly	3.6
Mental health	3.5
Hospitals etc	3.5
Medical research	3.5
Youth work	3.0
Housing	2.8
Animals	2.8
Overseas disasters	2.7
Environment	2.6
Training for employment	2.6
Education	2.6
Overseas development	2.3
Women's organisations	2.2
Religious organisations	2.2
Sport	2.1
Museums	2.0
Arts	1.9

This table is taken from the **Charity Household Survey**. It shows how people rate the various causes that they might be presented with. The greater the number, the higher the importance they give to that cause.

3.4.7 Techniques and skills

Chapters 4 and 5 give a fuller understanding of the techniques and skills required of an effective fundraiser. See in particular the following sections:

4.2 Direct mail	4.11 TV and radio appeals
4.16 Trading	4.1 Local fundraising
4.12 Giving at work	4.4 Capital and big gift campaigns
4.9 Schools	5.14 Marketing
4.10 Gambling	5.15 Public relations
4.6 Events	5.13 Market research
4.7 Committed giving	5.2 Working with volunteers
4.8 Membership	5.6 Saying thanks
4.5 Legacies	5.7 Using the phone

CAF's Charity Trends and the CAF Charity Household Survey give statistical information on the giving habits of individuals.

3.5 Giving by other institutions

Many people work and play in large groups and in the last decade some of these groups have played an influential role in supporting both local and national charities. These groups may have money, influence and the human resources to support you. And when they do back you, they can play a major role in the success of your charity.

3.5.1 Overview

There are many different organisations which are potential donors to your organisation. We are not able to list all the possible sources, but there are four main types: Trade Unions, membership bodies and local groups, and churches.

3.5.2 Types of organisation

Unless there are clearly suggested links between what you are doing and one of these bodies, this area of fundraising is not one of the greatest potential areas for fundraising. There are no clear statistics for the giving from any of these organisations as a whole. Although there are thousands of small trade unions and other groups, the potential for raising money is relatively small and identification of donors can be difficult except at a local level.

Trade Unions have a quite different basis for their giving. It is invariably an extension of their political stance and will be expressed by some campaign or sectional interest. For example, many unions contributed to the fight against apartheid by making donations to the voluntary organisations concerned with combating apartheid, in pursuance of resolutions at annual conferences. The structure of giving can be through a union HQ, the TUC itself, one of the local branches or from the membership at large. Giving can be in the form of gifts in kind, advertising in brochures or journals, appeals to the membership or cash grants. Unions have proved helpful in getting payroll giving off the ground in a number of workplaces. A good place to get started is by using personal contact at a local union branch.

Membership bodies such as the Women's Institutes, Young Farmers, Round Tables and Rotarians can be extremely valuable partners for your charity. Usually they don't make large grants themselves, but will encourage their membership to support a particular appeal. Each organisation has its own special characteristics and time taken in getting to know these will pay off. If you are not successful in attracting the attention or interest of the national headquarters then you may well be able to get the support of your local branches or get invited to speak at a function. Rotary Clubs, Round Tables, Inner Wheel, Soroptimists, Ladies Circles, Mothers Unions, Townswomen's Guilds, Scouts, Cubs, Guides, Brownies, sports clubs, dance schools, churches . . . . can all help. And many organisations have been able to develop significant support from these sources.

A wide range of church bodies give to charity. Many local congregations decide to allocate an annual collection to a particular cause – and it certainly does not need to be religious in nature. Groups within congregations often meet to explore particular themes and this will lead them, for example, to become interested in homelessness or poverty. On a higher level, churches have boards of social responsibility or their equivalent whose role is to support key areas of concern. And the Church Urban Fund, organised at a diocesan level, harnesses the interests of Church of England members in social action. Churches too have extensive networks that can be very supportive.

3.5.3 Getting started

1. Consider what support you are looking for. Is it money, or people's time, or access to a network of individuals, or facilities, or the influence to guide you towards particular organisations?
2. Review your own records for the evidence of past support from the organisations you plan to approach and from others in their and similar networks.
3. Check with your own committees and supporters to see if they are members of organisations who might be willing to help.
4. Draw up a short list of possible organisations who you believe have the resources or interest to support you.
5. Make contact locally or nationally.

3.5.4 Getting in touch

Getting in touch with any of these organisations is best carried out in as personal a way as possible. This will help allow for the very different approaches and interests of each, and will help you determine the opportunity, adjust your approach and identify the right person to talk to. In general an initial phone call will identify the best person to contact.

3.5.5 Three good ideas

1. Always plan a long time in advance. The bigger the request the longer you are likely to have to wait. For example, the National Federation of Women's Institutes plan their giving up to two years ahead.
2. Always take the trouble to research the organisation that you are approaching. Find out what their current interests are, how they give support and for what reasons. Most important, find out who the people that make the decisions are and make every effort to see them.
3. Take the trouble to get the local organisation on your side if you are going to approach a national body. Their endorsement can help.

3.5.6 References

In this book see:

And from elsewhere:

The Directory of Organisations, Yellow Pages, the local Volunteer Bureau, the local library...

4. TECHNIQUES

4.1 Local fundraising

Whether you are an established national charity or a small group just starting out, raising money through local events and collections can be an important and rewarding fundraising area.

4.1.1 Introduction

The vast majority of fundraising takes place across the country in hundreds of thousands of small interactions between volunteers working in a local branch of the charity or in a support group and members of the public. More people come into contact with charity this way than any other. In general, these occasions are fleeting affairs which leave little impression on the donor and convey nothing much about the cause. One of the challenges for fundraisers is to make more of these opportunities.

In this section we discuss some of the main types of event and focus on the management of this type of fundraising.

4.1.2 Management of local fundraising

Most organisations start as ad hoc groups raising the funds they need from amongst themselves and only later on from the public to cover their expenditure. As the organisation gets bigger and there is a need for more money, other small groups may be formed to raise more funds. At this stage the need for structure and management is born.

There are two main approaches: using volunteers and using staff. Some charities – those that have an established name in the main – find that they can work best by using paid employees concentrating on a small area of fundraising. The other approach is to build a group of volunteers who might undertake the same fundraising activities.

CONSTITUTION OF A LOCAL COMMITTEE

The following are some of the headings for the constitution of a local fundraising committee. These responsibilities are not to be taken lightly.

- The committee and the charity
- Support to be provided by the charity
- Responsibilities of committee members
- Name
- Location
- Bank account
- Objects of the committee
- Structure including: patronage

- election of officers
  responsibility of officers
- Meetings and operation
  quorum for meetings
  frequency of meetings
  voting
  resignations
  termination of memberships
  annual general meetings
- Remuneration of members
- Alteration of constitution

FORMING A FUNDRAISING GROUP

My brief was to form a fundraising group in a large British city. Where should I start? My usual system is to check my address book and contact my friends for their suggestions. This time I knew only one person in the area. It was a priest I had known for thirty years and I felt sure that he would set me off in the right direction. I actually made an appointment to see him as I knew he would not make excuses on the telephone! Normally I would 'pop in', as it is amazing how helpful people can be face to face on the doorstep or over a cup of coffee. There is time on the telephone to think of all sorts of reasons why they cannot think of anyone with free time.

This meeting produced a detailed social survey of the city and highlighted the extremes of poverty on one side of the road and affluence on the other, in a large and busy parish. It was a fascinating morning but I left knowing that anyone at a loose end would have been snapped up for the much needed social work of the parish.

I studied the map and decided to work first of all on a concentrated residential section.

I wrote to an MP I had met some 25 years ago. I wrote to the High Sheriff whom I had met at a function in the city. I wrote to a business man in my home town who is on various boards in the city. I had the Provost of the Cathedral to an extended lunch at home.

All communicated back most helpfully, but only one suggested any specific people to visit. I followed this up and it led me to a wives' group who I don't think wanted me to pounce on their people as they met for purely social reasons. However, through this contact I did call on one person who would be free to help in a couple of years. Too long to wait, alas! In driving around the lush and tree-lined roads I felt that there must be someone in there longing to help the cause.

At this very time I was invited to speak at a Rotary luncheon. Hopes were high. Unfortunately the meal was so delicious and the fellowship so great that my allocated time to speak about our charity was severely cut, so the actual one-to-one cultivation didn't happen (no-one 'offers' on these occasions!).

The break came in a totally unexpected way. I was arranging a visit to a city child-care project by a group I had formed in another town a few months earlier. I explained that I would send a map to show location of the project. "Don't worry" was the reply, "I was brought up in the city". This was the cue to act. "Do you know anyone at a loose end who could help me form a fundraising group in the city?" I inquired. I obtained the name of a relative and other members of the group within earshot provided me with another name.

I set off with new enthusiasm having ascertained that the first name would probably be in on a certain morning. I waited tactfully outside in the car for a while as it is not good to call too early or at meal times. I then knocked and although the lady had been rung by her relative I received a strict telling off for calling unannounced. I apologised and, grasping a diary, suggested that we might find half an hour for a chat sometime. "Half an hour" was the horrified reply! "Where have you come from?" I explained and said it was about 45 miles away. It must have sounded like the other side of the world as I was invited into the kitchen for coffee "as I was here". Immediately we got on like a house on fire. We might have known each other all our lives. How easily I could have fled at the first tirade! Names and suggestions flowed and an agreement that she was willing to be part of the new group in spite of numerous other commitments.

The next visit was quite alarming also. I was invited into the hall. "I was wondering if you know anyone who would be free to join a fundraising group?" I proffered. "Are you asking me – or asking me if I know anyone?" I kept my cool and said "Well, I was really asking you if you knew anyone but if you are able to help as well that would be wonderful!" Not only was she willing to help but she continued to rack her brain, and make suggestions. She rang people. She rang me. I visited most of the people she suggested. Some I just spoke to on the telephone. All agreed to help.

The most exciting introduction was to a very active person who had that very month given up work (although young!) She was an obvious candidate to take the chair. Soon we had twelve people and were able to have our first meeting over a kind invitation to lunch. This is always a highly charged occasion. Are people going to get on well together? Is anyone going to offer to be Secretary? There was only a tiny hint of any possible incompatibility. The three officers I appointed smartly after some undercover work beforehand. The democratic vote follows once they are established – at future AGMs!

The first function, which made £3,000, was fixed for a few months hence and all members worked well together and enjoyed themselves. Husbands proved a strong and background force to the all-female group. My initial request was to hold two functions a year, to use the Christmas catalogue and perhaps to distribute some collecting boxes. Flushed with the success of the launch, the next two events within the first 13 months raised £1,200 and £1,400 respectively. The future looks good.

Recruitment is the key to success. In the case of staff appointments you must consider what sort of people are going to be attracted to the hours and pay you are offering; and whether there are such people around. Anyone you take on should be carefully screened.

As far as recruitment of volunteers is concerned, screening is just as critical. You may need to find people to serve on small committees or support groups or you may be looking for just one person to take all the responsibility for a particular area of fundraising. In the latter case you will need to spend time identifying those people who can bring something to the job (use of their homes, contacts, ideas, initiative, etc). It can easily take up to a year to identify suitable people. For very local groups, you will have to depend much more on the group's own existing contacts, and as you organise events, you will find that more interest will develop in what you are doing and more people will be prepared to volunteer their time. At this stage good publicity in the local press or radio can bring further support. If you are part of a national organisation or network, ask for their mailing list for the area. These will be people who are already interested in what you are doing, so when you approach them you may find them prepared to give their support.

THE CHARACTERISTICS OF A GOOD FUNDRAISING LEADER

1. The leader must be an efficient and capable organiser.

2. Leaders must be able to plan an event in every detail.

3. Leaders must be able to communicate with their helpers. They should enjoy working with people and should be able to lead without causing offence.

4. A leader must be able to motivate others and inspire them with enthusiasm and zeal.

5. Leaders must be good judges of people. They must get to know the committee and helpers well and be able to recognise and use the talents and abilities of individual members of the group. They must also be able to understand each person's strengths and weaknesses in order to be able to direct and guide them in a way that they can accept and enjoy.

Source: **Complete Guide to Fundraising**, Sterrett.

One final aspect of the management of local groups needs to be highlighted: how they are constituted. There are a range of issues that will sooner or later arise in the life of a voluntary support group. Are they a separate group with their own constitution, or are they a branch of a main organisation? To whom does the money they raise belong? What can they say in public? And what role do they have in the determination of where their money is spent? There are many different ways in which local fundraising groups can be constituted and each has important legal consequences. One way of developing an effective relationship between the local fundraising group and the main organisation is to provide them with a constitution which sets out their purpose and operating structure. Model constitutions are available from NCVO.

Sometimes you may find that an individual or a group decides to raise money on your behalf. In certain circumstances you may feel that because of the nature of the individual or group or because of the fundraising method adopted, the good name of your charity will be at risk. A charity is able to apply to the Court to obtain an injunction to prevent unauthorised fundraising, having first served notice on the unauthorised fundraiser requesting that they cease the fundraising forthwith. This provision was introduced in the 1992 Charities Act.

4.1.3 Local fundraising activities

The value of creating voluntary support groups and locally based fundraising is the richness of different ideas that can be applied to generating funds for the organisation. There is little value in trying to explain in detail the hundreds of different fundraising ideas. However we list here a number that work well at a local level. *(Sponsored events and collections will be dealt with in more detail in Section 4.1.4 – 8.)*

Church or school fetes	Garden open days
Town or village carnivals	Heritage walks
Halloween parties	Treasure hunts
New Years Eve parties	Cycle rides
Firework parties	Sports events or tournaments
Picnics and outings	Tugs of war
Bread and cheese lunches	Fun runs
Dinner dances	Auctions
Discos	Craft fairs
Tea bars	Jumble sales
Coffee mornings	Bring and buy
Bridge and whist evenings	Sales of work
Bingo	Advertising calendars and diaries
Fashion shows	Valentines cards
Charity races	Car boot sales
Film premieres	Competitions
Concerts	Raffles and lotteries

4.1.4 Organising a sponsored event

For most fundraisers, sponsored events are the answer to their prayers. You can sponsor just about anything so long as it moves! It can be a good way to get the involvement of a core group of people by getting them to do something that they quite like, and to get a wider group of people to sponsor them.

Sponsored events rate as one of the most popular voluntary activities for the participants, as well as one of the most frequently used ways of raising money for charity.

The aim in setting up a sponsored event should be to find something sufficiently popular and trouble free, and something that you can build on and repeat year by year to achieve greater returns. The best sponsored events have been built on small beginnings, and now have the organised expertise and a band of loyal helpers to generate a substantial annual

SPONSORED EVENT CHECKLIST

1. Choose a good activity: one that people will want to do and is novel enough to warrant others sponsoring them.
2. Set a date and venue: make sure you give lots of warning to allow for preparation.
3. Get the relevant permission: from the police or the local authority.
4. Involve as many other organisations as possible: Rotary, scouts, guides etc.
5. Organise local publicity: get any celebrities and media signed on if possible.
6. Seek local commercial sponsorship: for costs and any prizes needed.
7. Produce sponsor forms: give examples of what amounts you expect and get good amounts first.
8. Prepare for the day: ensure you have all the stewards, equipment and information for the event.
9. Tidy up afterwards.
10. Thank all the participants.
11. Chase all uncollected pledges.

income. A sponsored event can also be used to get across an important message about your cause.

The first thing to do is to consider who you are likely to be able to attract. Younger people may be interested in disco marathons, but will not be interested in a sponsored knit. For older people, it would be the other way round. If your target audience is young families, can you think of something that will involve them all during the weekend? Walking, cycling and swimming are all popular, but only your imagination is the limit to what is possible. You can expect three types of person to join in: those people who have done so before and who know it will be a lot of fun; those people who, for whatever reason, are supporters and sympathisers of your cause; and those people who just enjoy the particular activity you have chosen (cycling, walking etc).

Most sponsored events of any size have a natural captive audience. That is, they are initially derived from the membership of a particular organisation. Thus the Nicaragua Solidarity campaign used its mailing list of members to promote its successful London to Oxford bike ride. Beyond this, a network of family and friends became involved, and over the years was responsible for the growth of the event. In the early days, posters and local radio will help spread the word widely; these should be targeted especially at institutions where you might expect sympathisers to live or work – schools, colleges, trade unions amongst others. Some people, especially parents of school age children, are heartily fed up with the events they are persuaded to support. Despite this, sponsored events do still succeed in generating worthwhile levels of funds.

Organisation takes place in three stages: in advance, including agreeing the route and getting any permission or insurance necessary, the promotion and preparation of the forms and other materials; organising volunteers to help on the day, to mark the routes and provide the required support; and afterwards when the money is collected. The work involved can be considerable, and so you must ensure that you have enough help to do it.

Before the event

Preparation of the forms requires a little thought. They must spell out exactly what is being done, but they also provide an opportunity to state why the money is needed. The key purpose is to provide the opportunity for sponsors to commit themselves to a generous amount of sponsorship. They need to know how many miles (or things) they are likely to be paying for. Is there a maximum for example? Most sponsors do not know what is expected, and are guided by what others have written before. Thus you should try to put some preferred amounts in the form of 1p, 2p, 5p, or 10p per mile. If you do it per kilometre, you may get more, so do think creatively about the units of sponsorship. Equally many people may prefer to give a direct contribution. The form should allow for this too. The form must provide you with all the information you need to collect this money later. So don't make the lines so short that sponsors' addresses are illegible!

On the day

On the day, you will need to have information at the start of the event to advise performers and public what the route is and the facilities are for refreshments and support. This provides a further opportunity to ram home a message about your work. You will need to have sufficient helpers to staff the various check-in procedures and to mark the route.

After the event

After the event, the key activity is to collect the money and to thank those who actually took part. Collecting the money is difficult. This must be the prime responsibility of those who got the sponsors in the first place. You should aim to keep a register of all those who were collecting sponsorship and this should include their phone numbers. Follow up letters may be needed too. Offering prizes for the highest sponsorship brought in can provide an incentive for people to collect their sponsorship money.

4.1.5 Organising a house to house collection

House to house collections are very popular with national and local charities as the main way of asking everyone in a given area to help. They present a great many opportunities to develop support, if collectors are well briefed.

First you will need to obtain a permit to collect from the District Council (or in London, the London Borough), unless your charity has already obtained a Charity Commission exemption. You will need to specify the date or time scale of the collection, the localities in which you intend to collect and the manner in which the collection will be conducted. A licence may be refused on several grounds including the possibility that it will cause inconvenience to the public, that it is on the same day or the day immediately before or after another collection, that the expense is too high or too little will be generated for the cause, or that the promoter has not acted properly in past collections. You only need a licence for a collection in a public place (which is a place to which members of the public have access) or when you are collecting in more than one location. A collection restricted to a private house, school office, public house or hospital would not require a licence. If you are organising a national collection (throughout the whole or a substantial part of England and Wales) then you can obtain an order from the Charity Commission authorising the collection. For details of the rules on collections in Scotland and Northern Ireland, consult the Scottish Council for Voluntary Organisations or the Northern Ireland Council for Voluntary Action. The detailed requirements for conducting a collection are set out in the regulations attached to the 1992 Charities Act. These cover such things as who can collect money and how the collection has to be run.

Before even applying for a permit, you should plan how you will run the collection. Local knowledge should help you decide which sorts of houses are likely to be responsive to your appeals. Consideration should

1. Check dates: holders of Home Office permits have set dates for their collections. Avoid these.
2. Seek authorisation: from police or local authority or the land owner.
3. Identify areas or locations for collections. Go for middle class housing or busy shopping streets.
4. Recruit volunteers: use past lists or use friends of friends to find more.
5. Prepare materials: include collecting devices, leaflets and flags.
6. Brief volunteers: either collect them together or prepare written materials to indicate times, places, procedures, etc.
7. Organise money systems: collect money in person, or arrange bank systems to ensure money is accounted for.
8. Thank volunteers.
9. Record money, reference to locations and numbers of volunteers for next time.
10. Bank all proceeds.

be given to the affluence of the people who live there and the length of the approach to each house. For larger collections you may want to collect everywhere.

An important factor is the group of volunteers that you have. Typically you may want one volunteer to take responsibility for one street, either their own street or one nearby. Volunteers can be recruited on a networking basis or, as in the case of an increasing number of charities now, by telephoning them. If they can be trained, they should be. For example, they can be told when to call, what to say, what difficult questions to expect, and so on. You may be able to do this by arranging a meeting, by briefing people personally, or by preparing a pack containing all the necessary information.

Their main function will be to deliver an envelope on which there is some message, possibly with an accompanying brochure or letter from the charity. After a short interval of days, the collector should return to collect the envelopes. At this point they will encounter responses ranging from ignorance to enthusiasm. There will be those who decline to help you and those who choose to be abusive. Most people will be polite. Some will be interested in what you are doing. This is an ideal opportunity to recruit a new member or volunteer, to give more information or to sign them up for a covenant. Equally for those who just return their envelope, make a note of their address. You have identified a new donor and you will therefore want to keep in touch.

Some people will offer a range of reasons or excuses in justification of why they will not give. In most cases these are people who find it hard to be seen not to give without a clear reason; if you stay to demolish their argument you will find another argument springing up hydra like in its place. In the meantime, you may be missing other supporters elsewhere in the street.

The returns should be handed in at one central point and opened under the supervision of two people. A local bank may agree to help with this. You should also try to keep track of how much money is coming from each area for future reference.

There is always the possibility of fraud being perpetrated on your charity by someone carrying out an unauthorised collection in your name. All collectors should therefore have a permit from you to collect. If you receive any reports of unauthorised collecting, you should investigate this as fast as you can, as any bad publicity will damage your organisation and the voluntary sector as a whole. And under the 1992 Charities Act you now have the power to prevent unauthorised collections by seeking an injunction from the courts.

4.1.6 Organising a street collection

Running a street collection is in some ways more difficult than a house to house collection. The differences lie in the fact that volunteers find it a less agreeable way of spending their time and you, the organiser, have to provide enough collectors to cover the population.

You will need a licence. As for a house to house collection (see Section 4.1.5), apply to your local district council. Give plenty of warning, as others may have laid prior claim to important collection dates and sites. If you have an annual flag day or collection week, you will need to apply each year.

You will need plenty of volunteers to carry out the collection. The choice of location is important to ensure that collectors have access to the maximum numbers of people. The high street or shopping centres are usually best, though collecting at well populated events may also work well. Draw up a rota for each collection point which uses people for an hour or two. They can then link this with a visit to shops and pubs in the area.

To make the most of your location you need to train collectors to be a little assertive. Although collectors are not allowed to solicit on the streets, they should not shrink back from passers-by. The collector who is prepared to vigorously rattle the tin, who is prepared to look people in the eye, and who is prepared to station themselves in the middle of the thoroughfare will do very much better. Street collection requires a positive attitude.

Equipment is an important consideration. You will need a sealed collection device that is convenient to carry, convenient for the public to put money into, and easy to get the money out of again after the collection. The main choice is whether to go for a more expensive box that can be reused, or whether to use a cheaper disposable box. This will depend on your future plans. A number of commercial suppliers, including Angal Products, now provide a range of fundraising devices which can be personalised with your charity's name and logo.

VICTIMS OF KHOMEINI REGIME

REFUGEE FAMILIES AND CHILDREN NEED YOUR HELP TO SURVIVE

The problem of Iranian refugees has caused serious and growing concern. Facing hunger, homelessness and illness, the lives of these destitute refugees are under grave danger. This is why your **support** is needed to save lives of thousands of innocent families and children who have fled the oppressive conditions created by the Khomeini regime.

IRAN AID

Charity Registration No. 326460

This is the leaflet that is used by **Iran Aid** to canvass support on the streets of Britain. Exiled Iranians approach people on the street and explain what has happened to their own families and what the fate of the many refugees in Pakistan is. They then invite you to sponsor a refugee family for food and water by the day. The price given for a day is around £15, and the sponsor form will often have sponsorship of up to £100. Unlike sponsorship, you are then asked to make a cheque payable straight away. The combination of fundraisers who speak with clear personal involvement and commitment and the very specific amounts asked for, make this a powerful way of fundraising.

4.1.7 Static collections

Static collection devices can provide a regular source of income for any charity, but considerable care needs to be taken.

Locations for static devices can range from pubs to motorway service stations – in fact anywhere where people are paying for things. They must be on private property, although the street outside a shop may well be satisfactory. There are two types. First those that appeal to children; these need to be visually appealing and have some sort of moving part that is operated when the money is inserted. For example, the RNLI box which launches a lifeboat. Adult boxes on the other hand need to be functional and have a good design or label, which clearly expresses the cause or need.

Finding locations for static boxes can be the work of a persuasive volunteer. However the challenge is to arrange for the money to come back reliably. One approach is to make the box the responsibility of the proprietors of the establishment, for example in a pub. In this case it is the responsibility of this person to send in a cheque when the box is full. This will be inappropriate in places such as shops, where the turnover of staff is high. In such places, volunteers should arrange to make regular collections or keep in touch by telephone.

If boxes are not looked after regularly they will be vandalised or stolen. Larger devices should be chained so that they cannot be removed by over enthusiastic supporters! It is always worth checking up regularly on the devices to see how they are displayed, and taking the opportunity to chat to the shopkeeper and enthuse them about your cause.

4.1.8 Mass collection schemes

A local collection scheme which has been tremendously successful in the past, but whose results have declined in the last decade, is the cascade or penny-a-day collection. This is based on the chain letter principle. The collector is recruited to collect from ten people in their locality; the collector remits their money to a further coordinator who collects from ten collectors and so on. Recruiting collectors or donors can be done by teams of recruiters or by charging the collectors with the task. In return for a contribution of maybe 50 pence each month, donors are given a basic newsletter.

4.1.9 The future

Two things will effect the durability of collections and other local fundraising schemes. These are demographic and competitive factors.

In the 1990s there will be an increasing number of older people in society, and it might reasonably be expected that they will have time on their hands to contribute to local charitable and fundraising efforts. This will provide a greater pool of volunteers for charities in future, and those organisations that are geared up for this will benefit enormously.

Equally, as more and more national charities extend their fundraising through local schemes, some sort of donor resistance may develop, thus there will be increasing benefits to those who get in first and organise themselves professionally.

4.1.10 Spin off

The great strength of locally based fundraising schemes is that over time they can cover very large sections of the public. Not only does this have advantages in fundraising terms, it can also have a great educational or publicity impact. Imagine the impact of a national AIDS campaign that contacted every household, not just to raise money but also to provide information. You could provide information on the disease, gain publicity for the organisation concerned and of course raise funds. Equally important is the converse, where sloppy volunteer work which is replicated across the land will quickly bring an organisation into disrepute.

4.1.11 Skills and resources

The key resource for this area of work is to have a supply of well trained, enthusiastic volunteers to extend the work well beyond what would be possible for paid staff.

To this should be added good organising skills to mobilise the people, to run a good scheme and to operate across a large area.

4.1.12 References

In this book refer to:

- 3.4   Giving by individuals
- 5.2   Working with volunteers
- 5.7   Use of the phone
- 5.9   Recruitment, training and secondment

Other resources:

For equipment consider Angal Products

Raising Money Locally, leaflet from DSC, Organising an Event, leaflet from DSC

The Complete Guide to Fundraising, Sterrett

Fundraising A to Z, Kirkfield

ICFM guidelines on collections

Starting and Running a Voluntary Group, NCVO

4.2 Direct mail

The mail provides one of the most flexible and powerful tools in fundraising. With an appropriate and continuing level of investment in your supporters, a direct mail programme can provide both regular and quick income. The key though is investment. Unless you already have an active and enthusiastic list of supporters, you will have to spend time, effort and money to build this up. So direct mail should not be seen as a source of immediate income.

4.2.1 Introduction

The essential feature of this medium is the ability to direct a personalised message to chosen target audiences quickly and relatively cheaply. It demands the use of a list, a 'communication package' and a system for dealing with the response. The main areas in which direct mail is of value to the fundraiser are firstly in 'cold' mailings to people with whom you have had no previous contact, then in 'reciprocal' mailings where you swap your member list with that of another organisation and use their list to recruit new members for your organisation; and finally in 'warm' mailings to your existing members and supporters. The skills and techniques that are used will be of much wider relevance and, for example, will be useful when producing literature, writing to members of parliament, your own volunteers or any other group for reasons that may have little directly to do with fundraising.

SIX WAYS TO PERSONALISE YOUR MAILINGS

1. Get a computer or volunteers to handwrite or personalise the salutation "Dear Mrs Smith".
2. Type the address onto the envelope. Use an ordinary postage stamp on the envelope.
3. Make handwritten notes or underline parts of your letter even if they are then going to be printed!
4. Make sure that the response form has the donor's name on it.
5. Use a reply envelope that is handwritten and has the sender's name on it.
6. Handwrite the whole of your appeal letter.

Your message to your potential donor must appear to be a personal letter from you to them. Though it is not easy to address 2,000 or 200,000 people in a personal way, these are some ideas that may help. As soon as your letter is seen to be a stereotyped message recipients will feel quite at liberty to discard it.

4.2.2 Donor mailings

Sending letters to your own donors can be the most profitable way of raising money. Though not everyone can expect to raise £1 million by mailing 80,000 people, it has been done. The principle is to get these elements right:

> THE AUDIENCE
> THE MESSAGE
> THE TIMING

The high response that you can get from donor or warm mailings is the main reason for collecting the names and addresses of donors in the first place. When you include the longer term benefit of covenanted donations and membership subscriptions, you may expect to raise up to £10 for each £1 spent. Writing to your own supporters demands a number of special requirements. These are the people on whom to a greater or lesser extent your organisation depends for its success. You are therefore communicating with one of your most important audiences. Get the message right and you will succeed in raising money; get it wrong and you risk poisoning this particular well for a period.

There are varying views about how often you can afford to write to your own donors; some still feel that twice a year is an invasion of privacy, while other organisations are in touch at least once a month (especially when all types of mailings are included). Trustees often take a very conservative view of this and effectively prevent further growth; a test is sometimes the only way to prove the point that more mailings are valuable. If you find it cost-effective to mail more frequently, then do so.

A SAMPLE MAILING PLAN FOR A YEAR

Donor Group	Feb	April	June	Aug	Oct	Dec
Covenantors			R			A
Standing orders			R			A
Recent major donors	A	A	R	A	A	A
Recent donors	A	A	A	A	A	A
Old donors			A			A
Enquirers			A			A`

An example of how a small charity might structure its mailing programme, taking into account the need to appeal more often to good but uncommitted donors, to report back to major donors with an annual report, and to appeal rather less frequently to enquirers or lapsed donors. Each of the segments in the plan will demand a different package even if appeals are going out at the same time.

A - appeal sent out
R - annual report sent out

If not, then don't. You need to develop a programme; and you need to have a good idea of the mailings that will follow when you are planning the next one.

Most organisations will be using direct mail to seek money directly. There are a number of variations on this theme that can be profitable, help vary the approach, and make any high frequency mailing programme less repetitive. Inviting existing donors to make a covenant is often extremely effective, even though the response rates will be much smaller than for a single donation. Asking donors to organise an event or participate in a local collection can help get new things going locally. The majority of Oxfam shops started with an appeal for volunteers in the locality. Suggesting to existing donors that they make out a legacy to your organisation, will obviously not produce cash now although you can give them an extra option of making a donation as well or instead. But most of the time you will want to be asking donors to give immediately.

There are great attractions to using mail as a medium for communicating with your supporters. Perhaps the most important advantage of the medium is its ability to help you target particular groups of supporters. Depending on the sophistication of your mailing list, you will be able to subdivide it into different segments, separating out your covenantors from people living in Wales and from those who have given large gifts, for example. This gives you the power to address a different message to each group. Indeed, there is a great danger in ignoring the information that you have. If, for example, you appeal to everybody on your donor list for a donation, you might well expect criticism from your existing covenantors who are already giving regularly. Surely you knew this, they will ask. The best way of dealing with the infinity of possibilities is to have a general message and produce a series of variations – probably only needing to change a paragraph of the letter – to suit the group chosen.

Typical components of a warm mailing to your existing supporters can vary widely. A well used model consists of five parts:

- **An outer envelope:** with a window to carry a name and address on the reply device. This can be overprinted with some teaser copy to encourage recipients at least to open the letter.

- **A letter:** which should be regarded as the main communication, and which should be written as interestingly and personally as possible (see also Section 5.4).

- **A coupon:** or some reply device which summarises what the appeal is, gives examples of expected donation levels, carries any codes and donor identity so that you can keep track of the response. This is what the donor returns with the contribution.

- **A reply envelope:** which can be extremely helpful in securing a gift and helps get over the undoubted inertia of the donor. Use Freepost if you can. Making it simple for the donor to reply will increase the response considerably.

- **A brochure or leaflet:** which helps provide illustrations of the need which has been highlighted in the letter. This is not always necessary

IMPROVING YOUR APPEAL RESPONSE

1. Try personalising your communication.
2. Mail a separate appeal to large or regular supporters recognising their giving and asking for an appropriate response.
3. Review your letter and introduce more human examples.
4. Try putting in a pictorial leaflet. If you already do try omitting it.
5. Ask for specific amounts which will achieve particular things: "£5.65 will buy a new syringe", for example, and mention this in both the letter and response device.
6. Put a stamp on return envelopes. No one likes to waste a stamp.

Here are six ways in which you could increase your response rates or average donation values. Before committing yourself to any of these you should attempt to test the idea first.

but can be helpful in building a clearer picture for the donor of what you are writing about.

Another advantage of this form of appeal is that you can make it as long as you like. There are several schools of thought about how long a letter ought to be; there is little doubt however that even the skimpiest mailing package can include a great deal more information than an expensive advertisement in the newspaper. Beware though of producing mailing packages that are too full of words. There is a great danger that they will go unread.

The power of the medium comes not only from the ability to target your message precisely, but also from the possibility to send the same message to very large numbers of people, which provides an economy of scale. As with all so called economies of scale, there are some dangers. The whole idea is to make the medium personal; the ideal is to be able to write a letter by hand to a friend. As the numbers on your list get larger then the opportunities for making it personal get smaller. The cost, for example, of producing a handwritten greeting on 5,000 letters or even 500, becomes very great and it is much easier to print "Dear friend" for every one. This depersonalization will inevitably have an impact on your returns.

Response rates on warm mailings can vary enormously: from as low as 7 or 8%, while some parts of a donor list might produce 30% or more.

REDUCING YOUR MAILING COSTS

Discounts available from the Post Office are as follows:

mailsort 1	on sorted post	on residue
delivered within 1 day	13%	0%
mailsort 2		
delivered within 3 days	13%	8%
mailsort 3		
delivered within 7 days		15%
under 250,000 letters	25%	
under 1 million letters	28%	
over 1 million letters	32%	

Mailings that are delivered in postcode sequence to the post office will qualify for a discount on the postage. Some will be sorted 'direct' while postcodes with only small numbers in them have to go into a 'residue' and qualify for a smaller discount. Full details of the scheme are available from the **Post Office**.

4.2.3 Cold mailings

It's all very well to dream about the returns you could get if only you had 10,000 supporters on a computer mailing list. Somehow these people need to be identified and won over to your cause. One of the main ways voluntary organisations do this is through the use of cold mailings. 'Cold' because the person in receipt of your letter has not demonstrated any warmth to your cause before.

The practice then, is to create a mailing list from directories or to rent lists from someone who specialises in this; to put these lists together with any other promising lists you can obtain, and then to mail an appeal package as before.

The difference between the two activities lies in the cost and the message. Because the people you are contacting are not your existing supporters, you can expect a rather poor response from them. Thus to get the same amount of money you may have to mail to ten times as many cold names at ten times the expense. Additionally, the cost of the mailing is increased by the cost of renting the list. This often forces mailers to look for a cheap way of circularising the large numbers necessary to get a response of any size.

> ### ISSUES IN COLD MAILINGS
>
> 1. Whether to do it at all. There is a vocal group of the public which regards the trade in mailing lists as nothing short of sin. These people will contact you from time to time and complain in the most vocal way. Be prepared with your response.
> 2. Waste is created by the extremely low response rates. If 1% of people respond to you then 99% throw all that paper away. At a time of concern about green issues this may appear wasteful to many. Using recycled paper may help, despite its greater cost; targeting your lists better will help all round; and suggesting it is given to a friend may also be useful.
> 3. Whether you have the capacity to invest in this form of fundraising which may require a large expenditure commitment, a significant degree of risk and a payback period of several years.

Because most of the recipients of a cold mailing will not know much about you, your message needs to have a slightly different approach. The degree of understanding of the issue will be that much lower, and this may demand a rather more simplistic approach to describing your cause and what it means. It also means that they will not know your particular organisation, and so they will need some reassurance about the value of your work. This might take the form of providing endorsements from well-known people; or you might present the answers to frequently asked questions, like the amount spent on administration; or you might highlight your achievements and successes. Not all of the people on the list will be new. Some may be duplicates of people who are already your supporters. If you can't find a way of removing these duplicates, this can create sticky situations when you find you have sent what is perceived as an inappropriate message to your own chair or other key supporters.

Though cold mailing response rates may rise to 4 or 5% in special situations, usually 0.5 to 1.5% is the likely range. Since it costs at least 30-40p to send each letter, without the benefit of a few high value responses, cold mailings rarely pay for themselves. Why do it then? Simply to get those new supporters to keep your donor list alive. You are balancing the cost of acquisition against the likely lifetime value to you of those who respond. If half the donors continue to support you at an average of £30 per year for five years, this is a valuable asset. And some may go on to leave a legacy. You have to calculate the cost of donor acquisition with the expected lifetime value to determine what is a reasonable donor acquisition cost.

When starting from scratch, a programme of direct mail can be extremely expensive in the short term. Depending on the sort of response rates you get, you may find that the programme only begins to generate any profit after two or three years. However, at that point, the profits should gradually build up, given regular investments into the programme. Local appeals may have a significant edge here. It may be easier to find suitable local lists, and the local connection can generate additional interest in the work. The question here is how to develop this medium cost-effectively without access to expensive professional advice and design work.

4.2.4 Reciprocal mailings

The problem of low response rates to cold mailings has been overcome by an approach used commonly in US for years – reciprocal mailings. The idea is that your best potential donors are people who have recently given to you; the next best are those giving to similar organisations. These people are likely to have an interest in your cause and are known to respond to direct mail appeals. And vice versa. The theory is that if you mail to the supporters of the nearest similar charity and they do the same to yours, you both gain. And that's how it usually turns out in practice. Typically response rates of from 2.5 to 10% can be expected.

The way to carry out such activities is helpfully described in the ICFM guidelines which ensure good practice and protection for your supporters. (See Appendix 6.4.) The best results will be obtained by choosing to swap lists with organisations that are closest to your own, even though they may be your competitors. Before you do, make sure that your organisation backs you in doing this. Most organisations will want to devise a simple policy to safeguard the interests of themselves and their donors.

> **ISSUES IN RECIPROCALS**
>
> 1. The first issue relates to the ethics of the idea itself. For most, the objection is to letting names of supporters out of your hands. The recommended way of doing this ensures that you keep firm control of your own supporters' names. However, you will have to argue it out with your trustees (who will usually take a cautious view).
> 2. If you do decide to do it, do you come clean with supporters and tell them what you are doing or do you keep it quiet? The Data Protection Act dictates that you must register yourself if you plan to do this. But you might wish to insist that any mailing from a reciprocal organisation to your supporters carries a slip or message to the effect that they are being mailed as a supporter of yours.

4.2.5 Management

The management of your mailings and the maintenance of your donor list is of great importance. The first thing to look at is the way you intend to communicate with your supporters. This should be planned a year or 18 months ahead. You should segment the list into different groups depending on when they became a supporter, how much and how they gave, and other relevant characteristics. Since each group will be receiving rather different messages from you, it is important to plan the overall mix of these. For example, what are you going to say to your regular supporters (covenanted, standing order and payroll deduction)? Are they to be taken for granted and not written to? Or thanked and otherwise left alone? Or treated just like any other supporter? The illustrated mailing plan on page 75 gives an idea as to how different groups might be treated. It also indicates some of the themes that might be chosen to give a balanced view of the organisation's work.

Another task of the manager is to ensure that the mailings are producing the expected results and coming within budget. Control can be exercised in a number of ways, which are not mutually exclusive. First, costs must be monitored through the normal process of budgeting. You should get competitive quotes for all items of expenditure and your suppliers should keep within this. Costs will normally be referred to as per thousand mailed for comparison purposes.

DEALING WITH COMPLAINTS

1. Complaints are often due to duplicated mailings being received: de-duplicate your mailings.
2. Some people hate getting unsolicited mail and will tell you so. Use lists that have been run against the DMPS list and tell the recipient to join the Direct Mail Preference Service.
3. Your own supporters will complain of the waste of money involved in mailings. This is an inherent part of the process. If they think they can raise money more effectively, invite them to do so.

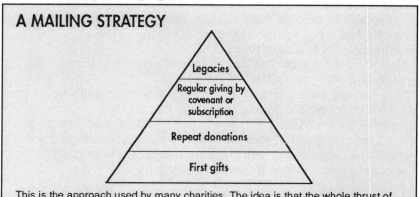

A MAILING STRATEGY

Legacies

Regular giving by covenant or subscription

Repeat donations

First gifts

This is the approach used by many charities. The idea is that the whole thrust of appeals should be to move individual supporters up through the pyramid. Getting the first gift may be done on a continuous basis with cold mailing, advertising or other mass appeals. Regular appeals thereafter should aim to upgrade supporters to the next level of the pyramid.

Income can be best estimated by breaking down the results achieved on the last comparable occasion for each segment of the mailing list. Though costs will inexorably rise with inflation, there can be no such certainty on the income side. Every extra penny given has to be worked and planned for carefully. Useful measures of income are firstly the response rate (how many people from every hundred mailed respond). Response rates will vary from around 30% for the very best segments of your list to around 5% for the worst. Response rate is not everything: the other key component is how much each person gives (the average donation). A further measure which is the combination of these two is the yield (the money received per hundred mailed). It is usually better to focus on both – response rates and average donations – as you can do different things to improve each.

Improving response rates is part science and part judgement. The science is in the appropriate application of testing to your mailings. You can test almost any aspect of what you send and hope to be able to tell with a fair degree of certainty whether it can be bettered. You do this by sending a slightly different message to a small sample of the total that you are mailing, and then comparing the results. Test your letter, your message, how you personalise it, and test one group against another. Whatever you do, test just one thing at a time and ensure the group is large enough to give a good result. Testing is the way you learn from experience and improve your performance over time.

4.2.6 Using agencies

Another aspect of the management of your mailing programme is the way you use outsiders to help you. There are a number of types of agency who can help.

For the hard pressed, a direct marketing agency will carry out all the necessary functions for a fee. This has the advantage of getting the work off your desk, but against that it can be expensive in both time and money. The introduction of outsiders to your organisation inevitably involves a learning process that takes time.

Designers and copywriters are available freelance and can be used in conjunction with yourself or with other agencies.

Your mailing can involve a great deal of work sorting out which letters go to which people and putting everything into the right envelope within a reasonable time. Mailing houses will perform these functions at a much greater speed than you are likely to be able to manage, unless your mailing is quite small. An advantage of using a mailing house is that they can help you claim a postal discount for bulk mailings.

4.2.7 Getting the message right

Like any other printed communication, getting the message right is at least half the battle (the other half being sending it to the right people at the right time). For a mailing however there are a number of important components.

The proposition

Each mailing should have a central proposition. This might be "£21.60 can help a child in distress" or "urgent action is needed to save the rainforests of Brazil". This should be the visual and verbal theme throughout the mailing pack. This is not only essential for the recipient to help them get a clear message, but is also extremely helpful in creating the package itself.

Making the ask

The creative feel of the mailing must be subservient to the essential purpose of the letter which is to get someone to help you. It is often assumed that the recipient will know what you want. A good letter will repeat the request for help up to six or seven times. Then there can be no mistaking what you are really wanting from the reader.

Length

There is no rule about this. Eight-page letters can be great, and one-pagers lousy – or the other way round. The more important thing is to say what you want and to say it effectively. So you need to focus on quality rather than length. See Section 5.4 for more suggestions.

4.2.8 Lists

The market for lists is served by list brokers who keep details of what is available and have much the same commission system as an advertising agency. The choice of lists is usually left to a hunch or past experience. In order to identify good lists it is necessary to test them on a small quantity first as it is not usually clear whether people who subscribe to a magazine or buy a particular product through the mail, will want to support your charity in sufficient quantity to justify mailing them. Other ways to identify good lists in advance, are to find out whether the list is already mail order responsive; whether there are a high percentage of people on your own list of donors who are also on this list; and whether they seem to be the same sort of people as your typical donor.

Before you purchase or rent a new list, you should check a few things before deciding whether these people are more likely than the average to support you. Has this list been used recently? How old is it, and has it been updated? You do not want to be sending letters to out of date addresses. The other thing to check is whether it has been run against the Direct Mail Preference Service list recently, to remove all those people who have asked not to receive direct mail letters.

EVALUATING MAILING LISTS

Eleven questions to ask before you buy a mailing list:

1. Are the people your supporters or someone else's? If so, could you get them to endorse your appeal?
2. Are they mail order responsive? If this is a list of mail order buyers or postal donors they will be more used to responding in the post.
3. Is this a compiled list or a list of someone's customers/supporters? Compiled lists do not respond as well.
4. Are the people on the list similar to your own donors; by age, gender and attitude?
5. How up-to-date is the list and when was it last updated? Don't buy names of people who are no longer there.
6. Is there a name and a home address for each person?
7. Are these people buyers/donors or just enquirers?
8. Have these people bought or given recently? Can you take only the recent ones?
9. Is there any information on frequency of activity? The more frequent the better.
10. When was this list last mailed? The more recently the better.
11. What was the amount of money on average that was given/paid? Are these people likely to be able to give what you need?

Getting the right mailing lists is essential when you are trying to find new supporters. The difference between getting a good mailing list and a poor one may be as much as five times. Taken from Drayton Bird's **Commonsense Direct Marketing**.

Your own list

The most valuable resource you have is your own list of donors or supporters. Guard it carefully. You need to manage this resource in a number of different ways. For example, just like with a cold list you need to keep it up to date by removing all inactive or deceased supporters, and by the same token adding all new ones. The sooner you can do this the sooner these people will be able to receive further appeals.

Periodically you should review whether you are holding the names of people who are no longer active donors. One way of determining this is to segment the older parts of your list in one mailing. Look at the results. Where the yield is below that of a cold mailing you should consider dropping or archiving them.

If your list is held on a computer, how safe is it? Have you got a security copy of your file held somewhere else for safety's sake? You should produce regular back up copies of your files. If you lose it, you may never be able to recreate it without a massive investment of time and money.

4.2.9 Getting started

To get started with a mailing programme several elements will need to be in place: access to lists; the ability to write and design mail shots and to get the material printed; a mailing house; a plan; the money to invest; a budget; and a response system.

Access to lists is easily obtained through a list broker or direct marketing agency.

The ability to produce mail shots that work is something that lends itself to very professional help. This is dealt with in Section 5.1. If you don't have the facilities in-house to produce quality mailshots, then you might consider using freelance writers or designers or using a specialist direct marketing agency all of whom advertise in the trade press. Since you are spending a great deal on production of the material and on postage, it pays to send the best message you can – even if this costs money in professional fees.

Printers are not difficult to find. However with direct mail work you should pay particular attention to details like folding, delivery and paper qualities, all of which are important to mailing houses and can incur extra costs if you get it wrong.

You can send out your own mailings, but as the volumes get larger it will become attractive to use a mailing house. They can take a computer tape or a list of labels and, with the other ingredients, ensure that the mailing is put together and sent out when you want it.

Finally you need to be geared up to deal with the considerable numbers of people who will respond to you. This will involve a clear response strategy: producing the form letters for the different responses you will be making; responding quickly, hopefully in less than a week; and having the appropriate means to send a personalised reply.

4.2.10 References

From this book:
- 2.5 The donor
- 3.4 Giving by individuals
- 4.7 Committed giving
- 4.8 Membership
- 4.5 Legacies
- 5.16 Using computers
- 5.4 Producing effective materials
- 5.8 Involvement
- 5.11 Testing, evaluation and control

And from elsewhere:
- Advertising by Charities, DSC
- Royal Mail Guide to Mailsort
- Commonsense Direct Marketing, Drayton Bird
- Direct Mail Handbook, Exley

4.3 Sponsorship

Sponsorship is a way of harnessing your own financial needs with the opportunities to provide benefit for others, and particularly for companies. A great deal of what we now recognise as good voluntary sector work (from the opera to major fundraising events) is sponsored and would not be possible without this important source of funding.

4.3.1 Definition

Sponsorship needs to be carefully defined. We are not talking about sponsoring someone to lose weight or run a mile (see Section 4.1 for that); nor is it a jargon word simply meaning a gift from a company. What is meant by sponsorship in this context – and it is a useful distinction – is a partnership between two parties with quite different interests who come together in order to support a particular activity. The charity hopes to be able to raise funds, or to carry on a service that otherwise it might not be able to do; the company hopes to get its name across in a certain ambience or to promote its products and thus to reach its potential customers. The sponsor's contribution does not need to be money, though usually it is. It could also be gifts of goods (such as a car), or services (such as transport), or staff time, or staff fundraising, or the use of buildings, and so on.

4.3.2 The sponsors

Most sponsors are commercial companies. This includes those state industries that remain, but it is unlikely to include any central government department although local government and development organisations sponsor local events. There are three main opportunities for sponsorship.

Firstly there are those organisations that are anxious to promote themselves, to create a better image of themselves or to generate an awareness in the local communities where they operate. They are likely to be active in the sponsorship field. This could include those companies sometimes associated with the destruction of the environment and those companies which have determined that they want to project a clean image for positive reasons. This can be at both a local and a national level.

The next group are those who have a particular product or service to introduce or promote. In the first phases of product promotion public awareness is especially important if a product is to be rapidly accepted. It is therefore easy to see why companies might be open to proposals that give a particular product or service more exposure.

The final group, who should never be left out of any sponsorship proposal, are those companies who have been committed supporters of yours in the past. They often will not be able to sponsor you themselves, but might feel offended if they are not approached.

4.3.3 What can be sponsored

The beauty of sponsorship is the wide range of things that are in fact able to be sponsored. The limitations are the things you really don't want to

BRITISH TELECOM AND ITS SPONSORSHIP PROGRAMME

BT's non-commercial sponsorship programme is designed to demonstrate our commitment to improving the quality of life in communities throughout the country. The policy is to concentrate on the arts and the environment.

For the arts, the programme sponsors touring companies rather than major events in central London. Our support of the regional tours of the Royal Philharmonic Orchestra and the Royal Shakespeare Company enables their performances to be seen in more than 30 venues country wide – many of which would normally not have the opportunity to stage live performances.

Local events are also supported, many of which have attracted nationwide, and in some cases international, interest. One such project is the Lake District summer music festival in Ambleside, which combines children's workshops, concerts and master classes, and allows top flight musicians to work alongside talented amateurs.

Young people particularly are targeted. We support Artswork, to encourage children to take part in a wide range of creative activity. In the area of fine art, the BT New Contemporaries exhibition takes art school graduate work to the ICA and provincial galleries.

For the environment, the programme includes the sponsorship of National Environment Week and the Community Pride Awards scheme, both of which are organised by the Civic Trust. BT is working with Friends of the Earth on a recycling city initiative, which began in Sheffield and is rolling out to other cities across the UK.

A joint venture with East Anglia police forces, the Square Mile project, encourages teams of children to help clean a square mile of their environment. This project is now rolling out to other parts of the UK. Young people's involvement in other environmental activities is encouraged by the BT Young Environmentalists competition, and the Living Rivers scheme which aims to improve the condition of our rivers.

BT's own activities are monitored by environmental audit teams to ensure that our everyday operations are as environmentally friendly as possible.

An example of a well developed sponsorship policy from one of the UK's major corporate donors, **BT**.

do; those things that confer no benefit to a sponsor; and those that have to be done discreetly.

The most popular things to sponsor include projects, events, books, fundraising materials, leaflets and posters, hardware such as cars or computers, sports and theatrical events, competitions, and many more.

A good example of how sponsorship of a charity's programme can help a company, is the link up between Heineken (which refreshes the parts that other beers cannot reach) and the British Trust for Conservation Volunteers. BTCV were busy rechalking the Cerne Abbas giant – that anatomically explicit chalk figure in Dorset. The link is reputed to have produced outstanding press and TV coverage for BTCV whilst also reinforcing the company's advertising slogan. (See the illustration on page 51).

A trip to the headquarters of the Worldwide Fund for Nature will almost certainly reveal some staff cars in the car park which carrying the line "This car is sponsored by Fiat".

Similarly, TV commercials produced by charities often include a credit to their sponsors. Some were so short that the public might have been forgiven for not noticing, but at least an effort was made to give the sponsors credit.

4.3.4 Getting started

First, you will need to identify those items of expenditure or activities which are likely to be sponsored. Next, you should define the audiences that you may be able to reach with any of these activities.

Then, you can begin to define the companies who might be interested in what you have to offer. They may be local or national. You should work out how many potential sponsors you plan to approach, and whether you can do any research prior to submitting your proposal. Next, you will prepare the written proposal, so that you have this ready when you need it. This will outline the project, and highlight the benefits to the company of sponsoring it. Finally you will need patience. Sponsorship can take a long time to negotiate, and it is best to plan well in advance.

4.3.5 Issues

Setting up in the sponsorship business brings charities face to face with a range of dilemmas. It is one thing when a charity accepts or even solicits money from an organisation about whose activities it has some reservations; it is quite another when it actively seeks to promote the work of such a company, as it must do in a sponsorship relationship. This has been found to be a major stumbling block to campaigning charities and those which depend on a degree of consensus to work well.

In all cases it is strongly recommended that you develop your own sponsorship policy – agreeing in advance which types of company you are happy to approach and which you are not. How you handle the tax on sponsorship giving is also important (see Section 5.17 on Tax-effective giving).

4.3.6 The sponsorship package

Before you can approach a company seriously you will need to have prepared a sponsorship package. The main things you will need to cover in this are as follows:

- The exact nature of the project or item, and how it is likely to work.

- The audiences that will be reached and publicly obtained. Remember that the company will be interested in delivering messages to people who are their potential customers.

- The target area in which these audiences will reside. Is this a national or a purely local activity?

- The image that will be projected through the event, and how this will fit in with the sponsoring brand or company.
- The specific advertising opportunities that will be available on hoardings, vans, programmes, TV, and so on.
- Some of the other benefits that the sponsorship might confer on the company. The effect it will have on staff, on business contacts, and on government and other authorities.
- The costing. The specific sponsorship opportunities, and how they compare with other ways of reaching the target audiences.

4.3.7 Making the approach

There are a variety of ways in which you can make the approach to a company. Depending on the circumstances, different approaches will work. What can be said with confidence is that you can expect a large number of negative responses before you hit on the right partner.

If you are lucky enough to have a range of things to offer, the best approach is likely to be a visit to a company to give a presentation of your work. Only then will you be in a position to find out what the needs are of the company and how you might be able to meet them. If you are not able to arrange this, it will almost certainly pay to do some research before sending out anything detailed. A phone call to the marketing, public relations or community affairs departments will often elicit a wealth of information about who to send the proposal to, what types of activity they are currently preoccupied with, and what sort of proposals they consider. If this fails, you can send a complete or summary proposal to see if it sparks any interest. This route is much less likely to be successful.

There are a number of organisations which undertake the work of introducing sponsorship opportunities to sponsors. They will sometimes charge the charity a fee; sometimes they will charge a commission from the sponsor. Success can never be guaranteed.

4.3.8 Contractual issues

It is advisable to agree your sponsorship through some form of contract, though this can be just as effectively done in the form of a letter. A number of important issues need to be settled at this point which will form a major part of your discussions and negotiations. One of the most important issues to agree is how long the arrangement will run. Is it for one year, thus requiring you to find a new sponsor next year, or can you get a commitment for three or more years? Most successful sponsorship lasts for several years, and the benefit builds up over the sponsorship period. Clearly the fee to be paid is most important. You should specify exactly when this is to be paid, since the difference, both financially and emotionally, between a fee paid on January 1st and the following December, is considerable. You should also confirm whether the stated fee excludes or includes VAT (if you are registered for VAT or have to register as a result of undertaking the sponsorship). The question of costs is often forgotten. Who is going to pay for the additional publicity that the sponsor requires? You need to start out with a clear understanding of who is responsible for what, so that you can ensure that everything is covered and that you don't fall out later over misunderstandings. It is important to settle who is actually responsible for organising the various activities. If you have a clear idea of what you want, then you may be wary about letting anyone else organise it, as it is sure to turn out differently. On the other hand, you may not have the staff to organise a sponsorship of any size, and the use of an agency would be welcome. If money is being raised or goods are being sold by the sponsor to benefit the charity as part of the sponsorship, then the sponsor will be deemed to be a commercial participator. This then requires the sponsor to meet certain conditions laid down in the 1992 Charities Act (see Section 4.14). Finally there is the issue of competition. If the arrangement is a good one, most companies would want some reassurance that you are not going to go and offer the idea to their main competitor the next year. This can be overcome through long-term contracts and exclusivity clauses.

4.3.9 Skills and resources needed

The key skills that you will need to get sponsorship, are those of negotiation and good presentation. Good verbal and written presentation will help you explain what you have in mind to companies which have very little experience of your world. You will need to be able to produce well presented written materials, as well as having the ability to present them personally to a group of people.

Negotiation skills will come in to play when you have got their interest and need to wrest an advantageous deal. How not to give too much away and yet how to ensure you don't lose their interest.

4.3.10 Spin off

Perhaps the most important thing to come out of any sponsorship deal is the link with the sponsoring company. This can lead to a range of other benefits depending on how the original sponsorship goes. Staff support for your charity, future sponsorship, donations from the company charitable budget, use of company resources and facilities are all things you might expect to flow from a successful sponsorship.

4.3.11 The future

One of the future directions of corporate giving is sponsorship – particularly the extension of sponsorship from sport and the arts into environment, education and social projects. Getting your act together now and developing links with the major and local corporate sponsors – even if this effort comes to nothing – is an investment in your future well worth making.

4.3.12 References

Some useful publications:

Finding Sponsors for Community Projects, FOE and DSC
Conservation and Business Sponsorship, WWF
The Corporate Donors Handbook, DSC
The Major Companies Guide, DSC
The Sponsorship Manual, ABSA

In addition:

ABSA, the Association for Business Sponsorship of the Arts, which runs the Business Sponsorship Incentive Scheme awarding government money to projects attracting new sponsors, can also advise on arts sponsorship.

4.4 Capital and big gift campaigns

In the search for large sums of money, large and small charities now employ techniques for getting major gifts with increasing success, and have been able to raise sums from £50,000, up to as much as £50 million or even more.

4.4.1 Definition

Charities have been able to attract big gifts from time to time, but recently attention has turned on this as one of the principal components of a capital fundraising campaign. The techniques tend to be used in the context of a single large one-off appeal. Some charities have tried to apply them for their ongoing fundraising needs, but this has not always been successful. Typical uses range from the Campaign for Oxford which is seeking £200 million for the University, to a local school raising money to build a new classroom.

4.4.2 Campaign phases

A campaign to raise any sort of significant sum must be properly planned and is likely to go through a number of clearly defined phases. These are:

- The planning stage;
- The case document, which sets out and justifies the purpose of the fundraising;
- The business plan or feasibility study, which sets out the plan and time scale for the fundraising;
- The research;
- The recruitment of an appeal committee;
- The private giving phase, in which major gifts are sought;
- The launch;
- The public giving phase;
- The consolidation.

THE WISHING WELL APPEAL

Some of the key figures recruited to the appeal:

Royal Patrons
The Prince and Princess of Wales.

Chair
Chair, GEC.

Deputy Chair
Deputy Chair, British Telecom.

City Panel
Chair: Vice Chair, Kleinwort Benson.

Commerce and Industry panel
Chair: Chair, The Rank Organisation.

International Appeal
Chair: Deputy Chair, Midland Bank.

Marketing Panel
Chair: CEO, United Biscuits.

Special Events Panel
Chair: CEO, TVS Entertainments.

These are just a few of the well placed people this appeal managed to recruit. Each panel had a wide range of equally well-connected people on it. Not all appeals will be able to manage this, but it does help show that it is who you know that makes capital appeals successful.

The importance of going through these stages is not only to ensure that the appeal is properly organised, but also to allow a feasible time scale for the appeal and to link this in with expenditure plans and any implications for cash flows. It may take at least two years from start to finish, and a large appeal may well take longer. There is also the question of investment and risk. When plans have been approved and the staff have been taken on, trustees may begin to get nervous about the chances of the outlay being recouped. This is quite a common occurrence, and demands both an understanding of the appeal process and an act of faith in its value.

TABLE OF GIFTS NEEDED

Number of gifts	Value of gifts required	Total required
1	10,000	10,000
1	7,000	7,000
2	5,000	10,000
5	3,000	15,000
8	1,000	8,000
17 donors		**50,000**

This typical table of donations gives a clue as to the number of donors and amount of fundraising and research that you will need. You might expect a success rate of one in ten, meaning that you will need to approach 170 people.

4.4.3 Planning an appeal

The planning stage will involve a number of separate activities. These include:

- Establishing the feasibility of the appeal;
- Planning the structure of the appeal and reviewing the likely funding sources;
- Documentation and research to back up the above.

Many organisations will decide to take on a consultant to offer advice on how to conduct the appeal. One of the first steps a consultant will take is to conduct a feasibility study which will, apart from anything else, advise on whether the appeal is likely to be successful. This is an important process, as it will serve to highlight any inconsistencies or ill-conceived ideas.

The next step will come with the review of likely sources of funding. This requires some research and exploratory work, and some previous experience in this area is invaluable.

When you know how much money is required, you will be able to decide what structure might be needed to generate that sort of funding. The structures are likely to be of two sorts:

- The appeal committee and any similar structures for harnessing volunteer help;
- The professional office and back up support that will be needed.

A vital tool in guiding individuals as to the size of donations needed, is the table of gifts. The table on page 89 lists the gifts that were expected from a recent campaign. You will see that the top three gifts accounted for one quarter of the income and the top ten for nearly half. This is typical of these sorts of appeals and illustrates the importance of planning the leading gifts at the right level, and then going out and getting them.

A vital job that will need to be undertaken at this stage is the planning document. This will be the strategic plan for the appeal. It will include sections covering the following:

- A background to the charity;
- A description and justification of the project;
- The costs of the project;
- The individual components of the project, costed;
- The gifts needed to achieve this target;
- The plan to meet the needs and raise the money;
- The sources of money expected.

A final component of the planning phase will be to start researching those people who will play a major part in the appeal, both as donors and on the appeal committee. This is usually done by drawing up lists gleaned from a wide range of sources, and refining them and adding to them as the campaign progresses. This is one of the key activities which can determine the success or failure of the campaign.

4.4.4 Leadership

The leadership of the campaign is enormously important. The qualifications you look for in the Chair and Appeal Committee members are that they have the resources to **give major gifts** on the scale you need; that they have **important contacts**; and that they are able and **willing to ask others**.

The first stage is to identify people to help you plan the appeal. A group of two or three senior people with an interest in your work can be invited to act as a planning group. Their role is either to act as the formal leadership of the appeal or to select that leadership. They should be people who are well respected in the community and who may have not been associated with a similar appeal in the recent past. They should have plenty of contacts. One of their tasks will be to select other people to form the nucleus of the Appeal Committee.

To involve such people you may want to set up a range of small receptions or presentations at which the issues can be explored and at which questions can be answered and any doubts about the appeal can be removed.

One important issue is the motivation driving important people that makes them want to work for your cause. Research seems to suggest that almost every motive under the sun will be present. Some people find themselves genuinely supporting the cause; others find the approach from a peer in the community difficult to resist; others find the link with other business people attractive for their own purposes; some are motivated by the notion of some sort of reward or recognition at the end of the day; and some just like the challenge of achieving something rather unusual and worthwhile. All those involved at this level are likely to appreciate (and be used to) good management and back up support, spending the minimum of time in committee and ensuring that their time is effectively used.

4.4.5 The private phase

With the building blocks in place, you should be ready to begin the slow yet vital task of solicitation.

The first task is to get the commitment of those on your Appeals Committee. It is important that your early gifts are of a sufficient size to give a lead to those that follow. Through the process of developing and refining the appeal document, most committee members should now be aware of the scale of donations that are needed. They will have been engaged in discussions about what is expected of other prospective donors, and will be familiar with what might be expected of them.

Once they have made their own commitment, they should move on to the task of approaching others. For this purpose you will have already drawn up lists of prospective donors. They will be able to help by adding new names and deciding how an approach can best be made. The role of the fundraiser is to provide smooth administration; the task of asking for big gifts is best done by the committee member. Once you have identified who is the best person to approach a prospective donor, a wide variety of ways can be used. The one that will be selected is the one that the person doing the asking feels most comfortable with. Usually, big donations take time to be decided and this will be particularly true of big donations from public sector sources. A decision should not be expected within the course of a meeting. However, what might happen is a series of meetings – starting perhaps with a reception, followed by informal chats – that culminate in the prospective donor being asked to help and offering a range of possible ways. Not only can they be asked to give money, they can be asked to give support in kind and suggest contacts.

The objective of the private stage of the appeal will be to collect promises of between 25% and 50% of the appeal target. This will give a tremendous boost to the appeal when it is launched. Indeed, you should not actually launch an appeal to the public until you are confident of its success.

4.4.6 The public phase

The next phase commences with the launch. This can be done in any number of ways depending on how the campaign is structured. It should certainly involve a press conference and might also involve an event to which you invite prospective donors who have not yet committed themselves.

In the public phase of the appeal, much of the money will be raised from large numbers of people in smaller donations. This phase will have several objectives. The first is to take the appeal to a wider audience. The second is to assist the task of the big gift fundraising. And the third is to give an opportunity to those who were not able to give at a high level to give at a more modest one.

A press and public relations campaign is important to give your appeal a continuing profile. Some of the bigger appeals recruit PR committees and involve a range of PR professionals on a voluntary basis. You should certainly have someone working hard on public and media relations, as this will underpin your other fundraising activities.

Events are an important component of an appeal, so long as the organisation of the event is carried out by someone else. They can attract good media coverage. They usually involve a great deal of organisation, so can meet the need of your existing supporters who will want to do something for the appeal. They can reach a large audience who will get the appeal message direct.

Mail shots are also useful as they can be targeted to those that your personal approaches have not yet reached. It is important though that these be left towards the end, so that nobody gives a small donation who might otherwise have given a bigger one.

For the very large national appeals, a regional committee structure may need to be set up to harness the many possible appeal opportunities at a regional level. The regional chairpeople are appointed as part of the appeal structure, and they then recruit people in their area. Their role will mainly be in the public phase of the appeal helping to stimulate and coordinate events and to give support and publicity to the campaign in their area.

4.4.7 The issues

One issue of importance is the degree to which your trustees are committed to the project and to the appeal. It makes it extremely difficult to approach people for their support, if half the board are known to be half-hearted about the problem or favour some other approach. Establishing the importance of the appeal should form a part of the feasibility stage.

Another issue is the degree to which a major appeal will interfere with your ongoing fundraising work and future fundraising prospects. Naturally this depends on the strategy of the appeal and the relative sizes of your capital and revenue fundraising needs. For a £50 million a year charity raising £5 million of capital, there is likely to be a good deal of overlap. However, for a small charity raising a (relatively) big sum, the momentum and excitement and interest that is generated by the appeal will probably add to the regular income received rather than detract from it.

4.4.8 Skills and resources

A wide range of skills and resources will be needed. 'People skills' are probably the most important, since the first stages will demand a good deal of presentation, persuasion and negotiation. Planning and organisation skills are also needed. Research plays an important part of the process. You may need to acquire professional advice to help you in your planning. You will need to produce effective, though not necessarily glossy, literature. You will need sufficient staff to administer the appeal and an appeals office which can deal with the phone and maintain good donor records. It is important to recognise that no appeal is cost-free, and to budget for the necessary administrative and back up resources you will need to make the appeal a success. A properly planned and resourced appeal will stand a much better chance of success.

4.4.9 The future

As the state shifts the balance of responsibility for care and support into the community, charities are going to find themselves needing more and more capital funding. Schools, now self managing, will want money to develop their facilities; hospitals will want to purchase major new pieces of equipment; organisations caring for the elderly will need to extend their facilities to meet the needs of a growing elderly population. All this suggests that we will continue to see demand on the public purse accelerating. Inevitably this could result in a decline in responsiveness and a resistance to giving, but it also means that those seeking funds should be looking for ways of improving their effectiveness.

4.4.10 References

In this book see:
    3.1-3.5 Sources of funding
    5.15   PR
    5.14   Marketing
Also see:
    Building for Life, the Wishing Well Appeal
    The Giving Business, Business Matters, BBC Education
    The Fundraising Handbook, Redmond Mullin

4.5 Legacies

Legacy fundraising can often appear as a mysterious activity which generates large sums of money with apparently little effort. In fact, some of the largest legacy earning charities have clear and carefully planned strategies for developing their legacy income. Like other forms of fundraising, what you get out depends on what you put in.

4.5.1 Types of legacy

Four main types of legacy should be distinguished. All are of value in different circumstances, and as a fundraiser, you should be aware of them.

- **Pecuniary legacy:** This is a simple clause in a will where a gift of money is left to another individual or charity. "I leave £100 to my faithful companion, Rose" is one example. This is easy to arrange, but has the main drawback that over time the value of this form of legacy gets eroded by inflation.

- **Specific bequest:** A donor can equally give an object or specified item of property away in their wills – which would otherwise be sold and the money go into the estate for distribution. "I give my Bokhara rug to my favourite nephew, Jamie", for example. Such bequests are good in that they maintain a real value over time; though they can be problematic though if the Bokhara had long since been sold or thrown away after paint was spilled on it – in which case the beneficiary would get nothing.

- **Residuary legacy:** The usual alternative to those described above is to bequeath the residue of the estate after pecuniary legacies and specific bequests have been made. Most people will not have a clear idea of their net worth at an unknown time in the future. Thus "I leave one quarter of the residue of my estate to the Hospice" solves the problem. It is an ideal medium for charities: residual bequests are on average ten times as valuable as specific ones. This may either be because they keep up with inflation better, or because people simply do not know the value of their estate and seriously undervalue it. With the decline in the birthrate and an increase in property ownership, there will be an increase in the number of people without family to bequeath their estate to, who also have an estate of value. This is a real opportunity for charities.

- **Reversionary or life interest:** Where an elderly relative needs to be cared for a life interest clause is often used such as "My house is given to the Society with a life interest to my uncle Charles". This gives Charles the right to live in the house during his lifetime; and on his death, the unencumbered right to the property reverts to the charity. This can be a useful way of carrying out a responsibility to the supporter's family while at the same time ensuring a valuable legacy to a charity.

4.5.2 Promotion

This is one of the most problematic and little understood areas of legacy fundraising. How can you invite supporters to give you a legacy? Because the process of making a legacy is complicated compared with sending a donation, a systematic approach to raising legacies is valuable. This demands answers to the questions who, how, what and where before proceeding – and preferably the drawing up of a plan. The essential nature of legacies is that you make an effort now and, with luck, get a reward much later. There will usually be a time-lag of three or four years before you see anything at all for your pains. Thus you must be able to justify making an investment and be prepared to stick to your guns when early returns are not evident.

We shall review the choice of target audience; how people make legacies; what you should say to them; and when.

Target audience

A review of those people who have already made a legacy (if there are any) to your organisation will indicate the sex and location of your legators. It may also give an idea of whether they have been past supporters or members of the charity. As a general average, 60% of charitable legators are female and tend to have the title "Miss". Facts about their age are not usually known, but presumably will mirror the mortality statistics. There are several questions to answer in respect of targets: whether to go for existing supporters; to target the general public with a bias towards elderly females living in the South East; or whether to target legal advisers (such as solicitors who help in the drawing up of a will).

One aim of having a supporter base on which to concentrate your fundraising, is to build up a good understanding of them and how they might help you. If some form of regular giving is a natural successor to occasional gifts, then a legacy is a natural next step up from regular giving. What is more appropriate than to make your last gift your best? In the process of communicating with donors you will, over time, build relationships which will enable you to discuss potentially sensitive issues such as legacies. Approaching the public at large is unlikely to be as effective as starting with your own supporters. You might adopt a slow indirect approach, with regular mentions in a newsletter, or take the bull by the horns and write directly on the subject. One major charity embarked on this route some years ago with extreme caution. They invested in a mailing to 100,000 supporters inviting donors to send off for a range of new materials and to indicate their interest in making a legacy. The resulting 3,500 enquiries may represent a huge success or little more than polite interest; only time will tell. However the careful addition, as a defensive tactic, of the alternative of sending a donation if readers were unable to leave a legacy, yielded £100,000.

An alternative strategy adopted by many, is to focus on the general public. This can be done by posters, by cold mailing or through advertising. Although this has the benefit of lifting the awareness of your charity in general, it is an expensive way of getting the message across unless it is tightly targeted.

Yet another strategy is to concentrate on the intermediaries: the solicitor, the bank manager and the accountant. When wills are written, so the argument goes, these professionals are the ones who advise. They may be a source of information about charities, and certainly have their own preferences or prejudices which could act as a veto. In general, they are not often used to giving information on particular charities. There are a number of publications sent free to these professionals which contain legacy advertising by charities. Due care should be exercised in spending money on such advertising as it may not work and the pay back period can be many years ahead. Another approach, which is particularly appropriate at a local level for a local cause, is to communicate directly with local professionals through personal contact or by talking at meetings.

How to get the message across

There is a spectrum of possibilities which start from the very personal and moves to the extremely impersonal. The technicalities of the different approaches are dealt with elsewhere in the book. In order to discuss the intricacies of the legacy process in appropriate detail, donors should be met in their homes. This is not always easy to arrange but will undoubtedly be much more effective. The pioneering approach by Oxfam in the early 1970s involved setting up a team of volunteers primarily to visit solicitors and secondarily to visit Oxfam's larger donors to discuss will making. Others might prefer the greater control of using paid staff as is done successfully in the USA.

The less personal approach of mail shots requires a very clear set of objectives, a sensitive package and good fulfilment. Again it is desirable to link this with a follow up by telephoning donors who write enthusiastically or major donors who respond.

Finally the impersonal approach represented by advertising, needs to be well targeted, coded and analysed by medium and needs to carry a challenging message.

The message

Three types of message can be identified. Make a will (and don't forget us); remember us by adding a legacy or codicil to your existing will; or make a pledge to support us in your will.

The "make your will" approach leans on the fact that a high proportion of people die intestate (without a will) and the State effectively distributes their estate according to pre-set rules. Thus, it is in the family's interest to make a will if they wish to have any control over how the money is to be distributed and to minimise Inheritance Tax liability. According to a Charities Aid Foundation survey, 64% of the population have not made a will.

The "remember us in your will" approach must necessarily be directed at those 36% who have made a will. Will making is a complicated process, especially where there are significant assets and family interests to consider. Thus the value of this approach is that it gets to people who know what you are talking about and who could, at least in theory, do something quite quickly. Another advantage is that you can include a Codicil form in your mailing, which will alter the provisions of their existing will.

The "make a pledge to support us in your will" approach has several advantages. It allows you legitimately to keep the supporter on file and to keep in touch about it; whilst also allowing you to get a very direct reading of the effectiveness of your promotions; and most importantly it can imply some sort of commitment to the process (see the WWF example). It is always advisable to get people thinking of leaving you a legacy to send you a signed pledge form.

Other ways of promoting legacies

There are a number of barriers to making wills and leaving legacies. Some of them can be overcome by effective organisation.

Some people who do not already have a will are prevented from writing one by not having contact with a solicitor they trust. A number of charities get the local Law Society to offer names for supporters to choose.

Others do not have access to executors and feel inhibited about inviting a professional to do the job. Again, some charities will provide this as a service if they stand to benefit from the will. In a similar vein many charities, especially those with shops, offer a house clearance service, and will eventually benefit from this.

Perhaps the ultimate inducement is to provide assistance with the drafting of a will. This should only be done through the auspices of a registered solicitor, but is something some donors prefer as they feel it will minimise the loss to the beneficiary charity.

One usual step is to print sample wording for a clause in a will or a codicil to a will in leaflets, which can be used by a solicitor who is drawing up a will for a client.

4.5.3 Memorial giving

An important source is memorial giving. This is particularly appropriate for charities with a medical or health slant or where the deceased is known to have had a strong interest in the cause. Memorial giving is actually giving by the friends and family of the deceased in memory of him or her. It can be done in a number of ways. Small ads are regularly placed in the personal columns of the newspapers and can yield a continuing flow of donations. Donations in lieu of flowers at funerals can be influenced by funeral directors, as people arranging funerals will often go to their offices. A Deed of Variation, where all the beneficiaries of the will jointly agree to a variation in the will such that a bequest is given to a charity, can be negotiated in return for some form of memorial. This needs to be done within two years of death, and professional help in drawing up the Deed of Variation is recommended.

4.5.4 Getting started

The first thing you will need to do before you can expect anybody to decide to leave you money, is to produce some literature outlining your needs and showing them how they can do it. Important points to make are the tax exemptions for legacies to charity; the legally correct forms of words; and the importance by the charity placed on legacies as a source of income. These can either serve as materials to be mailed out or as response devices for enquirers.

The next thing that will be needed is an efficient administrator to keep track of legacies. Getting people to make a legacy is only the first step. A good deal of administration may be needed once the donor has died. The process can at times be extremely protracted especially when you are sharing the residue with others, or when the will is contested. It is important to have someone effective carrying out an accounting and chasing function as well as someone who can deal sympathetically with bereaved families.

Smee and Ford, a firm of legal agents, provides two services to charities which can be useful to any charity receiving legacy income. The **Will Notification Service** informs the charity when it has been mentioned in a probate will, so that the charity can notify the executors of its interest and press for an early distribution. The **Discretionary Will Service** notifies charities of situations where money is left for charitable purposes to be distributed at the discretion of the executors. Here the charity would send an appeal to the executors and hope that it would be considered favourably.

4.5.5 The future

The value of your legacy income will depend on a large number of factors; one will certainly be the age profile of the population and of your supporters. If your supporters are young, then your opportunities will be less than if they are older. But the population is likely to get older in the next ten years. You should thus prepare for the greater opportunities to raise legacies.

• The value of each legacy is very much dominated by the values of people's houses, which is usually their principal asset. Thus, when the value of housing rises ahead of inflation, you should expect legacies to get bigger and bigger. But if the value is depressed, the opposite will be the case.

4.5.6 Skills and resources

The skills you will need to set up an effective legacy promotion include marketing and a knowledge of the law. It is naturally important that you give correct advice and have a good link with solicitors.

In order to be effective you will need patience. You will need to spend money which will not produce a monetary return in the short-term.

4.5.7 Issues

One of the common issues confronted by fundraisers is how to decide how much to invest in legacy fundraising. The fact is that most people will, on average, die 3-5 years after having last changed their will. The average amount of each legacy may be between £1,000 and £10,000.

One way to do this is to use a percentage (say 10%) of your current legacy income for promotion. Another is to set a target for the number of pledges that you will receive each year. As time goes on you will find out both how many turn into legacies and how much it costs to get a pledge. The most common way is to look at what was spent last year and add a bit – not the most scientific approach!

To get an idea of the returns from any of your long-standing promotions, you can code the response so that you can identify a bequest with a particular promotion. You might use a variation of your address such as a room or box number. This will help you monitor your marketing methods, but is of debatable value when you are changing your promotions every few years.

4.5.8 References

From this book see:
    5.14 Marketing
    4.2   Direct mail
    5.12 Tax-effective giving
Read also:
    Legacies – a practical guide for charities, DSC
Useful organisations include:
    Smee and Ford, who provide a range of legacy related services (see Section 4.5.4)

4.6 Events

Whether you want to organise a concert in your home town, arrange a charity cricket match or celebrate your organisation's centenary in Hyde Park, you have to think not just about the fundraising potential but also about the possible risk of losing money from the event. You also need to be able to organise a successful event. For every event that attracts thousands of new supporters and gives everyone a good time, there is another that collapses, is rained off, or whose sponsorship collapsed at the last moment. While there is money to be made from a well run event, many absorb a great deal of energy and deliver only small returns.

4.6.1 Introduction

An event may be of almost any size and complexity; what all events have in common is that you will be publicly seeking support, and you will be giving your public something to enjoy in return for their money. This last point is important when planning the event. You should not just be creating an opportunity to take as much money as you can from those who attend in the short time they are with you. You should first of all try to give them a good time, but at the same time be generating cash and goodwill for your charity.

Some 10% of the public attend charity events. Some go simply because of the event. Many consider it a way of giving support to the charity.

DANCE THE NIGHT AWAY

On Saturday September 30th, 9pm-12pm at Summertown Church Hall, a 'Dancing Only' get together – bring a friend, your best bopping music on tape, snacks, drink and lots of energy!
Donation of £1 at the door. Proceeds to Waldorf Kindergarten.

Just to show that events do not have to be world class to raise useful amounts. One such event raised thousands.

People do not go to a charity auction feeling the same way they do about going to a commercial auction. They are much more likely to be generous with their bids. People do not go to a charity concert without expecting to be asked to give to a plate collection or to listen to an address by a luminary of that organisation. Their enjoyment of the occasion will in part be determined by the quality of the performance (get that wrong and you risk your reputation); and in part by the degree to which it has met their expectations as an event held to benefit charity.

You must be absolutely clear about the purpose of the event. Is it for PR, to get your name known; or is it to raise money directly; is it simply an opportunity to entertain volunteers and supporters; or is it simply to give an enthusiastic bunch of supporters something to do? The objective will help mould the exact form of the event itself and what you plan to get out of it.

4.6.2 The four ingredients

FOUR INGREDIENTS FOR A SUCCESSFUL EVENT

- The media
- The sponsors
- The charity
- The performance

Whatever your event, there are four principal ingredients. Get these working in harmony and you are well on your way to success. These are the media, the sponsors, the charity and the performance. With almost all events these four elements each have something to give and something to gain from a successful event.

The performers are those people upon whose skills and appeal the event is centred: the band that is booked to play at the ball; the auctioneer and auction house undertaking the sale for you; or the teams who will be playing in the charity event. They have plenty to gain from coming to your event. It might be that they need the fee, where they are not giving you a reduced or free performance. Beyond this, they have everything to gain by the good publicity that the event will generate both in terms of press features and reviews and any coverage on radio or television.

Sponsors who may be underwriting much of the costs have a good deal to gain too. They will be interested in reaching your audience and being seen to be supporting something worthwhile. The PR by itself is valuable; the association with an enjoyable and successful event is also valuable to the sponsor. Naturally, if you make the most of the next ingredient – the media – then your sponsors will regard the event even more enthusiastically.

The media are in business to report events such as yours, especially if it brings genuine talent to the fore or is of particular local interest. They may want to be the exclusive purveyors of the story if that is possible, and this can generate a good story or picture coverage. Whether the event is genuinely newsworthy depends on the nature of the event itself and or how creative you are in generating media interest.

The final ingredient is to do with you and your charity; to do with what you bring to the mixture. Without your involvement the event may not have a focus, nor perhaps even a reason for happening. The performers will not come to just any event, because they may have many other commitments. But a charity event, or an event for your charity, could be something that strikes a sympathetic chord with them. The sponsors too, are going to be very much affected by you and your reputation. The cause can provide the real heart of the activity. Your contacts with royalty or important patrons can be a further factor that really attracts sponsors.

4.6.3 Getting started

One approach to getting started is to examine the event from a marketing point of view. Who are the people that you are in touch with or that you can reach through a particular type of promotion? What are the characteristics of the people that you want to attract as helpers and as an audience? Are they young and active, or are they older with an interest in the arts? Sometimes you may want to start from the sponsorship end, and ask a potential sponsor what sponsorship money is available, and what needs to be done for them to release it.

An alternative starting point might be to think in terms of some of the major types of event and see whether any seem appropriate. A short list could include:

- Sporting events
- Musical events
- Balls and dinners
- Auctions
- Exhibitions
- Theatrical events
- Festivals and fetes

Most events are one-offs. More complicated are those that involve the co-ordination of multiple activities – for example a knockout or league cricket competition or a film festival. These should perhaps be left to when you have more experience.

Depending upon the nature of your plans, you may need some sort of licence. Check this with your local district council before you start any detailed planning.

4.6.4 Management

The ability and capacity to run the event well is crucial once the whole idea has been conceived and accepted by the parties involved. It will almost certainly take much longer and involve more effort than you think, but skimping on the organisation will lead to a threadbare event which fails to meet your objectives.

There seem to be three main approaches to running the event: do it yourself; get a professional to do it; or recruit a group of volunteers.

All approaches have their drawbacks and their advantages. Doing it yourself will help you learn how it should be done and provide vital experience to help you do it better next time. It will also give you a better

MAN'S LAST GREAT CHALLENGE

To raise awareness of MS and to help the many MS groups around the country to raise money, the MS Society linked up with Sir Ranulph Fiennes in trekking to the North Pole without support. They called it the sponsored event to launch all sponsored events. Sadly the walk had to be called off, highlighting the need to minimise risk in high profile activities.

ALLIED DUNBAR
AROUND THE WORLD
CHALLENGE

Help raise £1 Million
for

OXFAM

An example of an ambitious event designed to raise both money and awareness. The costs were sponsored by Allied Dunbar; the event was heavily promoted by Radio 1 and the Daily Mirror; and the performance was given by Simon Bates, the Radio 1 disc jockey. To ensure public participation and to help raise the money, a competition was launched in high street stores with prizes given by well-known companies.

understanding of the job the professionals do when they are taken on to run an event. If you haven't run an event before then you will be jeopardising the chances of success with your own inexperience. This can be countered by taking advice from more experienced people. Perhaps the single most important problem of doing it yourself is the opportunity cost that organising it will involve. What else could you be doing with the time; how much money could you be raising if you were not stuck with doing the organising? Almost any event will require constant attention to detail, and checking and double checking at every stage. If you are in the middle of a busy fundraising programme, then organising something that requires so much of your time may not be feasible.

An alternative is to engage a professional to organise the event for you. Very often the event will be run through some sporting or theatrical body in any case, whose job it is to organise this sort of activity. It could make sense to engage them to do all the organising. Perhaps you can persuade them to do it free as their contribution. If not, there are professional event organisers in the musical, sporting and entertainment fields, who put on events of all sorts. For a fee they can be engaged to take over all the day to day administration from you. Alternatively a public relations company could be taken on – again for a fee. If you are dealing with a commercial event organiser that agrees to run the event for you, with a certain proportion of the ticket price or of the proceeds going to the charity, then the event organiser will be a commercial participator (or professional fundraiser) and certain requirements will need to be met (see Section 4.14.8).

Finally, and this is the route chosen by many, you can establish your own voluntary committee to take all the responsibility for running the event. The key appointment will be the Chair. This need not be someone who knows how to run an event backwards, but someone who has the leadership qualities and the good management sense to link the commercial needs of the event to the requirements of the charity. You will probably then need to select a multi-disciplinary team that embodies all the skills necessary to make the thing work: from people with the sporting or musical background to deal with the programme, to the accountant who will tell you whether VAT is chargeable on the ticket sales and the legal requirements. You need to give yourself plenty of time to find the right people. An accurate budget is essential if you are to run a profitable event. At an early stage you will need to make an assessment of all the likely costs and the potential sources of income. At this stage you should include a good amount for contingencies. On the income side it is worth making a high and a low estimate to illustrate what may happen in different circumstances. This will set targets for you as well as highlight the risk involved. An additional idea is to set yourselves a financial strategy. You might decide, for example, to pay for no services and to get everything donated or sponsored.

4.6.5 Reducing the risk

One issue for the organiser is the degree to which in legal terms everything is cut and dried. Any event is likely to involve several different groups, each with the responsibility for separate but interlocking aspects of the event. If one fails, then it can put everything else at risk. The question then is how to ensure that what is planned actually happens on the day. Everything going smoothly depends on the planning, co-ordination and communication, rather than on any legal arrangements. However the intentions can be expressed best through some formal written agreement.

You do not need to use legal jargon to create a contract between you and a performer or a stadium owner. What you require simply needs to be written down and agreed by both parties. It is especially important that you agree how any money is to be split (both expenditure and income); who has the rights to the recording of the event; and who is responsible for which costs.

In the Amnesty International Secret Policeman's Ball, for example, much of the money was not made on the night but from the video and TV sales after the event. Agreement on this has to be down in writing, and where considerable sums are involved, the agreement should be drawn up by a lawyer.

This is a form of insurance; other insurance you will need to consider having are public liability insurance and insurance against the possibility of things going wrong, such as bad weather or a poor turn out. A final form of insurance is to get all the costs of the event covered by a sponsor, so that in the event of a disaster your low income is offset by equally low or nil expenses.

4.6.6 Promotion

The promotion of the event is what will turn it from a modest success into being really profitable. You should start from an understanding of who is likely to want to come to the event – your target market. It is to be hoped that it will be the sort of event that you have been able to get the media interested in from the start. For an important event, try to get the backing of one of the main TV or radio stations. Radio can be a powerful force in this area. For example, Radio One sends mobile recording studios to events; others may send their own reporter to do a programme live. This sort of link can create its own promotional momentum. The station will have an interest in giving frequent plugs in the run up to your event, mentioning the date and how to get tickets. Another possibility is to give away free tickets as prizes to be offered by the local radio station. You could invent a competition or let each station or newspaper devise its own to suit its own readers or listeners.

THE RAINFOREST FASHION SHOW

This is one of the many events that were organised for the Rainforest Festival. Heavily supported by glossy advertising in the brochure, some of the country's top designers produced and displayed special creations which were then sold by sealed bid. International models mixed with well-known supporters of the Arts for the Earth, and raised £21,000 for the rainforests in the course of one evening.

Few events get away without any paid advertising at all (though the 1990 Mandela Concert at Wembley did). Posters are the preferred medium, followed by advertising in the weekend press and the listings magazines. Local radio advertising or coverage can also be useful.

One way of helping with the promotion is to feature celebrities who may be attending the event or performing in it. This will be especially true of sporting or musical events where the performers will be one of the main attractions. Alternatively you can invite a celebrity to act as compere, to open the event or to present awards at an event. Being able to add famous names adds credibility to an event and will provide times at which people will want to be there during a whole day of activity. It goes without saying that the presence of royal patrons or visitors can also add a great deal to an event, though it will also add security and protocol headaches (see Section 5.5).

Selling tickets can be extremely hard work, and it is through having a full house that the event will appear successful. Give yourselves the best chances by having:

- A really attractive event;
- Plenty of ticket sellers who will take responsibility for selling all the tickets;
- A readily identifiable and reachable target audience.

4.6.7 Sponsorship

Events are ideal vehicles for sponsorship, not only because they offer a range of facilities and benefits that can be attractive to sponsors, but also because sponsorship can help reduce your risk and defray the costs.

Sponsors will need to know a good deal about the event and its intended and expected audience. How many people will come; who will they be and how will they be exposed to any advertising messages? This applies particularly where there are links with the media or you expect substantial press coverage.

You should have a clear idea of how much money you are expecting from the sponsor and what you can give in return. You might be offering special hospitality facilities, opportunities to meet royal patrons, opportunities to place the sponsors message in a prominent place, or the chance to publicise the sponsorship through advertising or public relations activities.

One of the key items that can carry the sponsor's message, and those of other advertisers too, is the brochure. Almost any event needs a brochure or programme, especially where there is a great deal of activity going on. The brochure should contain details of the programme, but it can also carry advertising. Space can be sold, generating a considerable income; and then each copy can be sold on the day.

Refer to Section 4.3 for more information on sponsorship.

4.6.8 Spin off

A great advantage of a successful event is that you can build up a clientele for future occasions. You will also be associating your organisation with a successful sporting or cultural event or another activity. You can also try to interest the people who attend the event in your cause. This can be done through the performers being well briefed and saying something at the event or during their performance, by using the opportunity to open or close the event with a speech from your patron or chairperson, or by having an article in the brochure.

With careful planning you can ensure that the names and addresses of all those who attend are registered and recorded, so that they can be used again for your charity: this might provide a good mailing list for donations, or may just be an invitation list for some future event.

Choosing a particular type of event can help you communicate to certain target groups. For example, if you want to appeal to working class males, you might consider running a charity football match and get considerable publicity for that event prior to your appeal.

On the down side, there is the opportunity to cause a lot of damage to your charity if things do not go right. "If they can't run this event properly, how can they be expected to spend my donations well?" will be the unspoken question. Just one more reminder of the risks associated with events.

4.6.9 References

In this book:
   4.3   Sponsorship
   5.2   Working with volunteers
   5.15 Public relations
For outside advice:
   Institute of Public Relations
   The ICFM Sub-Committee on events, (members of the Sub-Committee may be willing
      to offer advice.)

4.7 Committed giving

Committed giving is what really makes sense of your direct mail and other donor acquisition activities. If the donor acquisition process is unprofitable in itself but necessary to build a supporter base, the follow up mailing is what can be extremely profitable. Your aim is to obtain committed long-term support from as many as possible of your first time donors, and this is what makes the whole exercise so effective.

In this section we cover the main mechanisms for getting committed giving: covenants, standing orders and direct debits and link them to membership drives and legacy fundraising.

4.7.1 The covenant

The covenant is the key to committed giving with its built in time commitment and its tax claw back for the charity (and the higher rate taxpaying donor). It should only be used by those who pay income tax. The covenant itself is a legal contract in which a donor agrees to give to a charity a like amount each year, for a period capable of exceeding three years. The usual form of covenant is a set amount for a fixed period of four years. Once the covenant is properly signed and executed, the donor pays the agreed amount to the charity, usually by banker's order. The charity is then able to claim the basic rate tax back from the Inland Revenue. The effect of this, is that (at the current basic tax rate of 25%) a donation of £100 a year for four years is turned into £133 a year (or £533 for the period of four years).

Furthermore, a donor paying higher rate income tax can obtain tax relief from the inland revenue of an amount which is the difference between the higher rate and standard rate; using the example of a £100 covenant, the higher rate tax relief amounts to £20 each year.

HOW THE COVENANT WORKS

Mrs Brown, a 40% higher rate taxpayer, enters into a covenant to pay £100 out of her income to charity each year. The covenant payment is made net of income tax at the basic rate.

In order to pay £100 net of tax at the basic rate, Mrs Brown has had to earn £133. She will have paid £33 of basic rate tax and £20 higher rate tax. Total tax paid = £53 (40% of £133).

Of this £133, the basic rate tax of £33 will go back to the charity (25% of £133) and she herself will receive the higher rate tax relief of £20 (that's 15% of £133).

Hence the charity receives £100 plus £33 in tax relief, **totalling** £133, for which Mrs Brown pays £100 less £20 in higher rate relief, at a net **cost** to herself of £80.

4.7.2 Other types of commitment

Although the covenant is right at the heart of a committed giving programme, it is not in itself a means of making the payment. Both for covenants and for regular gifts, the payment system is important: the main methods are the standing order or banker's order and direct debit.

Although a standing order offers no tax advantage in itself unless linked with a deed of covenant, it enables regular payments to be made – on an annual, quarterly, monthly or some other regular basis. It can be drawn up to be open-ended with no fixed termination date. The payments are then made automatically and without any further effort from the donor. The standing order can be changed at any time by the donor contacting the bank.

The direct debit is different. Although it has in the past been the object of suspicion and consumer resistance, it enables the charity to receive regular payments by debiting the donor's bank account on pre-determined dates. It is possible to draw up a direct debit mandate such that the charity can vary the amount of the transfer (for example to pay an annual membership subscription, which may be raised from year to year). You need permission from your bank to operate a direct debit payment system.

4.7.3 Promotion

Not every donor wants to sign a covenant, but it is important to give every donor **the opportunity** to do so. For this reason, a clear promotion strategy is needed. This should include answers to these questions:

- How can you identify prospective committed supporters?
- How can you promote committed giving to our supporter base?
- How should you report back to committed supporters?
- How can you organise new appeals to existing committed supporters?

If you analyse the response to your appeals, you will see that a number of donors give more than once. They may give every few months or respond very promptly to one particular appeal. These are your priority targets for committed giving. They should be contacted, pointing out the advantages of giving regularly by deed of covenant and offered all the appropriate forms that are needed.

Promoting committed giving more widely involves a number of trade-offs. One strategy is to allocate one appeal per year to promote giving by standing order or by covenant. This will involve a loss of response from those not in a position to give regularly, but who might otherwise have made a one-off cash donation. Another approach is a drip-drip strategy, constantly mentioning the value of committed giving in each mailing, but by way of an afterthought or postscript.

A common problem is that once the support is committed, you then begin to take your committed givers for granted. This should be avoided at all costs. You should take every opportunity to keep them in touch with what you are doing. You might feel that once a donor has made a commitment it is an indication that they do not want to be asked for further support. A better approach is to view their commitment as being affirmation of the value and importance of your cause. The trick is always to recognise their commitment, so that they understand that whenever you approach them, you are doing this because of their commitment. Using this approach, covenantors and standing order subscribers can then be appealed to on a regular basis. This is especially true when there is an obviously good reason for the appeal, such as emergencies. Appealing to your list of covenantors, you might expect to get at least a 10% response rate (which is far better than you could achieve by cold mailing).

You will need to report back to your committed givers. You might produce a newsletter or a magazine or send a specially personalised letter from the chief executive. Committed donors are likely to want to see a minimum of expenditure on 'unnecessary' items, and so should not be approached too frequently or too lavishly. Friends of the Earth has a good way of reporting back to covenantors, which is to invite them to an evening meeting which is addressed by the senior staff of the organisation. These meetings are organised on an annual basis. This not only provides a good opportunity to say thanks, but also enables the most committed to become more involved, get more information and meet other supporters.

A few organisations have concentrated on using teams of trained people to visit existing supporters to ask for covenanted or other committed giving. This can be extremely profitable once a good system has been established and a reliable training programme set up. This method has been well used by Friends of the Earth and Action Aid among others, but only really works in urban areas.

PRESENTING THE COVENANT

If your personal tax rate is **25%**
You can covenant for a monthly sum of **£1.67**
On which we can claim an extra **£6.67 each year**
So we would receive over the four years **£106.68**

When any fixed term commitment comes to an end, there is both an opportunity and a need to ensure that as many people as possible renew. The usual way to do this is through sending reminder letters – one before the expiry and one coinciding with it. The telephone is also a valuable tool. It can be used to ask donors why they have not yet renewed; this both reminds those who have just not got round to dealing with it, and gathers useful information about those who have decided not to renew.

4.7.4 Variable covenants

These are generally used for covenanted membership subscriptions with payment by direct debit, where the annual covenant amount is tied to the level of membership subscription for the year. There are other forms of variable covenant, but the covenant must include some formula that determines how much is paid each year, and the donor cannot have any power to decide how much to give. In 1989, the Inland Revenue tightened up on the forms of 'escape clauses' which allowed the covenant to terminate; so if you are thinking of drawing up a complicated covenant for a large annual sum, it will be worth taking professional advice. Some common forms of variable covenant are:

- A promise to give when some event has taken place, for example, "I promise to give 5% of my income so long as my total annual income for the year to 5th April exceeds £20,000".

- A promise to give an increasing amount, such as, "I promise to give £500 per annum adjusted annually by the RPI".

- A promise to give a proportion of a specified slice of income, such as, "I promise to give 10% of my royalties from my book" (the title should be specified).

These are complicated to draft and to set up, and are thus not worthwhile unless for a substantial sum of money. You may need to consult a lawyer on the form of the deed. Also, because the amount of the payment each year will vary outside your control, neither a direct debit nor a standing order can be used, so they will be more difficult to administer.

In 1992 the Inland Revenue allowed covenants to run for an initial four years and then continue until the donor decides to cancel. The covenant has to be specially worded to allow this. If the covenant is tied to a banker's order or direct debit which continues indefinitely, and especially if the annual sum paid under the covenant is tied to the annual subscription rate, this provides the best mechanism for long-term committed giving.

4.7.5 Pricing

The question of how much you suggest to donors to give on a committed basis is of great importance, partly because of the long-term and cumulative nature of the arrangement and partly for psychological reasons.

"Just £5 each month will help pay the salary of one of our child care teams". This amounts to £60 per year, a figure many donors would find daunting if expressed as an annual sum. Thus there is a value in seeking **frequent payments** as they are more valuable to you and sound reasonable to the donor. This is something that can be tested quite easily in one of your mailings. The usual outcome is that requests for monthly giving are no less effective and have dramatically higher values on average. Many organisations use a table to illustrate the benefits of covenanting, showing how the regular sum accumulates over a period and with the added benefit of tax relief. You should emphasise the extra value of covenanting more than the value of giving over a long period or giving frequently.

Just like any other request for help, committed appeals can be linked to a specific part of the organisation's work. For example, rather than saying £5 will buy . . , you could say **£5 per month** will buy...

4.7.6 Getting started

First set a clear plan of what you want to do and what resources you are likely to need to do it. Next you will need to have a simple but legally effective covenant form for donors to sign. An example is shown in Appendix 6.5. It must have the twin advantages of being simple to understand and large enough to read and complete. But most importantly, it has to be acceptable to the Inland Revenue.

The next thing you will need to think about, is the administration of the resulting commitments and who is going to make all the tax claims. One possibility is to contract the administration to an agency such as the Charities Aid Foundation (several agencies offer this service).

4.7.7 Skills and resources

The marketing of committed giving involves the same skills as for direct marketing and is part of an effective donor strategy. Additional skills needed are administrative, since you will be coping with large numbers of regular payments and tax claims. At a certain stage you will almost certainly wish to keep your records on computer – possibly when you have 250 or so donor records. There are a number of purpose designed charity software systems available on the market.

4.7.8 References

In this book see also:

4.2 Direct mail
5.12 Tax-effective giving
4.5 Legacies
4.8 Membership

Useful sources of information:

Inland Revenue Claims Branch, Charity Division

Charities Aid Foundation

Community Computing

4.8 Membership

A membership subscription scheme is the method many organisations use to attract supporters to their cause. Some membership schemes confer benefits of a constitutional nature (such as the right to vote), while others provide more tangible benefits such as free or reduced price entry to properties or access to facilities. Membership is important not just for the subscription income it brings, but also as a means of recruiting people interested in your organisation.

4.8.1 Definition

The constitution of some organisations will refer to its membership. Members may have constitutional rights to vote on certain matters. They may also be responsible for electing officers at the AGM. Other types of membership may not include any such rights. Joining Greenpeace, for example, gives no rights at all to the member, who is merely a friend of the organisation.

There is another legal issue to consider. Payment of membership subscriptions can only be made by a deed of covenant (which increases its value through the tax that can be reclaimed) when limited benefits are offered to the member in return for the subscription. The general rule is that an 'ordinary small subscription to a charity' can be paid by deed of covenant if the value of the benefits offered to the member is not more than 25% of the cost of the subscription.

4.8.2 Introduction

There are three main benefits of having a membership scheme.
1. Membership offers a convenient peg upon which to hang commitment and long-term support. Organisations like Amnesty, Friends of the Earth and the Anti-Apartheid movement invite people to become members to harness their support for the cause. It is a badge of support for their campaign and it is the members who can be expected to be at the forefront of local action, while donors will be supporting the work of the organisation itself.
2. Membership opens up organisations to democratic control through annual meetings, giving the members some feeling that they control the direction of the movement.
3. The membership list is an ideal hunting ground for donations. Most membership fees are set deliberately low to attract the maximum number of people, and so not much money is raised through subscriptions alone. However, the members have demonstrated their commitment to the cause, so qualify themselves as perfect prospects for obtaining a further financial commitment.

Membership lists are usually held on computer, and appeals to members are invariably carried out using standard direct mail methods. Members may be asked to make contributions for special projects or in an emergency.

Since they are already contributing on a regular basis, the appeal should be seen as additional to the regular subscriptions that members are making, a completely separate contribution.

4.8.3 Promotions

The recruitment of new members requires a clear notion of who is likely to want to become a member and of how to reach them. There are a number of ways of recruiting members. The most frequently used mechanism is **direct mail**. The large national organisations have continuous programmes for recruiting members. **Promotions** link membership to some other relevant activity; giving free membership of the World Wildlife Fund to all purchasers of Fiat Pandas was a classic example of this, as is the linking of pond dipping activities at local shows to membership of local nature organisations. **Publicity** is the means of keeping the name and work of your organisation in the public eye, and the more people who know of your work, the more there are who will want to become members. Depending on the nature of your cause, somewhere between 50% and 90% of members will **renew their membership** from one year to the next. However for a membership of 10,000 this means that maybe 2,500 members will lapse each year. Through your membership renewal promotion, you have the opportunity to encourage as many as possible to continue membership. Invariably the cost of getting old or existing members to renew will be much lower than that of finding new ones altogether. Finally, a technique that has been used to great effect is Member-Get-Member (MGM). This is simply an invitation to an existing member to nominate or recruit another. Various incentives (such as a free entry prize draw or some form of gift) can be used which are offered either to the original member or to the new one.

The value of membership subscription income should be calculated, so that an organisation has a clear idea of the surplus income that will be generated by each member after the costs of running the membership scheme. From this it is possible to calculate a budget for promotion stated in the form of the cost per member recruited.

4.8.4 Administration

The administration of membership demands a high degree of organisation from your charity, especially if you wish to see the benefits in your direct mail fundraising.

In particular, there are two issues which concern many organisations. One is how to deal with the task of inviting members to renew their subscriptions. This can be done on a fixed date each year (with annual membership running from say 1st January), or it can be done for each member a year after the original subscription was taken up. Any significant membership scheme is likely to demand a reliable computer system to make it work well. A key point is the ability of the system to identify renewal points so that you can mail not only on the point of renewal but

YOUR INVITATION TO JOIN GREAT ORMOND STREET WELL WISHERS

"Well Wishers" is a special group of caring people. People who care enough to lend their support to these critically ill children. As a member of this group, you will receive our free regular newsletter. Each issue will bring you news of the latest research, treatment breakthroughs and real life stories of outstanding courage, determination, hope and success. It will give you an insight into the day-to-day running of the hospital. It will also keep you in touch with other Well Wishers.

After the huge success of the **Wishing Well Appeal**, this idea was created to maintain funds flowing into the hospital by setting up a 'membership'.

also both before and after to stimulate the highest possible renewal rate. The other point that causes grief to many fundraisers is the inability of the system to merge donor information, which is collected when members make additional donations, with their essential membership data. It is essential not to keep two separate sets of information so you are able to look up one person in one place to find out how and when they have supported you. With the current generation of high speed computers running sophisticated databases at a relatively low price, it is now quite easy to find a suitable system.

4.8.5 Pricing

MEMBERS OR DONORS

- Given the choice the majority of people will join, but this depends greatly on which recruitment media are used.
- Joiners give a smaller average amount than donors.
- Large numbers of people will simply be directed by the format of the coupon and do what it asks.
- Even when strongly encouraged to join, a hard-core of 20% or so will still choose not to, but will donate instead.

This is what **Friends of the Earth** discovered about giving donations or joining as a member when supporters have the choice.

One of the key issues in membership marketing is the way membership is priced and styled. Membership fees have to take into account the possibility of attracting large numbers of people who are prepared to be identified with your organisation. They need to reflect the costs of servicing the membership (from membership cards and AGM costs, through to member magazines and mailings); and they also need to give room to special categories of people, such as old age pensioners and benefit claimants at one end of the spectrum and those wealthy supporters, benefactors and corporate members, for whom an individual subscription would be too low. Many organisations have several categories of membership with different levels of annual subscription for each.

Life membership is a chance to get a single large payment in one go, offering the chance for a member to be seen as an important benefactor of the organisation. Other categories of membership can be created such as a sponsor or a patron, or special categories like those produced by the Royal National Lifeboat Institute's 'Shoreline', for people who can be expected to give more. One organisation has three categories – Friends, Good Friends and Best of Friends.

A change in the annual subscription rates can be a very laborious process. Some organisations review their subscriptions every two years or so at their AGM and take a conservative view of the need to increase rates. This means that membership fees can often lag well behind inflationary pressures and costs.

Membership subscriptions do not usually provide much surplus income for most organisations. Appeals to the members, especially if they are focused on a special need, can be extremely successful if the appeal is pitched right. Equally, the need to communicate regularly with members is such that it provides frequent opportunities to solicit for donations and to encourage regular giving. One effective point at which to ask for donations is when a member is about to renew their subscription. If it involves a cheque or standing order being sent, then there can be a line just above the 'total' box saying something like "I enclose my donation of". Another way of taking advantage of this opportunity is to ask people to make membership payments by standing order. A standing order expressed as a monthly contribution always sounds small. It is therefore not difficult to get the amount increased (as an extra donation). Two or three pounds a month sounds little to pay for an £18 annual subscription! The final step may be to get repeat subscriptions paid by direct debit, thus facilitating regular increases in the annual subscription rates to allow for inflation.

4.8.6 Spin off

An important purpose of having a membership is the indirect benefit it can bring. If an organisation wishes to mount a campaign, its members are the first who are usually called on to participate in it. Indeed, the Government is said to take very seriously membership numbers as a degree of the public support for a campaign or issue, and many campaigning and single issue organisations now have membership in excess of the national political parties.

4.9 Schools

Fundraising from children and in schools is virtually synonymous, since schools are about the only place where children can be approached. If you want to harness large numbers and the enthusiasm of young people, you will have to work through the schools in your area. Not only that, you will be approaching an institution that has been heavily targeted by other charities, and one whose interests are different from your own. Raising money from children in schools has grown in popularity to the point that schools are now restricting access and looking to their own needs and to the educational interests of their pupils. What children are likely to have is time rather than money. So if you are able to obtain access, raising money *with* young people can both be effective and help you lay an important base for future support.

4.9.1 Ethics

Raising money from children is a delicate matter for a number of interconnected reasons.

The first is a simple legal issue: people under the age of 18 are not able to enter into legal agreements and should not be expected or invited to make contributions of any contractual nature (such as a Deed of Covenant).

The second issue is what you can expect children to do in school. This is well covered in the Institute of Charity Fundraising Managers (ICFM) code of practice on fundraising in schools. (See Appendix 6.4) Obviously the role of school is to prepare young people for their future life. Though charity and charity appeals are certainly part of an outside world which is relevant to them, exploring this may be best done by classroom work rather than through some fundraising event. The school must be the judge of what is appropriate, and many now have quite tough stipulations on accepting charity appeals.

A third issue is the pressure that children apply implicitly or explicitly on their parents to give money or participate in an event. In most cases of fundraising with children, the money that is generated is contributed by parents and close relatives or neighbours. Parents may react negatively to the number of times and the purposes they are asked to give to through their children, and may even prevent their children from taking part.

4.9.2 Making approaches

Approaching children through their school has to be arranged through the head teacher. Most will be receiving a large number of approaches, and will want to ration the number of activities taking place in the school. Although the local education authority plays little part in determining what happens in the school, some charities find it useful to be able to say that they have sought approval from the education authority.

It is unlikely that you will be able to involve a school more than once in any one year, so you will probably need to contact as many schools as possible in order to get a reasonable number helping you. A personal visit is the ideal approach. If this is not practical, a telephone call will be better than a circular letter which is likely to find its way into the bin.

4.9.3 Ideas for fundraising

No school is going to want to have you in, if the only thing you plan to do is raise money. A useful guide is to make your activities:

• First fun;

• Then educational;

• And only then about fundraising.

The usual starting point is to offer to give a talk about your organisation and the needs that it aims to serve. This would probably be to a school assembly. You will need to make your presentation as attractive and interesting to the children as possible because this introduces the next step – the invitation to fundraise. This will either be taken up by the school or by particular classes if it fits into some other aspect of their educational programme.

For infant and junior schools you will need to offer very clearly set out ideas if they are to succeed. Help the Aged, for example, has a series of quizzes for different age groups which are changed every year or so, and are designed to fit in to the curriculum as closely as possible. Sponsored competitions are popular as they give the child the opportunity to learn and to obtain sponsorship for the number of questions answered correctly. For secondary schools, the children themselves are in a better position to decide how funds should be raised.

SOME FUNDRAISING IDEAS FOR SCHOOLS AND YOUNG PEOPLE

Auctions
Carol singing
Contests
Discos
Litter picking
Picnics
Raffles
Rag days
Recycling
Sponsored events
Summer fete with:
    face painting
    name the teddy
    high jumping
    puppet making
    treasure map
    book stalls
Tea bars
Treasure hunts
Tugs of war

WHAT'S SO SPECIAL ABOUT BARNARDOS?

Barnardo's and the Children's Society are among those who publish excellent materials designed for young people to thank them for their giving or to give them ideas as to what their money will achieve.

4.9.4 Follow up

A number of the larger charities produce publications for children which are sent to young people in response to enquiries or as a thank you for a donation. Young Gateway, a four-page section of the Children's Society magazine sets out to motivate children to become further involved by showing what other young people around the country are doing for the charity. The Red Nose Club does the same for Comic Relief. Barnardo's, on the other hand, have devoted a 16-page full colour leaflet to informing children about the work of the charity. Laid out in cartoon format it demands the child's attention and includes a well designed quiz. These undoubtedly build a strong loyalty to the organisations concerned and are an important ingredient of their fundraising programme.

4.9.5 Issues

There are two main considerations that arise out of raising money through young people.

First is the impact of getting it wrong in some way. If you are seen to be asking too frequently or to be applying too much pressure, then this will be felt by parents. They will be especially sensitive to this, and any mistake will cause a loss of public confidence in your cause generally.

On the other hand, the advantages of having a large number of young people involved or at least aware of your work, will stand you in good stead for the future, especially if you are able to maintain contact over the years.

4.9.6 School fundraising

Not only is there an increase in competitive pressures, with more and more charities competing to raise money from a smaller and smaller number of schools and young people, but there is a whole new sector of organisations raising money through schools – the schools themselves. As the local management of the school budget gets established, schools will appreciate that the only way to expand or improve the quality of their service or provide for extras will be to raise money themselves. Naturally schools will have first call both on access to the parents and children, and also on their loyalty. Raising funds for the school itself can be carried out in a whole range of ways that are covered elsewhere in this book. Fetes, discos, sales, Christmas cards, tapes, performances and entertainments, and 100 clubs have all proved themselves to be popular and effective.

4.9.7 Skills and resources

To make a sensible approach to schools, you have to be able to make an interesting presentation to the children and to illustrate your talk with

HECTOR'S NATURE TRAIL

Using a preprinted sheet, **Help the Aged** have combined educational content with having fun by offering children a nature trail in which they have to answer 40 nature questions, work out anagrams, and so on, having got sponsorship from family or friends. The sheet comes with clear instructions to teachers and comes in a range that are suitable for different age groups.

slides or a video. To follow this up, you need to have well written up sets of ideas or activity sheets that even the youngest children can follow.

4.9.8 References

For a range of useful ideas see:
> The Complete Guide to Fundraising, Mercury
> Fundraising for Schools, Kogan Page
> ICFM code of practice for schools, ICFM – (see Section 6.4.1)

4.10 Gambling

Raising money through competitions or games of chance has had a chequered past; yet some organisations do very nicely from running lotteries and raffles on an almost continuous basis or occasionally to raise money locally.

4.10.1 Introduction

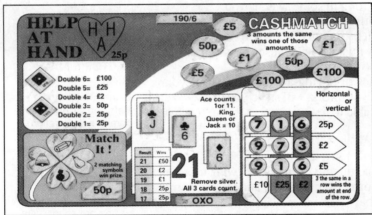

There are three main types of activity. The first is the lottery, which is a sale of tickets, each giving an equal chance of success, where no skill is involved. A sweepstake such as the Irish Hospitals Sweep (though operated outside British law) rates as a lottery, as does a tombola or a raffle or a money game (usually run with scratch cards). These are all governed by the lottery laws. The second is the game of skill – a true competition – where there is a prize: spot the ball is a good example of a game that is supposedly a game of skill, and as a game of skill not chance it can be operated outside the lottery laws, although under the guidelines of the British Code of Sales Promotion. In either case, a keen observance of the legal niceties is important here. The third is the free entry draw, which may be part of a sales promotion or offered as an incentive to members. Because no stake money is involved, this again falls outside the lottery laws.

Scratch cards like this can be popular for fundraising. The numbers come silvered over and are scratched off at the point of purchase. The cost of the tickets is high and thus you would need to be able to distribute large numbers. These are governed by the normal lottery rules.

4.10.2 Legal requirements

There are three main types of lottery, all governed by the Lotteries and Amusements Act 1976. There are legal requirements on the level of

116

prizes that can be offered, the amount of expenses that can be charged and the way the lottery is organised. These are outlined in the ICFM code of practice (see Appendix 6.4).

If you are planning a small event like a bazaar, then a **small lottery** will be appropriate. This has to have the following requirements: the lottery (or raffle as it may be called) must be ancillary to the event; it must be promoted only at that time and place; prizes must be goods not cash; and no more than £50 can be spent on the purchase of prizes – donated items don't count. If all these conditions are met, then no registration is required and you can simply use cloakroom tickets.

Next is the **private lottery**. This requires that you promote the lottery or raffle only to the members of a society or those on the premises; that all proceeds are used for the work of the society; and that properly prepared tickets are issued. Again no registration is required.

For bigger lotteries, if sales exceed £10,000, you need to register with the local authority or with the Gaming Board. In either case, there is a fee to be paid for the licence, strict rules have to be observed, and accounts for the lottery have to be produced and submitted to the registration authority after the lottery.

In 1993 a new lottery law will be passed enabling a National Lottery to be organised under the supervision of the Department of National Heritage. This will be an extremely large-scale affair and the large proceeds predicted will be distributed amongst heritage, the arts, sport and charitable purposes.

For a competition where skill is involved in determining the outcome, no registration is required and there is no limit to the prizes that can be offered, as these fall outside the lottery laws. It is important to verify that there is a real element of skill, so that the activity is not deemed to be a game of chance. Likewise, for sales promotions where no entry fee is required to enter the draw, no registration is required whether or not the activity involves skill or chance.

4.10.3 Prizes

Clearly the attraction to many in entering a raffle or competition is the chance to win a prize. The prizes on offer should relate to the audience who you hope will buy the tickets.

For most small scale competitions, the audience is relatively easy to assess. In the school fete you can be fairly sure that parents and their children will predominate. In which case toys, food and drinks are safe prizes. It is in these sort of events that the prize is least important: people will often buy a ticket for the fun of it and because they wish to support the cause. However for a larger event, the choice of prizes is more important. In a recent Save the Rainforests raffle, the first prize was an Amazon adventure for two donated by a travel company, with a second prize of an expedition to Mount Everest. These were targeted to appeal to an audience interested in the rainforest and in the environment generally. An unusual and imaginative prize will almost always be more attractive than a money prize.

This is a good example of a charity raffle. It combines, on the reverse, details of all the prize donors and an opportunity to make a gift to FOE. On the front are the key prizes that will certainly be attractive to FOE supporters and consistent with their ethos. They run several of these raffles each year.

Prizes can be in the form of donated goods or services or bought using money donated by a sponsor. Try to get everything sponsored or donated, as this reduces the risk of the venture and increases the amount you raise from the lottery.

Identify what you can offer a sponsor. Can you put their name and phone number on the tickets? Can you describe their prize in glowing terms in any posters you produce? Can you mention their generosity in your newsletter? Link this to the numbers of tickets you expect to sell and this should make an attractive proposition to any sponsor. Remember that the actual cost of a £1,000 tour may well be only £500 or even less to the company donating the holiday.

In approaching sponsors, you will want to prepare an outline of your plans. For large raffles, organisers are now producing a special brochure describing the activity and highlighting the advantages to donors and sponsors. Next you should phone, write or arrange to visit potential sponsors, and this should be done well before the event. The Anti-Apartheid Movement contacted 100 companies in order to reach their target of getting prizes donated by 25 companies planning for a 1-in-4 success rate.

4.10.4 Promotion

Everything hinges on the selling of the tickets. If the prize is right and the price of each ticket is not too high, then raffle tickets are best sold on a personal basis. Whether you have a captive audience at an event or a dispersed membership, selling those few extra tickets will make all the difference. Most of the costs of a raffle are in the preparation and printing; hence it makes good sense to do everything possible to sell all the tickets you have planned to sell. First approach your own constituency. Though many people dislike inertia selling, mailing raffle tickets to supporters is just about acceptable and can work financially. On receipt of these your supporters will either go out and sell them, buy the tickets themselves, send them back to you, or do nothing. Few will return them – only around 1%. In one large raffle, 20,000 members were each sent 2 books. This resulted in around 100 returns and a total sale of 96,000 tickets. The result was expenses of £12,000, yielding total receipts of £60,000.

Your supporters may have access to other networks. Groups of medical workers could sell in hospitals; trade union members could sell to other members; and employees to colleagues at the workplace. This can be very cost-effective. Similarly, if you are organising a large public event, you can sell books of tickets at the event by personal solicitation. A small team of volunteers can go around a showground or a conference hall, and ask everyone they meet to buy a ticket or a book of tickets.

Some organisations are now offering incentives for the sale of lottery tickets. Since it is likely to be your own supporters who will sell the tickets, you need to find a prize that will appeal to them and offer it to the person who sells most tickets. One organisation offered a computer, though they found it difficult to tell whether this made any difference. The use of the telephone can be a powerful way to find people to sell tickets.

4.10.5 The draw

In a small raffle the prize draw is a key moment of drama. It is important to build the timing of the draw into your plans. At the event, it should be announced that the draw will take place at a certain time. This time is critical, because after it people will begin to drift away. It is a fixed point in the programme that most people will stay for. Indeed it can be a time of great excitement: the opportunity to collect a prize from a celebrity. Thus the recruitment of a suitable presenter can add to the success of the raffle and the event. As the time of the draw approaches, announcements should be made to encourage last minute sales.

For a larger raffle there are different opportunities. Few members of the public will attend the prize draw, though you must announce where and when it will take place. This is a time for looking forward and for building bridges. Some organisations use it to invite the sponsors in to meet senior staff and trustees, and to enlist their interest and support for next year. Equally there is a good opportunity to publicise the result of the raffle in newsletters, and so build interest in any future lottery. Get a photographer to take photos of prize winners and some of the prizes.

4.10.6 Issues: to gamble or not

Organisations with a religious tradition may find this area of fundraising ethically difficult. They may not want to be involved in a form of gambling. It is not really important whether there is any actual link between addictive gambling and entering a lottery. What is important, is to be clear about the attitude of your trustees before starting to organise any game of skill or chance. Try to get your management committee to agree a policy on this to ensure that there is no disappointment or friction later on.

4.10.7 Getting started

To get started you will need:

• To be clear exactly what sort of activity you are proposing (in legal terms) and what the legal requirements are;

• To have a clear target audience which will help determine your preferred prize or prizes;

- To be able to get hold of a set of desirable prizes without buying them; you will need persuasive powers to get appropriate prizes donated by sponsors;
- To have a plan for selling the tickets, and selling them in sufficient quantity to generate a handsome profit for you.

If you are planning an instant lottery, scratch cards can be obtained from Norton and Wright or from Dale Promotions. Lottery ticket printers can be found in local yellow pages or through the Lotteries Council. Licences, where required, are obtainable from your Local Authority (or from the Gaming Board for large lotteries).

4.10.8 References

See also the following sections:

    4.3   Sponsorship
    4.14 Commercial promotions

And elsewhere:

    ICFM code of practice for lotteries (see Section 6.4.4)
    Lotteries and raffles, NCVO (out of print)
    Norton and Wright
    Dale Promotions
    Lotteries Council
    The Gaming Board of Great Britain

4.11 Television and radio appeals

Broadcast appeals can play an important part in your fundraising. In the changing world of broadcasting, new opportunities for raising money or getting support are opening up almost daily. These cover both television and radio and include both paid for advertising and free coverage of one sort or another.

There are currently four nationally available terrestrial TV channels. Channel 3 is divided into 14 regions with separate coverage in London for weekdays and weekends and a separate company responsible for early morning programming on a national basis across the regions.

Additionally those with a satellite dish can receive the 6 channels broadcast by BSkyB. In some areas some people are able to receive their programmes through cable networks, with the cable station able to produce its own programming to its subscribers in addition to providing subscribers with the broadcast and satellite channels.

Radio is divided into three: commercial stations, BBC and BBC local radio, and community radio. At the time of writing, there are some 44 commercial stations, 30 BBC stations and a growing number of community radio stations.

4.11.1 Television appeals

Because of the nature of the medium and its huge audiences, TV is the most powerful way of getting a message across and of raising money. But it is difficult to use TV to raise money directly. The opportunities for free appeals are limited and paid for advertising is expensive. However, there are many opportunities to get a message across in ways other than a direct appeal; these can, if well co-ordinated, enhance your other fundraising work.

LIKELIHOOD OF ARRANGING BROADCAST APPEALS

Type of appeal	large national charity	small national charity	local charity
The Week's Good Cause (radio and TV)	no	yes	possible
Editorial mentions	yes	yes	yes
TV specials	no	possible	yes
PSA's	yes	yes	yes
TV adverts	yes	possible	no
Radio adverts	yes	yes	yes

The Week's Good Cause

This is the name used for BBC radio appeals, but the mechanisms are similar for TV appeals. To get an appeal you must first apply either to the BBC or the ITC. Both are advised by a joint committee (the Central Appeals Advisory Committee) about which appeals should be given air time. Some appeals are allocated TV time on the monthly slots, usually on Sundays, and others are allocated the weekly radio slot on Sunday mornings.

You may apply for an appeal both to the BBC and to the ITC once every two years. If you are lucky enough to get an appeal slot, you might expect to raise anything from £130,000 to as little as £5,000. There are also opportunities for local appeals in Ireland, Scotland and Wales, where the sums raised will be much less.

Public Service Announcements

Viewers of network TV can hardly fail to notice what look like rather unpolished efforts to recruit volunteers for local charities. These are known as Public Service Announcements (PSA's). They are an extremely good way of recruiting volunteers, and they are free. Approach your local independent TV station.

Editorial appeals

Each year, and especially clustered around Christmas, some magazine and news programmes feature an appeal. Usually they do this only once a year and they always plan well ahead. Blue Peter is the best known example, supporting charities that appeal to children. In their case money is rarely sought – stamps, clothes and other convertible items being the usual object of the appeal. Local and regional news programmes have similar appeals.

To get your charity featured, you must make yourselves known to the producers of the programmes, and in the first place to their researchers. This should be done at least six months in advance. Where there is a link between the audience and the appeal, you are more likely to be successful.

Special fundraising telethons

Telethons were a feature of the 1980s and look set to continue to raise relatively large sums. They are to an extent a counterbalance to the pulling power of the large charities, as most of the proceeds go to smaller and local organisations. Children in Need began appearing annually as a TV appeal supported by radio in 1980, followed in some style by Live Aid in 1984, Comic Relief in 1986 and ITV's Telethon in 1988. Children in Need consistently raises over £20 million each year. The Telethon and Comic Relief are organised every other year and raise slightly larger sums (although 1992's Telethon raised a disappointing £15 million). There are opportunities for charities to be featured as part of the broadcast, but the main chance is to apply for and get a donation of money after the event, in exactly the same way as from a charitable trust. The chances of success are high.

Mention should also be made of the Disasters Emergency Committee (DEC) which provides an opportunity for the major overseas charities to get air-time when there is a major disaster. Members consist of Oxfam, Save the Children, Christian Aid, CAFOD and the British Red Cross, supplemented by Help the Aged and Action Aid from time to time. This is a self selecting club which has been notoriously difficult to get into despite, or perhaps because of, the very high sums raised (from £500,000 to £10 million).

Advertising

Charities have been able to run TV commercials to raise money since September 1989. Gradually some of the major – and some smaller – charities have joined the ranks of TV advertisers. The main problem is the high cost. Though relatively little experience is available yet in UK, there is plenty in other countries that suggests that paid for charity advertising is likely to be a growth area. It can also be used effectively to promote events and charity shops; Oxfam's TV commercials were deemed to have lifted shop returns in excess of the advertising costs. Commercials can be used to promote sponsorship schemes, an example of this being the Christian Children's Fund. They can support charity weeks and flag days, and raise funds directly off the screen.

Very few are paying their way at this stage. However, in the future the costs of air-time may come down, which could make TV advertising more attractive.

Credit card donations

The 1992 Charities Act covers credit card donations or payments for goods in response to a charitable appeal on TV (and also on radio) where the appeal is made by a commercial participator (see Section 4.14.8) or a professional fundraiser (see Section 5.1.7). If the donation or payment is over £50, there is a cooling off period. Donors have the right to cancel the donation or return the goods for a full refund less any administrative expenses. Credit card payments are increasingly used by charities as a response mechanism because of the immediacy of response and ease of payment. Note that the cooling off period does not apply to donations or sales in response to an appeal made by the charity itself.

4.11.2 Radio appeals

Radio must surely rate as the most under-exploited fundraising medium, as it holds many opportunities for the imaginative and energetic fundraiser.

- *The Week's Good Cause:* This has been mentioned above.

- *Public Service Announcements:* The procedure is the same as for TV.

- *Advertising:* The situation is the same as for TV, although the commercial stations are local (with national stations now being licensed). The costs and audiences are both much smaller than for TV.

- *Editorial Coverage*: Radio is a medium which, especially at a local level, has a great deal of potential for charities. News and current affairs programmes can give you coverage and will often accept speakers who will talk about your needs. They may not let you make an overt appeal, but the line is a narrow one! Equally for a local charity they may be prepared to consider doing some sort of on-air appeal event or activity for your benefit. This could range from a straight appeal, to radio auctions, to plugging an event. You should get in touch with the programme producer to explore all the possibilities here.

For national organisations these local initiatives may not be practicable. One thing that can be done is to produce tape recordings, possibly using a celebrity's voice. These can then be mailed to radio stations who may use them to fill any gaps in programming. It is very difficult to identify the value of doing this.

- *Phone ins:* It is always possible to phone in to a chat programme or to get your supporters to do so to express a point of view, promote an activity or make a request.

4.11.3 Choosing a strategy

The best opportunities for obtaining media support depend very much on the size and nature of your organisation. There is nothing to prevent you going for as many of the free options as you can, though the time involved will certainly be a limiting factor.

4.11.4 Advertising on TV

Because television advertising is immensely expensive, it is important to identify realistic objectives for an advertisement. If you simply wish to promote a message, then you may well succeed; but beware here of the ITC rules on what you are allowed to say. Alternatively you may want to lend support to activities going on in the regions or around the country. The Children's Society and Christian Aid have both used TV advertising to support their national fundraising weeks. This can give your volunteers moral support and make the public aware in advance of a flag day or house-to-house collection. So far, there is little evidence of the cost-effectiveness of doing this. TV advertising can also be used to support other appeals such as press advertising or direct mail. Again there is currently little evidence of the outcome of doing this.

The medium can be bought in a wide range of ways. Individual spots can be purchased, but are extremely expensive at peak times. However the evidence suggests that off-peak times are better for charity advertising, such as afternoons and late at night. In this case, packages of spots might be purchased at a good discount.

The choice of media depends on your objective: if it is to get a message across to a national audience then the independent network, breakfast TV, or a satellite channel can be used. If you are to test in one region, then use just one independent TV station.

The message itself is difficult to get right. On the one hand, if it has little impact, you risk wasting the chance to bring your charity to the attention of millions. If you attempt to make it too strong and emotive, you risk having the ad turned down by the regulators. They are still feeling their way, and are likely in the future to relax control somewhat. Make sure your advertising agency checks carefully with the appropriate authority before committing you to too much expense.

TV commercials are not only expensive to run, they also cost anything from £15,000 upwards to produce, depending upon whether you can do the shooting in a studio or need to take a film crew to the Amazon. To cut down on costs, you can try asking the professionals to donate their services free, use existing film or slide based material, use a personality (preferably in a studio), find a partner to share the cost, or get the advertisement sponsored.

RESULTS FROM RECENT ITV APPEALS

	Date	TV Co.	Amount Raised – £	Presenter
National Deaf Children's Society	Jul 89	YTV	8,336	Bryan Mosley
Council for Music in Hospitals	Jul 89	YTV	2,248	Joan Wallace
Church Urban Fund	Aug 89	Cen	2,515	Wendy Richard
VSO	Nov 89	–	12,097	Jan Leeming
Army Benevolent Fund	Dec 89	Cen	9,708	Kenneth Kendall
Royal Nat Mission to Deep Sea Fishermen	Jan 90	Cen	3,517	Michael Bentine
British Home and Hospital for Incurables	Jan 90	YTV	47,022	Gwen Taylor
BRECH	Feb 90	Gra	21,252	Ernie Wise
Nat Osteoporosis Society	Apr 90	Gra	5,320	Linda Evans
Immigrants Aid Trust	Apr 90	Gra	5,200	David Steel
British Deaf Association	May 90	Gra	2,576	Paul Nicholas
Old Pheasantry	Jun 90	Cen	4,620	Lord Tonypandy

4.11.5 Advertising on radio

Advertising on radio has the advantage that it is very much cheaper in comparison with TV and is much more localised. However, it also reaches a much smaller audience. Although it lacks the visual element and is local, it can be especially useful for supporting local or regional events. For example, a concert can be promoted on local radio stations in the catchment area. Shops, or indeed a charity week, can be usefully promoted on radio too, as the information does not require any visual treatment.

Radio time is bought in exactly the same way as TV time and national packages are also available. It would be quite normal for your advertising agency to place adverts with a dozen or so radio stations to cover one part of the country.

The creative possibilities with radio are considerable, but require the help of professionals. Radio lends itself well to competitions, to celebrity voices and to repetition. The cost of production may be from hundreds of pounds to a few thousand. If you have to distribute tapes widely, this will be an additional cost. You can expect well-known voices to give their time free if properly approached.

4.11.6 Getting editorial coverage

The cheapest way of getting publicity for your appeal is to use the editorial power of the media (see also Section 5.15 on public relations). If you are doing something newsworthy, you might try to get coverage for this as a news item. TV and radio news, locally and nationally, require a large number of 'stories' each day. If yours can be one, then you could gain everything that a commercial can give you for a fraction of the cost; indeed if you are mentioned on the news, it gives extra kudos and respectability. It is generally reckoned that editorial coverage is worth at least seven times the value of the equivalent paid space.

News items are picked up because they are relevant locally, because you have announced an important new piece of information (resulting from your research, perhaps), or because you are doing something unusual. If all this is accompanied by film or taped interviews, then it makes it easier for the broadcasters.

The first contact should be with the news desk, and this will start the ball rolling. There can never be any guarantee that you will get coverage, but the producers of the programme will help you identify whether you have something of interest to them. Offering good spokespeople always goes down well, and this can be a very powerful way of getting your organisation's cause across.

Although the media do not like direct appeals to the public in programmes, any appearance or interview is always an opportunity to make an appeal. You should always have worked out exactly how you can mention your specific needs, or give a phone number to call. This can help ensure that your appearance will not only build general awareness, but will also give the public an opportunity to respond directly.

4.11.7 The Week's Good Cause appeal

You can never guarantee that you will get on *The Week's Good Cause* appeal; but since there is nothing to be lost, you should apply every two years. It takes very little time to do this. If you are successful, the publicity and support can be considerable. If you obtain an appeal slot, you next need to think about how to make the best of it. The first step should be to meet the producer who will be allocated to you by the broadcasters. You will want to discuss with them the approach to the appeal, the presenter, and how the script will be developed. Clearly it is not expected that most charities will have the required broadcasting skills available to them so the broadcasters will offer these services. However you may feel that it is more appropriate to develop your script in-house, based on a more intimate knowledge of your organisation. An important decision is who will be the presenter. Actors are very suitable, as they can bring most scripts alive. The person should also be credible to the audience; and so, for example, the choice of Moira Stewart, a BBC1 news reader for a BBC1 appeal, helped the Anti-Slavery Society to raise over £90,000. The broadcasters will be able to suggest possible names to you and help you make the approach. Production of the appeal will be organised by the broadcasters, who will provide a producer with the appropriate skills. All that remains for you, the fundraiser, to do is to ensure that you have enough staff or preferably volunteers who will be able to handle the donations and enquiries that arise.

4.11.8 Arranging special appeals

Most charities will be content to use the existing appeal slots or apply for money from telethons already raising money and with a system for allocating it.

A few may want to consider creating their own special event. There are several reasons why this may be difficult. One is that the broadcast authorities are not keen to encourage or allow appeals (or what may amount to appeals) for individual organisations. The second is that to get TV coverage, the activity needs to be of major news or entertainment value in its own right – for example the Amnesty world concert tour and Anti-Apartheid's two Nelson Mandela concerts. Arguably these were not successful in raising money in the short term, but they were extremely successful as recruitment and information vehicles. They only succeeded at all because they promised good television and excellent entertainment.

4.11.9 Other electronic media

There are a number of other media that can be considered for appeals, but whose impact is unlikely to be great.

Oracle is the ITV text system (parallel to the BBC Ceefax) which puts messages on people's screens. It takes advertisements. As more and more sets have this facility, it is possible to envisage successful fundraising using this medium, especially if it linked to an ability to key in credit card donations.

Prestel is a similar system, which works in an entirely different way. It is run by British Telecom and consists of huge numbers of pages of information on a wide range of subjects. Information providers (regard them as programme makers) provide sets of information (British Rail provides train timetables, for example) which viewers can search or browse through. The whole system is carefully indexed to ensure that if you are looking for information on health care, say, you can find it quickly. Working with the information providers who use Prestel, you may be able to find opportunities to get your message across. Opportunities for doing this will only be found by extensive browsing on the system. You may be able to persuade information providers to organise an appeal for you. Save the Children did this a number of years ago as a joint promotion, where users of services offered by one of the information providers were encouraged to make donations to their appeal. The system provides for two methods of money transfer: one is the ability to make credit card payments on screen; the other is the frame charge fee where each time a subscriber accesses a particular frame of information, they will be charged anything up to 50p. The drawback about Prestel is the very small number of private subscribers, believed to number only around 30,000.

A final medium should be mentioned for completeness. That is the opportunity to communicate provided by facsimile machines. A recent court ruling has stopped this as a safe form of advertising. It is unlikely that in anything other than in direct communication will the fax be of much use to fundraisers.

4.11.10 Getting started

Radio and television offer lots of opportunities to both national and local charities, whatever their means. It is an area well worth exploring. The first thing is to work out a strategy. What can you do with the given resources and what is likely to work for you. That done, then make the time to contact those organisations which may help you. Finally try to co-ordinate your approaches with your other fundraising and promotion work to create extra value from everything that you do.

4.11.11 Skills and resources

To make a successful application to Comic Relief, Telethon and Children in Need you need skills in preparing proposals. The first step is to get a copy of the guidelines for applicants and an application form.

To apply for a radio or TV appeal you simply need an application form.

To get editorial coverage, you will need considerable skills in presenting your case and negotiation. These should not be underrated.

It will be helpful to have proof of your good reputation and work; this can be in the form of newspaper cuttings, well-known supporters, endorsements and so on.

4.11.12 The future

Broadcasting is in a period of substantial change. There is fragmentation of audiences through the use of video and the increasing penetration of satellite and cable. The awarding of new franchises for commercial TV operational from 1 January 1993 will also have an impact as will the renewal of the Charter for the BBC in 1996. At the same time the cost of airtime is likely to reduce, and for the first time the media owners will start pursuing the advertisers.

The radio network is also undergoing considerable change too. The introduction of Community radio in particular must present a major opportunity to local charities to get their message across and to raise funds in their locality.

4.11.13 References

In this book, see also:
> 5.3   Writing a fundraising proposal
> 5.15 Public relations

Refer also to:
> Charities and Broadcasting, DSC. This lists radio and TV stations and describes their community contributions
> Fundraising and Grant Making (ITV Telethon 88), CAF

Broadcast Charitable Appeals (a report on the potential of local radio), DSC
Comic Relief
ITV Telethon (local charities should contact the Telethon Trust at their regional commercial TV station)
Children in Need Offices:
England
Wales
Scotland
Northern Ireland
BBC Appeals Office
ITC Appeals Office

4.12 Giving at work

Giving at work has experienced a renaissance over the last few years with the advent of tax deductible payroll giving. Some 8 million employees are employed in organisations which have introduced a payroll giving scheme. Of these, only around 172,000 employees appear to have signed up and make regular weekly or monthly contributions to charities of their choice – so the potential is (in theory at least) considerable. Will you be able to exploit this? The advantage is that donors make an open-ended commitment to support the charity, which can generate a substantial income in the long-term. Those charities who have put some effort into promotion have received returns of up to 5:1 on their canvassing costs.

4.12.1 Give As You Earn

The tax-effective payroll giving scheme involves the employer registering with one of the approved payroll agencies. Once this has been done, employees can support one or more charities of their choice by making a regular deduction from their pay by signing a Payroll Deduction Coupon and sending it to the wages department who will note it, make the appropriate deduction and pass the form on to the payroll agency. The agency collects together all the payments, ensures that the beneficiary is a charity and pays over the donations to those charities chosen by the employee. The employee does not pay tax on income donated in this way. The scheme has had considerable backing from the Government and the limit for donations that an employee can make is £600 per annum. The scheme is promoted under several different names, the best known

GETTING IN TO A COMPANY

"Instead of starting with local managers, I begin by making contact with the head office concerned, and locating the person whose role covers the scheme. I then seek permission to get in touch with their regional office in order to help promote the company's GAYE scheme. With this backing, regional managers are also willing to back further contact at local level. Finally, at the workplace, the scheme is well received because the preparation has been done thoroughly and all present are aware of the reason for my visit. In other words, the workforce is far more likely to be convinced of the value of the scheme if those in managerial positions have given their personal support for it beforehand."

These are the suggestions of the **Telford Community Trust**.

being **Give As You Earn** (GAYE) run by the Charities Aid Foundation and **Work Aid** run by the Charities Trust. The Agency may make a deduction (normally around 5%) from the deductions, to cover the cost of administration.

4.12.2 Promotion

Before getting into payroll fundraising, you need to decide on your promotional approach and whether to go it alone or join with others in a consortium (see Section 4.12.4).

There are three approaches to promoting your cause to employees. The method adopted initially by some charities was to look to their own supporters and to ask for them to support the charity as usual but using a slightly novel mechanism. This method – conducted in the normal way through the mail – was found to be extremely cost-effective in generating long-term support. Not content with just seeking support from existing supporters, charities then started asking these people to ask others within their places of work. This has proved more difficult as many supporters are not comfortable being fundraisers. The next approach that developed with the advent of the first consortia, was the canvassing campaign. This involves gaining access to employees to mount a promotion, hand out literature and encourage people to sign up. Barnardo's and Save the Children have been doing this for many years. The difficulty has always been to get employers to open their doors to fundraisers who want access to the workplace. A consortium representing a group of charities often finds this easier.

The final approach is to sit back and hope that your charity is well enough known and that when anyone is completing a form, they will include your charity. This approach will only satisfy the most complacent, since any request to give, though it must give the donor freedom of choice to select any charity, will result in returns almost exclusively for the charity organising the promotion.

4.12.3 The employers

Over 2,700 companies, local and health authorities, government departments and other employers have signed up for the payroll scheme. With branches and subsidiaries, this

---

GETTING THEM AT THE WORKBENCH

The Bell Team has taken consortia into over 100 work places. An introductory pilot comes after long hours devoted to getting details correct. The Bell approach does not depend on toys and gimmicks, more on making sure that everyone employed in a company is confronted with the opportunity to give regular charitable donations.

Barry Sheffield, with a background in industry and in agency charity work, who organises company promotions, prefers to have people approached at the workbench; the dining room or canteen appeal can miss out several people. In shift working establishments it can mean a long day for the Bell team – very early morning to late at night.

But the results seem worthwhile. For every £1 spent on a payroll drive a (recurring) donation of £1.50 is secured. The relationship does not stop at securing the signature on a form. Almost at once the new donor gets an appreciative letter from the charity. The intention is that the relationship can be built upon.

Taken from an article in **Charity** magazine describing one commercial organisation's approach to payroll promotion.

GROWTH OF THE PAYROLL DEDUCTION SCHEME

	1987/88	1988/89	1989/90
Employers in scheme	1,800	2,408	3,566
Employees participating	50,629	110,945	180,818
Total receipts (£million)	1.2	3.9	7.3
Average annual gift (£)	23.7	35.2	40.3

This table shows clearly the steady growth of payroll giving in terms of people giving, companies participating and amount given.

must extend to 20,000 or more locations, and the figure is growing all the time.

Some larger employers have organised special promotions to encourage payroll giving amongst their own employees. These involve matching employee giving with company giving or undertaking special promotions for selected charities. Some have rules for access to employees. It is unlikely that you will be given permission to make direct workplace approach except via an open day or as part of the employer's own promotion of payroll giving. Some will have arrangements that leave the choice to elected committees which decide who is given access. Most will have no clear policy. Approaches to committees can best be arranged by the people on the spot.

4.12.4 Consortia

A number of consortia have been formed to ease the problem of access to companies and to share the cost and the risk of promoting payroll giving. As many of these have failed as have succeeded.

A consortium can be structured on a geographic basis (local Gateshead charities), a functional approach (Third World charities), or to include a range of different charities (the Charities at Work Consortium). All can be made to work. The consortium does not itself have to be a registered charity but should be registered with the Inland Revenue. Though a constitution is important in any multi-agency venture, good co-operative working is essential.

4.12.5 Agencies

The agency provides the distribution service for the donation. It makes no difference to the donor which agency the employer uses. The choice of agency is decided by the employer. Half will not have any existing arrangements. It

THE CHARITY CONSORTIA

Charities at Work
Cancer
Combined Charities Fund
Darlington Partnership
Blind Care
Action for Neurological Diseases
Bevaid
Wiltshire Charities Consortium
Scotcare
Triangle
Disability North East
Charities Together
Scottish Disability
MK Care Scheme
Charity Northwest
Paygive North
Capital Giving Portfolio
Active 8
Charities in Action
Five to One
Sheffield Children's Charities
City Life Line
West Hants and East Dorset Charities
Barnet Children's Consortium
South London Family Focus
Fairshares
Breakdown
Deaf Accord
Ex-Services Disabled Homes
New Horizons

These are the consortia that are currently registered. For more information you should contact **CAF**.

may be worth having a good link yourself with one of the main agencies, so that if you find an employer who has not yet introduced a scheme you can suggest an agency to them.

4.12.6 Loan scheme

To help develop payroll giving, the Charities Aid Foundation has set up a loan scheme to encourage charities to employ staff specifically to canvass for payroll giving for a one year period. The loan is repayable out of the proceeds raised. This is a carefully controlled way in which smaller charities can get into payroll giving with little commitment.

4.12.7 Skills and resources

The key skill required to develop payroll giving is the ability to present your case face to face and at meetings. You will need a small team of people provided with good 'point of sale' materials and payroll deduction forms for the employee to make the required deduction (see Appendix 6.5).

4.12.8 References

Further information from:

Charities Aid Foundation, for information on the Give As You Earn and loan scheme
Six Steps to signing, a fundraiser's guide to GAYE published by the Northern Ireland Council for Voluntary Action
The Payroll Giving Association, for details of standard coupon formats that you must use for your deduction forms

4.13 Advertising

4.13.1 Introduction

Taking space in a newspaper or magazine can be a powerful if expensive way of promoting a message or raising money. You can raise money off the page directly, or indirectly by recruiting members, volunteers or those seeking further information. It can be extremely successful in raising money at the time of a disaster or when an issue has hit the headlines. You can also use it to build awareness of your charity, or indeed to invite people to support you with legacies. Advertising can be carried in the pages of the press (national or local, display or small ads), in magazines and journals (general interest or specialist), as a leaflet inserted in a magazine, or as a poster. TV and radio advertising is covered in Section 4.11.

4.13.2 Press advertising

There are several key factors about the use of the press as a medium for advertising. The cost is high, even for a limited space. As a result, the

NINE QUESTIONS TO ASK BEFORE YOU ADVERTISE

I find it useful to start work on appeal advertising by thinking of myself as a person to person fundraiser; about to set off, ringing the doorbells of potential donors. Like a salesman (for that's what I am), I ask myself these questions:

- Which are the best door bells to ring?
- How have I identified them?
- What kind of people live behind these doors?
- What's the best time to 'call', remembering the clamour for their attention?
- What's their lifestyle; their attitudes, discretionary income; knowledge of, and sympathy for my organisation's work?
- How do I best get a hearing?
- How do I get them to open the door and invite me in?
- What shall I ask them to do and how can I most successfully get them to do it?
- How do I retain their continued interest and practical support?

Not until I have answered these questions am I ready to see how my charity's need can be translated into the 'calls' I'm going to make in printed advertisements.

I'm not writing to a mass audience. I'm writing to individuals; to the reader, my press ad (like my mailing), must come as a personal message, telling her or him of a need, so that it evokes a personal reaction and response. But the initial impact needs to be swift, or it will never retain attention.

From **The Printed Fundraiser** by Harold Sumption.

---

messages that can be afforded tend to be very much shorter and must be more striking to be noticed. Press advertising has an advantage over other fundraising methods in that you can select your audience by reference to the known readership of the paper or magazine; you can also predict with more or less certainty whether your issues are likely to be given editorial coverage and, if so, whether or not this will be done sympathetically. At best, an advertisement in the press will give a 5:1 revenue to cost ratio. Most organisations cannot hope to achieve this and many lose substantial sums through advertising. It is likely that what you can achieve with advertising, can also be achieved more cheaply with effective and well-targeted public relations (see Section 5.15.).

Disaster advertising

Possibly the most exciting aspect of using this medium is its flexibility. You can place an advertisement extremely quickly. Thus if a disaster happens one day, you could be appealing for help the next day at the breakfast table. What is a disaster? It is not what you think is serious, it is what your public is being told is serious by the paper itself and by other news media. Timing here is all, and one estimate is that 30% of your response is likely to come from getting the timing right. The difficulty with this use of the medium is getting enough information soon enough to be able to go to press safely. A famine overseas is an obvious example;

HOW BIG A SPACE SHOULD YOU USE?

Space size	Responses
1/4 page	48
1/2 page	71
3/4 page	87
full page	100
Double page	141

This table illustrates what research and practical experience has shown about the disproportionate effect of using small spaces in advertising. The responses are those you would expect to receive indexed against a full page. You should bear in mind that you may be able to get a larger space for a greater discount and thus counter the advantage of taking a smaller space.

Taken from **Commonsense Direct Marketing**.

less frequent are domestic disasters and those that occur regularly, such as Crisis with its Christmas appeals.

Acquisition advertising

This is all about finding new supporters who can then be put on your mailing list and profitably appealed to. This is the rationale for the many organisations who do not break even on the initial proceeds of their advertising. They regard it as an investment in their mailing list, which eventually does much more than break even. As an example, the Woodland Trust takes small spaces in the papers to invite you to send £1 to plant a tree. Many of those responding go on to give more substantial sums on a regular basis. You should decide before you start how much you can afford to pay to find a new supporter. Some organisations are happy if they can find new supporters for £50 each. But the precise sum for your organisation will depend on how much you can expect to raise on average subsequently from each supporter.

Awareness advertising

If no one knows about you or if you want to launch a new campaign, then your objective may be to build awareness rather than just raise money or generate support. This form of advertising is both expensive and difficult to measure, and often demands the use of very large spaces. Although this approach is much used by large companies, is it the best way of using very limited charitable funds? Many would say that the use of public relations will buy a good deal more awareness, if used well, than any amount of advertising. The advantage of paying for the space is that what appears is exactly the message you want at the time and frequency you want.

Legacy advertising

This is a bit of a hybrid that demands some careful thought. On the one hand, the likely value of a legacy is very high, while on the other you can rarely determine whether the advertising has succeeded, partly due to the length of time that will elapse before you receive the legacy and partly due to the difficulty of linking the legacy with a particular promotion. There are a number of specialist media for the legacy advertiser targeted at solicitors and others who advise on will making. A good deal of pressure is exerted on charities to advertise for legacies. Before you say yes, read Section 4.5 carefully.

4.13.3 Loose inserts

One of the main problems with buying space in newspapers is the size constraint. The purchase of 20 cms across two columns in a national broadsheet may cost in excess of £4,000; the cost is high **and** the space very limited. The use of loose inserts gets over half of this problem. Depending on the publication, anything from a small leaflet to a catalogue can be inserted or bound into the publication.

The same considerations and uses apply to inserts as to advertisements. There are two main differences between an insert and an advertisement. The first is the space available to you. There may be restrictions on the weight of the insert, and the print cost will vary with size. The cost of using a larger format is quite small, and this means that inserts are an ideal medium to describe your work and the different ways of supporting your organisation. They can work extremely well for membership and covenant drives, sponsorship schemes, and those appeals that demand space. The other major difference is that inserts take time to arrange and produce. Thus they cannot easily be produced to take advantage of topical events in the same way as an advertisement.

4.13.4 Posters

Posters fit least well into the fundraising area, but are nonetheless a useful promotional medium. They can range from the huge 96 sheet hoardings visible on main roads right down to A3 size and smaller posters for use in windows and notice boards.

An example of a simple loose insert that falls out of so many magazines. These have the advantage over a space ad that they have much more room to develop the story needs and that they can have a built-in envelope or response device. Like ads, they can be targeted to appropriate prospects and can range from very small to very large distributions.

Commercial posters

A whole industry exists to plaster huge images of products and ideas across the land. Posters are a potent communications medium. Their impact depends on size of image and the extent of coverage. Naturally it requires a great deal of both to get a message across. And this is expensive. What charities can do is to use the medium in small bursts to highlight a week or the launch of a campaign, either nationally or in a chosen area. Or, like political parties at election time, they can rent a site for a day to promote a poster which will generate controversy and media coverage.

It is also significant what posters cannot do. By and large posters cannot be used in rural areas – most sites being in town and cities. Perhaps more significantly, posters do not allow for any direct response, except via a phone number. In any event, the time over which people see a poster, either in a car or walking around a town, is extremely short. In neither case are they well-placed to respond to your appeal. Thus, at best, posters can only act as an awareness medium to support other activities.

Free posters

For a long time the poster industry has organised itself to offer free poster sites to charities on the basis that it's better to display something than have empty and torn billboards. These are usually the less good sites and those that are unbooked. They are likely to be 16-sheet and 4-sheet sizes. The former are the smallest sites that go on building ends; the 4-sheet sites are at pedestrian level.

THE GREAT WHALES

Since commercial whaling was banned in 1986, the whaling nations have killed over 13,000 whales. Now they want to lift the ban.

In that time, Greenpeace has exposed and opposed the slaughter and has won international support for a permanent ban to end all whaling. Because of this, the whales may still have a future.

THANK GOD SOMEONE'S MAKING WAVES

The purpose of this ad is to find a new supporter for **Greenpeace**. Ads of this sort are not usually expected to do better than break even and often do not even do that. Their real purpose is to build a mailing list which can generate returns of over £5 for each £1 spent.

The things to consider with free sites include:

- Are these sites available when you want them?
- Where are the sites themselves, and are they in the right place?
- Is the cost of printing posters too high to make it worthwhile?
- Would it be useful to produce cheap run-on posters in addition to those required for the sites?
- Can you get the posters sponsored?

Mini-posters

In a different league from the commercial poster industry are the small posters which are used to publicise almost anything locally. These are attractive for fundraising, since they can be printed cheaply and posted free.

Depending on what you are promoting, mini-posters can be targeted at whoever you want. They can be put in windows, in local shops, on library notice boards and in community centres. Distribution can be done by volunteers distributing thousands of leaflets and creating highly visible campaigns at little cost.

4.13.5 Evaluating the results

Fundraisers should always try to evaluate the effectiveness of advertising. The way of doing this is by using a coded coupon, reply address or phone number on the advertisement. The coding should be done for the campaign as a whole and for each separate promotion in the campaign. This is the only way you can find out which medium works best for you. Results can then be measured in terms of:

- Income raised per £ of media cost;
- Cost per new donor recruited;
- Cost per legacy notification generated (for legacy advertising).

In the case of awareness advertising, research can be conducted before and after to measure the increased awareness generated by the campaign – however, this can be expensive.

4.13.6 Issues in advertising

- **Seeing it through other people's eyes:** In fundraising, it will be necessary to illustrate the cause in some way. Images of the beneficiary and their needs will often provide the most powerful means of generating a response. The question then arises as to the effect this might have on the beneficiaries themselves or on public attitudes towards the cause. The views of British children of the Third World are cited as an example, with images and attitudes formed by disaster advertising. It is noteworthy that organisations dealing with the problems of disability use very much less harrowing pictures, especially when they are controlled by the people who themselves suffer the disabilities. An alternative approach is to use very positive images.

- **Free or fee?:** There remains the option of declining to pay for advertising. A number of campaigns have been developed using free space whenever it becomes available (for example, the advertisements by the Friends of John McCarthy). The disadvantage is that you have no control over the intensity or timing of your campaign. The same approach can be applied to getting the services of an advertising agency. Most claim not to make money on charity accounts; they may be prevailed upon to take on your account free.

4.13.7 Getting started

Once you have decided to use advertising, there are two key decisions to take. How to design and produce your advertising and how to place it. Both can be done by you, but you will never be able to purchase media as cheaply as a registered media buyer or an advertising agency. Developing the creative approach and producing the design, has traditionally been the role of the advertising agency. They may be less than interested in taking on very small clients; check first. However, selling fast cars may not make them as sympathetic to the nuances of your work as a friendly local designer who is familiar with what you are doing.

4.14 Commercial promotions

For larger charities, commercial promotions can be a welcome addition to their income, bringing in large amounts of money relatively painlessly and exposing their name to millions of people for little or no cost. The principle can also be extended to local promotions for local charities.

4.14.1 Definition

This type of fundraising is an arrangement that benefits both your charity and a commercial partner, usually a company. It is rather like sponsorship, but the relationships are reversed – you are linked to the company's products rather than them to yours. Included in this section are on-pack and licensing promotional deals, competitions and awards, the use of phone lines, and self-liquidating offers of your own products. What they have in common is that they present an opportunity to raise money for your cause and to project your charity to new audiences, and they require that you work with others in achieving it.

SAVE THE WORLD WITH WORLD SAVERS

"1989 has seen the launch of **NatWest**'s biggest sponsorship to date – a guaranteed £3 million link with **WWF** over three years. Launched in January, the World Savers scheme offers accounts to children, paying a premium rate of interest, which can be opened with a minimum of £5. A donation of £1 from the Bank's own funds will be given for each World Saver's account opened, and 0.5 % of the total balances will be donated annually."

A classic example of "you buy this product and we give an extra £1 to charity".

4.14.2 On-pack promotions

The driest boy and girl is a Pampers Boy and Girl.

An example of the value of a charity's name being used to mutual advantage. After some debate over the environmental friendliness of disposable nappies, it was well worthwhile this manufacturer receiving the approval of the **World Wildlife Fund**. In return, WWF have developed a close relationship with P&G worth up to £200,000.

There are many variants of the on-pack promotion. They start with the need of a manufacturer to promote a product or service at a particular point in time – to the wholesaler, the retailer or to the consumer. The basic mechanism is that with every purchase of the product or every label returned, the manufacturer gives a specified amount to the charity, sometimes with an upper limit on the total that will be given. Good practice requires that the amount be specified on the pack, and that there should be no conditions which affect the donation. Manufacturers like this sort of arrangement as they can predict quite accurately what it is going to cost to achieve sales at a given level. Fundraisers like it, since it presents their cause to literally millions of shoppers, and because they can usually expect to recover a substantial sum. Variations on this theme include the consortium promotion which includes a galaxy of well-known charities included together in one promotion. Most schemes are on a national basis with a nationally known charity. For example, every Pizza Veneziana sold by the Pizza Express Chain generated 25p for the Venice in Peril appeal. But local and smaller scale promotions are also possible. A local Indian take-away donates all the proceeds of the sale of a lentil dish each Friday to selected charities supported by the owner.

4.14.3 Licensing

When a charity has become a safe household name, branded goods manufacturers are interested in using an association with the name of the charity to enhance its brands. Out of this is born the licensing deal. This differs from the on-pack promotion in that the promotion is likely to involve a fixed number of uses of the logo or name over a given period. Precisely where and when it is used is then up to the manufacturer within the agreed limits. The outcome is then not directly related to the level of public support, but is agreed at the outset as a fee.

4.14.4 Competitions

Another variant is the on-pack promotion that involves a competition. The competition is usually a prize draw which is essentially a game of chance and may involve a tie-break question. For the fundraiser these offer several benefits. The promotion can be related somehow to the charity. If it's an overseas charity, the prize could be a trip or some of your trading goods; if a domestic cause, the questions could be built around creating a better understanding of your cause. Money will accrue to the charity either through a contribution for every entry or from an agreed fee for the use of the charity's name.

4.14.5 Self-liquidating offers

The self-liquidating offer is the rather grand name for promoting one of your products so that its cost is recovered. You offer one of your products – say an attractive t-shirt – to a manufacturer to feature on the back of a pack. There are several advantages of such an arrangement. Depending on the pricing, you may end up making a profit on a large number of sales – something that charities do not often manage by selling such goods themselves. Whether or not you do better than recover your costs, you can certainly expect to distribute a large number of items bearing your message. Finally, there is the number of people who see the promotion but who do not buy. You should also note the possibility of retaining the mailing list of purchasers – or those redeeming packet tops – as a suitable list for subsequent direct mail fundraising or trading.

4.14.6 Getting started

Getting started on promotions of this kind is quite daunting for a small charity and exacting for anybody. It is one of the areas where professionalism will pay dividends.

The first step is to decide whether it is worth waiting until companies or their agencies contact you, or whether you want to take the initiative and contact likely partner companies. In order to do this, you need to be absolutely clear about the nature of your cause, the extent to which you can associate it with a given industry or company and your attractiveness as a cause and an organisation to commercial partners.

Ideally, you need to research the industries and companies that are likely to make good partners. What products do they make, what are their marketing objectives and who are their competitors? With this information, it is worth trying to meet the marketing director to present the possibilities and the advantages of an association. It is preferable at this stage not to have too detailed a proposal in mind, so that you can react to what you find to be the company's own preferences and needs. Though this will not be possible if it is the first promotion you are arranging, you should take along examples of how other companies have benefited from an association with you.

Finally you need to consider what to do when you are approached by an agency pitching for business. These are independent sales promotion agencies. They may have a good idea that involves your charity; having got your interest, they then have to sell the idea to a company. Probably nine out of ten of these ideas come to nothing, and you may find you have to put in considerable effort.

This promotion by **Operation Raleigh** appeared on the back of a cereal packet. For every eight tokens sent in, the manufacturer gives £1. Apart from the millions of people seeing this every morning, continuity is guaranteed by the distribution of mini comics in subsequent cereal packs.

4.14.7 Issues

Getting into the promotions business brings charities face to face with a range of dilemmas, just as sponsorship does. It is one thing when a charity accepts or even solicits money from an organisation about whose activities it has some reservations; it is quite another when it actively seeks to promote the work of such a company or be publicly associated with its goods or services, as will happen in a promotion.

You are strongly recommended to develop your own policy on what commercial associations you are prepared to enter into.

How much you should expect from a promotion is also a difficult question. Your name is effectively being sold to the company to enhance theirs. It may be worth a great deal to them to be linked with you; on the other hand the value of your reputation may be very high too. Ultimately that is what you will lose if the links you make are unsound. Any negotiation should start from what you think the association is worth to them and whether it is worth your while to enter into the promotion at that price.

The income generated from the arrangement will almost certainly be trading income (from the sale of good will), rather than donated income; and you may need to take professional advice on how to structure the arrangement (see Section 4.16.6).

4.14.8 Charities Act requirements for commercial participators

Part II of the 1992 Charities Act seeks to control fundraising, and one part is specifically aimed at commercial promotions. The Act first defines a 'commercial participator' as anyone engaged in any form of business other than a fundraising business where they engage in a promotional venture (an advertising or sales campaign or any other venture undertaken for promotional purposes) in which it is represented that donations or proceeds from sales are to be given to charity. If the commercial organisation carries on a fundraising business, then it will be a 'professional fundraiser' and similar conditions will apply. If it is the charity itself, through its connected trading company, which is undertaking the promotional venture, then the conditions laid down by the Charities Act do not apply.

There has to be a proper written agreement between the commercial participator and the charity. What the agreement must cover is laid down in the Charities Act regulations, and advice on the wording of the agreement can be obtained from the Institute of Charity Fundraising Managers. The commercial participator is required to make a clear and accurate statement in their promotions stating the institution or institutions that will benefit and in what proportions, and how the institutions will benefit (the amounts of any donations to be made or the proportions of the price of any goods or services which are to be given to the charity). It is an offence to breach the requirements.

4.14.9 Skills and resources needed

As with sponsorship, the key skills that you need to get promotions off the ground are those of negotiation and good presentation. Negotiation skills will come into play when you have got their interest and need to wrest an advantageous deal. How not to give too much away, yet how to ensure you don't lose their interest. Good presentation both verbally and visually, will help you explain what you have in mind to companies which have very little experience of your world.

Marketing and public relations skills will help you identify where the opportunities for your organisation lie.

4.14.10 References

British Code of Sales Promotion from the Institute of Sales Promotion

4.15 Credit cards and financial products

The Financial Services Act carefully controls the links between charities and financial services companies. However, there are still a number of ways in which charities can exploit their goodwill and their supporters' loyalty by promoting or recommending the products of financial services companies. In this section we look at three different types of approach: the sale of investment products; the sale of insurance; and the sale of credit cards.

4.15.1 Investment and savings schemes

The unit trust business has been traditionally hungry for business and some have looked for promotional opportunities with charities. The arrival of ethical and green unit trusts has presented a further opportunity, as the ethical angle makes them natural partners for some charities.

The charity supporter is asked to make an investment (and typically this might be around £500 or more) in a unit trust. Some part of the initial commission (and possibly of the annual management charge) is then donated to the charity. An extension to this idea is the Mencap scheme, set up some years ago, where the Charity launched its own investment trust which is quoted on the Stock Exchange. Managed by a professional firm, the Trust is owned by the investors with the profits being shared with the charity.

Another type of scheme is organised by banks and building societies from time to time. For example, the Girobank offered to give £10 to charity for each investor who opened a new savings account. In this particular case the investor was given the choice of several charities.

4.15.2 Insurance schemes

If the typical charity supporter is in the ABC1 socio-economic group, then there can be few who do not have some sort of insurance on their car, house, personal effects, their lives or health. The providers of these services spend a great deal of money promoting them. This is the perfect climate in which to develop a link between the charity and the insurance company. Life assurance is as much an investment product as an insurance one. Nevertheless it provides a good opportunity for human charities to make the link between looking after the life of the charity's beneficiaries and their supporter's family and dependants. Another type of scheme promotes a commercial household contents insurance policy. Charities are asked to provide the insurance company with the names of people who want to insure their effects, and some of the commission is paid to the charity.

In setting up a scheme, there are two possible approaches. The first is to decide exactly what you want to do and how much commission you require, and then find a broker to work with. The other approach is to link up with a commercial scheme, which also involves a number of other charities, where the returns are likely to be lower.

The Girobank/Oxfam Visa card can help the poor every time you use it.

This was one of the leaders on the many charity cards now available. Most work on the basis of £5 to the charity for each new card taken out plus 25% of all the transactions. Over a period this has built up to large sums for the charities, but still requires a good deal of promotion by the charities.

4.15.3 Credit cards

A relatively recent development has been the growth of charity credit cards or 'affinity cards'. The idea is that most of a charity's members or supporters are likely to use a credit card. For most people one credit card is similar to another and will be accepted in the same places. So why not a charity card, where part of the credit card company's takings are donated to charity. There are now a wide range of schemes. There are two distinctive types.

First are those cards which a particular charity has set up in conjunction with a specific bank: Oxfam with the Girobank; NSPCC with the Bank of Scotland. In schemes like these the money comes to the charity in two ways. It comes through an introductory fee in which the bank gives the charity a fixed payment (£5 or so) for each new account set up. The charity also receives a regular commission of around 1/4% of the cardholder's transaction amounts. As the usage of credit cards for everyday purchases continues to climb, so these commission payments will increase.

The other type of credit card is one which benefits a range of charities. The Green Card is promoted for the benefit of a range of environmental causes. Though the card is not associated with any one charity, charities can benefit from distributions made by the related Green Card Fund.

The market for credit cards is changing with an annual fee now being levied on some cards and differential prices being charged in some shops for card and cash transactions. This presents new problems and opportunities for fundraisers in what has previously been a growth area.

4.15.4 Promotion

The promotion of these schemes presents an interesting challenge. You will almost certainly need a mailing list or a well developed network of supporters. It is the access to these names that the financial services companies are really interested in. The commonest approach is to mail as wide a range of supporters as possible (you should always try to negotiate an arrangement where the company pays the full costs of the promotion). You will need to agree who is funding the mailing, the period you promote it over, how much information on the scheme needs to be provided in the mailing and what return you get from this scheme.

For a charity that is already engaged in a busy mailing programme, there can be a considerable opportunity cost as the supporter switches from one means of helping to another. It is important to have a clear idea how profitable the arrangement will be to the charity.

4.15.5 Issues

There are important issues that the fundraiser needs to be aware of in a sea that is unusually full of sharks! First is the age old question of the company you keep. With any of these schemes you will be beholden to an investment or brokering company; your success will only be as good as the reputation of the company concerned and the performance of its financial product. The other business links of the company are important too. For example, the banks may have interests in the developing world which could compromise your charity.

Another issue arises with credit cards. You may find that the enthusiasm and commitment of a supporter is greater than their good sense. This might result in them getting into debt beyond their ability to repay. The consequences of indebtedness are not pleasant, and may draw you into areas where you have little competence and which are difficult to deal with. The general question of credit cards encouraging indebtedness is an issue you should review. This is just one example of how a charity can become involved in a debate about the quality of the product or service. Clearly there is nothing the charity can do to encourage or discourage an insurance company to meet a claim on a policy. But the supporters of your charity might not feel that way, and they may feel either that you have sold them an insurance policy on false pretences or that you don't care about what happens to them, if they are having problems with their claims.

The presentation of a financial service to your supporters is governed by the Financial Services Act. Your relationship with the financial services company will be subject to the 1992 Charities Act, as they are deemed to be a 'commercial participator', and you will have to fulfil the requirements of the Act (see Section 4.14.8).

4.15.6 Skills and resources

The most obvious resource needed is access to a significant number of supporters. This can be through a mailing list or through a branch or regional network. To be effective you will need to understand how direct mail works and the costs of promoting a scheme before you launch it. And as with other commercial arrangements, you will need sharp negotiating skills to ensure that you get the best out of the partnership.

4.15.7 References

Elsewhere in this book, refer to:

4.16 Trading

One of the most visible aspects of charity fundraising is the trading they engage in. For the biggest charities, this can raise large amounts; for the smaller, it can be a useful way to get started with volunteer fundraising.

4.16.1 Overview

Over 2,500 charity shops populate our high streets, and the number has been increasing rapidly. Next in importance are the many millions of gift catalogues sent out in the mail each Autumn. Trading may seem an attractive fundraising option, but in fact represents a long hard slog at relatively low margins, a high input of capital and drain on management time. The best shop chains get a return of 4:1 on their costs, and catalogue returns can be between break even and 2:1. But many organisations lose rather than make money from their trading – sometimes considerable sums – and this is one of the major areas of worry to the Charity Commission. Beyond these larger-scale activities, there are a range of other smaller-scale trading ventures, from running stalls to selling Christmas cards, which can add useful income to an organisation, particularly when the activity is undertaken by volunteers.

4.16.2 Shops

Most shops are simply a retailing outlet to generate trading profits for the charity. Some aspire to do more than this by being an information centre for the cause. To maintain a shop for whatever purpose requires a considerable management effort. The following are some of the key factors in running a successful shops operation.

- *The location:* Finding the right location is essential. The shop must be sited in such a place as to attract passing trade; it must be near enough for the voluntary helpers; and it must be accessible to those wishing to donate stock. You have to balance these needs with the cost of rental.

- *The staffing:* Most depend extensively on voluntary help. The usual pattern is to employ one professional manager for a shop of any size, who will be at the centre of a team of 20-40 volunteers. Some shops add a separate voluntary committee which takes responsibility for the running of the shop. The training, recruitment, supervision and management of this whole group of people is a key determinant of success.

- *The goods:* Most charity shops sell second-hand goods donated by well-wishers. The quality and the quantity of goods given are important factors in the shop's success. Some have to be cleaned, repaired or checked before they can be sold. All have to be sorted and priced before they can be displayed. In shops like Oxfam's, the second-hand goods are leavened by supplies of overseas handicrafts. In others, supplies of domestic Christmas cards or other new goods help to keep up the impression of quality. The proportion of new goods to donated goods being sold, can have VAT and rates implications and also affect the way the shop operation is structured (see above).

- *Control:* There continue to be a number of weak points in the chain in which charities can be denied the full value of their efforts. Usually the human elements are weakest in shop chains and need constant attention. Increasingly, charities are feeling the need to have security devices, electronic tills and frequent stock takes.

4.16.3 Catalogues

In catalogue trading new goods are offered to supporters usually by mail order or, as in the case of Traidcraft, through local agents. Successful charities may earn as little as a 10% profit from trading in this way, and often it is the associated donations that purchasers add to the purchase price that bring any profit at all. Christmas cards are a useful entry point into this sort of activity.

- *The goods:* When selling goods in this way high standards are needed. The goods are described in print and have to live up to their description. The goods should in some way reflect the values of the organisation either in the use of materials or through design. Some organisations manage to find products relevant to their work: Friends of the Earth with recycled paper products, for example. The goods must be conceived of as a range, and the items must appeal to the target market. The goods must be available in sufficient quantity to meet likely demand, or a serious loss of confidence will arise.

- *Promotion:* Unlike a shop where customers can walk in off the street, a catalogue needs vigorous promotion. The mechanism normally used

GOODS THAT CAN BE BRANDED
- Christmas Cards
- Calendars
- Diaries
- Biros
- Envelope Labels
- Address Books
- T-shirts
- Wallets
- Torches
- Mugs

A few of the many articles that are sold by charities to raise funds and promote their name. Paper items have the advantage of enabling you to print some sort of message about your work on them.

Traidcraft is unusual as a catalogue for a number of reasons. It is clearly differentiated from most catalogues in that the object of its work is to sell Third World handicrafts and because it has a clear Christian orientation. Not only do they send out this catalogue, they use it for their network of representatives selling goods all over the country. They recently built on their success by selling shares in the company to the public.

is direct marketing, the aim being to build up a list of regular purchasers. Although some sales will be gained by word of mouth, most will be through sending a catalogue to previous purchasers or to a list of your supporters or other likely customers.

- *Control and administration:* The management of catalogue trading activity is quite difficult. It involves a major buying operation, with all the control and timing worries that are associated with that. Then there is the question of how to finance such a fluctuating business, where the purchases may need to be paid for well in advance of the revenue being received. Finally there are the warehousing and order processing systems required, which for catalogues of any size can be a major logistic operation.

- *Agencies:* One approach is to use the services of an organisation that offers an off-the-shelf catalogue service. First you need to be sure that your supporters provide an adequate market to make the trading worthwhile. You should identify what you can bring to the operation, and what part of the process you need help with – product selection and purchase, the administration and fulfilment of orders, or the promotion. **Webb Ivory** (a commercial organisation) or **Barnardo Publications** (part of Barnardo's) both have a standard range of products which are regularly packaged into semi or totally personalised catalogues, for a range of charity clients to sell to their supporters. This tactic can enable you to get into trading relatively cheaply and without too much risk. As you find out about what your supporters want, you should be able to migrate away from this sort of arrangement to something that suits your needs more exactly and repays your efforts more fully.

4.16.4 Other trading activities

A great deal of other activity takes place in the voluntary sector that is trading of one sort or another. Most is not usually well organised, but all can be developed to become useful sources of revenue.

- *Sales of materials:* Many organisations produce saleable items either as an intrinsic part of their work or for publicity purposes. In either case, these can be priced to generate a profit. Books and reports can be popularised both through good design and by effective promotion. The sale of one publication can be used to build up a mailing list for the sale of others. This form of trading can extend now to the sale of expertise, consultancy or training. Other items such as posters, t-shirts, and stickers, have always been marketed as a profitable part of voluntary work. The key here is to recognise that it is the design as much as the message that will create success. The ideal approach is to have all the production costs underwritten, so that all the sale proceeds generate clear profit; alternatively every effort should be made to reduce costs and to encourage sales. Losses are often made in this area because of goods failing to sell.

- *Recycling:* A further type of trading is in the recycling of commodity goods such as paper, aluminium or glass. This can be an ideal activity for young and energetic volunteers, but has been shown over the last few years to be very vulnerable to changes in the price of the commodity, which can overnight turn the operation into a loss maker. You will need to consider issues such as promotion of any scheme, collection points, storage facilities, the labour force to make the collections, and contracts and prices for the collected materials. A discussion with Friends of the Earth will usually reveal what is going on in your locality and what opportunities there are.

4.16.5 Getting started

There are two easy ways to get started. One is for the organisation that has a good team of volunteers or can easily recruit people. Local shops will from time to time become empty, pending sale or redevelopment. Try out your shopkeeping skills on a temporary basis, and take whatever lease or licence to occupy that is available. If this succeeds, you know you could make a go of it, and then be prepared to pay a proper rent. Alternatively you could look for an office which has a retail outlet below it. Another approach is to start by setting up stalls at local events, staffed by a few volunteers and selling either new goods or donated items. If you can then attract a ready supply of helpers and goods to sell, you may be ready for the next step. Most importantly, don't expand too quickly.

A good way to start a catalogue may be to copy what the Ex-Services Mental Welfare Society has done. They designed a small range of distinctive Christmas cards and offered them exclusively to their donors. After three years they are earning a good profit, and encouraging the Society to consider selling a wider range of gifts.

Finally is the consortium approach. The **Charity Christmas Card Council** and the **Charity Christmas Card Scheme** help charities promote Christmas cards. The **1959 Group** is a consortium of national and local charities which operates temporary card shops around the country. Webb Ivory or Barnardos can help in building up your own catalogue operation.

4.16.6 Issues

The first issue is whether you can make a profit out of trading, or if it is the most effective way of using your volunteers. Too many charities enter this field over-optimistically, and end up losing money.

If you do trade then there is the question of what goods you should sell. Will you sell furs if they are donated and risk the objections? Will you sell cosmetics tested on animals or use plastic bags that are not bio-degradable? There can be no generalised advice here except to have a clear idea of the audience you are serving (both your supporters and your customers).

In selling anything to the public on any scale, there are attendant risks. For example, the quality of service in a chain of shops may fall below the standard expected by your public. It is not difficult to make mistakes, if there is a heavy dependence on volunteers who are left to go their own way. Equally the goods that are for sale, must be of an appropriate quality and fulfil the legal requirements for the sale of goods; if not, then this may rub off on the perception of the organisation of the charity as a whole.

In reporting the results, there is the problem of how to deal with expenses. When compared with other fundraising activities, trading will look unprofitable in terms of the costs associated with it. Deduct the costs from the revenue and suddenly it looks attractive. The question then is how you should publish the results of this form of fundraising to meet your legal reporting requirements, and show good management of the organisation's resources.

Trading, when this is not a primary purpose of the charity (such as charging for the charity's services), or the sale of goods made by beneficiaries of the charity (e.g. in a sheltered workplace), or the sale of donated goods (which is considered fundraising), is not considered to be a charitable activity. For this reason, charities create their own subsidiary companies to carry out the trading. Any profits are covenanted back to the charity, in this way avoiding any liability to corporation tax. This is an extremely complicated area and it is important to seek proper legal advice if you propose to enter this field.

4.16.7 Skills and resources

There are a number of key skills and resources you will require. For a shop you will need a supply of willing volunteers, suitable premises and some cash. An ideal skill is some retail experience from working in a high street shop. For a catalogue, you will need the resources to hold large stocks of goods, the money to finance the stock holding, and you will need to understand the direct marketing side of building and promoting a catalogue. You will need retailing skills and some caution in order to prevent getting landed with scores of last year's diaries. You will need good financial sense and stock control in order to manage the activity successfully.

4.16.8 References

See also in this book:
Books:
    The Charity Trading Handbook, Charities Advisory Trust (out of print)
    Charity Christmas Cards, DSC
    Museum Trading Handbook, DSC
    Waste Not: (organisations, index of items, useful addresses on recycling), CAF
Useful bodies:
    Charities Advisory Trust (which also operates the Charity Christmas Card Scheme)
    Charity Christmas Card Council

Friends of the Earth
Webb Ivory Ltd
Barnardos Publications Ltd
1959 Group of Charities

4.17 Personal solicitation

Meeting and speaking to potential donors in person is a much neglected area of fundraising, and one that comes into its own with a larger capital appeal. It has much potential for many organisations.

4.17.1 Introduction

There are many different ways in which face-to-face or personal solicitation can be carried out. Besides a one-to-one meeting, broadcast talks, making a presentation at public events or private meetings, personal visits, and telephone calls all fit into the process. All give opportunities for persuasion. Apart from broadcast appeals, which are covered in Section 4.11, all have the possibility of questions being asked and reassurances given. Thus what sets this apart from other methods of fundraising, is the degree of personal projection of the cause and the interaction between the charity and the donor that can take place.

4.17.2 Presentations at events

Many organisations have the opportunity to provide speakers for meetings, or conferences and fundraising events. This is an opportunity to speak directly to the people present about the work of your organisation and its needs. With an experienced speaker, this can be a good opportunity for raising money too. The presentation has to be carefully thought out. The main problem is to work out how your audience is going to respond, and if it is someone else's event, you may need their approval. After you have spoken, the audience may want to get home quickly or to move onto something else. The seating pattern may inhibit them from coming forward for written information or a donation form.

One good signal of your need to raise money can be made by organising a bucket or plate collection. Place collectors at the door or at the end of each row; but don't forget to announce what you are going to do in your speech! This will not generate serious support. To do this, make sure that there is a register of people who have attended or, if it's an invitation event, make sure someone notes who actually came. Those who attended can then be personally visited or written to afterwards.

Other people's events bring you new audiences. You can also organise your own. One idea is to invite a mix of existing and potential supporters to the home of a well respected donor for a dinner or a reception. All the new people who attend should be told to expect a follow up visit from you afterwards.

4.17.3 Warm visiting

Warm visiting involves face-to-face meetings with those who have already supported you or with those whom you have some form of contact. There are two methods of doing this. The first is the soft sell approach where you do not overtly solicit for help. Some larger charities employ individuals whose job it is to visit all their major donors. Though the visitors are ostensibly there to meet supporters and to thank them for their past support, they can actually collect substantial sums and act as a prompt for legacies, covenants and other ways of supporting the organisation.

The second is making personal presentations on the work of the organisation to potential new supporters. Possibly the best way of preparing for such a meeting is to think of it as making a presentation to an audience of one. It will involve fixing an appropriate time and place for the meeting; the charity's offices are often the best place to meet many potential supporters. Even if there is little more than filing cabinets, people and telephones in evidence, it does give people a flavour of the organisation. Alternatively, some people will feel more comfortable meeting in their own homes.

Any visit should be prepared with care. Though it may seem to be overdoing it to rehearse a presentation to just one person, this can pay off. You should try to predict what questions will come up. Use a colleague or friend to help. You will need to be well armed with written information. So go prepared with photos, brochures, budgets and plans so that you can use these as prompts. Short videos can be useful too. Finally, remember to leave some prepared material. Most people will not make up their minds immediately, and will be guided or reminded or helped to respond by what you have left with them.

Throughout the meeting, you should give them the opportunity to put questions. If you are not getting much feel for how the meeting is going, ask some questions. Do they feel it is an important issue? Do they think the project will achieve what it is setting out to do? At some point you need to make the ask (for money). There are many different approaches to this. One is to say that you want them to consider helping in one of several ways. The direct approach dispenses with such niceties and explains the urgency of the need, and simply asks for the money – but always try to ask for a specific amount. The final, and probably most effective way, is when someone who has already given support is making the ask, and mentions what their own donation has been.

4.17.4 Cold visiting

Much more daunting is extending these principles to visiting people cold, with no previous support or giving as a background to the visit. Though this sounds a thoroughly unpromising way of winning friends, it can work very well in the hands of trained visitors. This is unlike house-to-house collecting, in that you are asking for a covenant or some other high value method of giving, and thus the process needs to take place inside the home rather than on the doorstep. But like a house-to-house collection, it does require a licence to collect. A few organisations use teams of young volunteers who make visits on their behalf. The visitor chooses a likely middle class area and calls unannounced in the evenings. They ask if they can talk to the householder about the cause. Typical experience suggests that better than one in a hundred visits result in a covenant or something similar. You need to put in a lot of footwork and be prepared for the usual rejections. It is a particularly suitable method for raising money and support for local community projects where donors can see the need and the benefits on their own doorstep.

4.17.5 Getting started

1. First identify those people in your organisation who are really good speakers and presenters. These should be the people to use when there is an opportunity to meet an important potential donor or address a meeting.

2. Collect good pictorial and other visual material that can form the basis of a presentation.

3. Identify some of your existing donors who might be receptive to a direct approach. Arrange to visit them.

5. SKILLS

5.1 Getting help with your fundraising

The task of the fundraiser is to raise as much money as possible with given resources or, if objectives are more limited, to raise the required amount at the least cost. Inevitably in this process fundraisers will need help, both technically and with the hard slog of raising the money. You cannot be expected to master all the fundraising skills you will need. Nor, particularly in a small organisation, can you be expected to do everything yourself – and you will usually need quite a lot of help. The purpose of this section is to identify a number of the avenues which you can explore to help you do more and do it better.

5.1.1 Employing a fundraiser

The selection and recruitment of a fundraiser to your organisation, as a full-time post or on a part-time basis is covered in Section 5.9.

Before you embark on this option, a number of questions need to be answered. The recruitment of staff is a major commitment that should not be taken lightly. Not only will you need to pay their salary, but you will need to manage and support them to get the most out of the appointment; and of course they will need the essential tools to do their job.

The first consideration is timing. If you decide now to recruit someone, it may take anything from two to six months before that person starts working for you. The budgeting, the advertising, the selection and the notice period all conspire to lengthen the process.

The next question is that of money. Not only will a fundraiser, like any one else, need a basic salary, but there will also be all the usual extras including National Insurance and overhead costs. For any fundraiser to be effective they may also need a computer to store information, a vehicle or other means of mobility, a telephone and secretarial support. Lastly, there are the materials they will need: printing costs, mailing costs, money to run events, and so on.

Linking these two points is the question of training. For if the salary you offer is quite small, then you may need a lengthy training and induction period before the new fundraiser will begin to be effective.

In the event that you do not want to commit yourself yet to hiring a full-time fundraiser on a permanent basis, there are several other options. The first is to consider whether you have a volunteer with the time and skills to be trained up as a fundraiser. The next is whether a part-time appointment might be more appropriate. Depending upon the job to be done, the hours might suit a parent with young children, for example, or someone wanting to work only a few hours a week. Alternatively, you might want to look at a fixed-term contract for, say, one year. You can always re-appoint or extend the contract if things are going well, but you will not be committed if they do not.

5.1.2 Independent fundraising consultants

As a part of the trend towards independent working, the number of people leaving larger employers to work for themselves is considerable. This applies as much in the fundraising field as in any other field, and presents you with a number of opportunities.

What sorts of work might such freelance consultants do for you? There are two main areas. First, there are the consultants who will make an appraisal of an area of your fundraising and advise you what to do about it; then there are those who will not only do this, but will expect to be involved in the implementation of the work programme.

You must decide what sort of help you really need, because there is no such creature as an all-purpose consultant. Each has strengths and weaknesses which you need to identify. Some will offer specialist skills in a particular area, such as corporate giving, direct mail, payroll giving and so on. Others will have more general, managerial or strategic experience to offer.

Since consultants are expensive (you may pay anything from £200 per day up to £100 an hour or even more), you need to be sure you are going to get good value. Ways in which you might do this include getting a full CV from a number of consultants; discussing what similar jobs the person has done before; or seeking references from other charities on the consultant you select. These will help ensure that you find the right person. Then you have to determine the best way of working with them. This should be reviewed under headings such as terms of reference; remuneration; how long the consultancy will take; what arrangements for expenses are needed; and presentation of results.

If you are not certain what value a consultant (or a firm) can bring to you – or of how much you can afford to pay them – you can ask for a feasibility study first. This should be a short paid investigation of the major issues involved and an early indication of what might be achieved. Such a study would carry no further commitment from you.

Finally you may need to know where to find such people. Many work with little advertising of any sort and find new clients through recommendations. One possibility is to ask around, particularly amongst your colleagues in other organisations. Alternatives are to scan the trade press for authors of articles (a well-known way of advertising for business) and the small ads. The Institute of Charity Fundraising Managers has a list of freelance fundraisers and consultants along with a brief on each. So too does the National Council for Voluntary Organisations and the British Institute of Management. Their addresses are in Section 6.

IF YOU ARE CONSIDERING ENGAGING A FUNDRAISING CONSULTANT

1. Have you considered the alternative of taking on your own staff?

2. Do you know what kind of person you need: consultant, fundraiser, or co-venturer?

3. Check with other charities who have done the same sort of work recently.

4. Consult the NCVO and use the ICFM list.

5. Obtain a copy of the ICFM standard contract.

6. Draw up a short list of consultants and ask them about: their experience; availability; time they can give you; their charges; whether they support your targets; other organisations they have worked for.

7. Meet with them to compare their approaches.

8. Review their methods and whether they can realistically help you meet your objectives.

9. Find out exactly who will work on your job.

10. Consider whether you will have adequate control over the use of your organisation's name.

11. Ensure that all gifts are made directly to your charity.

12. Take up bankers references.

13. Enter into a written contract.

This advice is among that offered in the ICFM standard contract for fundraisers available from the **ICFM**.

5.1.3 Consultancy firms

In addition to individual fundraising consultants, there are the companies who specialise in particular areas of fundraising.

There are a few firms of fundraisers who offer a complete fundraising service. They can deal with the strategy and help with its implementation. The actual fundraising work might be carried out by their own staff seconded to your organisation or people recruited specially by you and trained by them. The more usual function of these firms is to show you how to do things rather than for them to do them themselves.

These companies almost always charge on the basis of a fixed fee, which is rarely less than £100 per hour. The high price has to be weighed against the undoubted experience that such people can bring. But the cost does mean that you have to know what you want from them and be able to use their contribution effectively; it also means that their help is most appropriate for major appeals.

A different source of help comes from organisations specialising in particular areas of fundraising. Things that you might expect to be able to find a specialist to do for you include the following:

- Advertising
- Capital giving

- Direct mail
- Design and print
- Mailing house and fulfilment services
- Covenant administration
- Payroll giving
- Promotions
- Annual reports
- Video production

5.1.4 Payment by results

Many charities think that it is desirable to hire a consultant on a commission or payment by results basis. Although this is done from time to time, it is not considered a sound basis for remuneration by any of the key industry bodies or by the Charity Commission. Their advice is that you should beware of fundraisers who offer this sort of deal. Particularly where the commission levied is high, they will be remunerating themselves at your donors' expense. For most consultants there is sufficient incentive to succeed without linking pay to results. Good recommendations and more work come directly from success.

The Institute of Charity Fundraising Managers (ICFM) and the National Council for Voluntary Organisations (NCVO) jointly publish a standard form of contract for charities who wish to employ consultants. Where the fundraiser is soliciting support on your behalf rather than simply providing you with advice or other professional services, certain conditions laid down in the Charities Act need to be met (see Section 5.1.7). The ICFM can also provide a list of those factors that should be considered by a potential employer of an external consultant.

5.1.5 Selecting an adviser

Whoever you decide to choose, there are a number of steps to go through.

First, be absolutely sure of what your problem is and what sort of service you actually need to help you solve it. Do you need someone to help you devise the strategy only? Do you need both the strategy and help with its implementation? Or do you have something specific you need done, and you just need someone to do it for you?

Second, write a good brief and a clear job description. This should cover what needs to be done, the timetable, and the specific objectives. Without this it makes selection extremely difficult.

Next, make sure you have a good selection of possible people or companies to choose from. Following this, comes the issue of remuneration. Is the budget and the basis of remuneration acceptable to you? What control over success and failure will you retain? How will expenses be charged? How much notice is required to terminate the arrangement if you are dissatisfied?

Finally, you should be sure to get references and follow these up to find out the quality of their work for other similar organisations. If you do not get good – or indeed any – references, proceed only with the greatest care.

You may want to use the ICFM model contract to highlight the issues you need to be considering.

5.1.6 Networking

There is an alternative source of information and help for a fundraiser. One of the remarkable aspects of the fundraising world is the way fundraisers have traditionally been free with information and advice to fellow fundraisers. This should be taken advantage of by newer and less experienced fundraisers.

The first useful network is the **Institute of Charity Fundraising Managers** (ICFM). It is a professional institute and exists to serve its members. There are a number of committees and regional groups, and members can get lists of other fundraisers in their area or with a particular expertise. ICFM organise an annual conference, an AGM and a dinner. It has a structured training programme of courses and meetings across the country for beginners up to experts.

For women fundraisers there is a group called **Women in Fundraising and Development** (WIFD). This group has a less formal structure, but is used extensively by its members to enhance their effectiveness as fundraisers.

A further group to consider joining is the **Charity Forum**. This arranges meetings in and around London on topics of interest to those involved in fundraising. Most meetings are arranged for lunchtime and are quite brief. They are useful not only for the content but also for the people you will meet there. Charities, not individuals, are usually members.

Finally, there are a range of conferences, workshops and other training events that take place throughout the year, at which you can meet many other fundraisers from both larger and smaller charities. The content of these events may not always be just what you are looking for, but the break-times can be valuable for meeting speakers and colleagues. Take special note of the conferences laid on by ICFM, the Directory of Social Change and the Charities Aid Foundation.

5.1.7 Charities Act requirements

Under the 1992 Charities Act a professional fundraiser is any person who carries on a fundraising business or any other person who solicits charity funds for reward, apart from the following:

- Charities, voluntary organisations and connected trading companies, the charity's staff and trustees;

- Volunteer fundraisers paid less than £5 per day or £500 a year (these amounts exclude any expenses remunerated);

- Collectors who volunteer or who are employed to collect for the charity or voluntary organisation;

- Radio and TV celebrities making solicitations for charity on radio or TV (but not other forms of solicitation).

In all other circumstances, where funds are solicited **for reward**, the person or organisation doing the soliciting will be deemed to be a **professional fundraiser**. This requires a written agreement between the fundraiser and the beneficiary organisation; advice on the form of this agreement can be obtained from the Institute of Charity Fundraising Managers. It also requires the professional fundraiser to give details of the organisation for which money is being raised (and if for more than one organisation, then the proportions in which the money will be distributed) and the method by which the fundraiser's own remuneration for undertaking the fundraising work will be determined.

If the written agreement does not satisfy the terms of the Charities Act, then it will not be legally enforceable. In such circumstances the charity would not be required to pay any fee or reimburse any expenses incurred and the fundraiser would be guilty of an offence. There are similar requirements for commercial participators who are defined as being those engaged in any form of business, other than a fundraising business, where they engage in a promotional venture in the course of which it is represented that contributions are to be given or applied for the benefit of a charitable organisation.

5.1.8 References

Refer to:

> Report of the Working Party on Malpractice in Fundraising, NCVO
> ICFM standard contract for consultants (see Section 6.4)

Sources of names of consultants:

> ICFM, as above
> NCVO, as above
> British Institute of Management

Networks to be joined:

> Directory of Social Change conferences and workshops, DSC
> Charities Aid Foundation conferences, CAF
> ICFM meetings, conferences and workshops. ICFM, as above
> Charity Forum meetings: The Charity Forum
> Women In Fundraising and Development

Magazines to be consulted:

> Precision Marketing (this carries stories on direct marketing and produces supplements on direct marketing agencies, mailing houses, etc)
> Professional Fundraising
> Charity (the CAF magazine)

Books to be considered:

See the bibliography in Section 6.2

5.2 Working with volunteers

Without volunteers, most charities would grind to a halt. Not only are head offices heavily dependant on the help of volunteers, but a large proportion of the funds raised are raised by voluntary effort.

5.2.1 Overview

The role of the volunteer is widely accepted and welcomed in the life of charities, and the range of their responsibilities can be very great. Volunteers actually control the organisation through its trustee body or management committee. In some cases, the volunteer force is almost totally responsible for the delivery of the organisation's service, the Samaritans being a good example. In other cases, the fundraising and publicity is carried out almost exclusively by volunteers – in Oxfam shops, for example.

Not only do volunteers save money for the organisation, which might otherwise have to pay staff to do the same thing, they provide the person with power to run the organisation and undertake any campaigning work.

In order to get the best out of volunteers, they need to be chosen well, placed with imagination, given work which matches their skills and interests, and managed with skill. They are not cannon fodder to be deployed in all the worst jobs. Rather, they can add hugely to the resources available to you and enable you to do more with less and do it better.

WHO VOLUNTEERS FOR WHAT

Activity	Household %	under 10 %	10 - 16 %
Jumble sale helper	24	5	9
Selling raffle tickets	23	4	10
Collecting things to sell	21	6	8
Sponsored event participant	21	15	23
Committee work	12		
Making things to sell	11	1	3
Selling event tickets	11	4	
Organising event	9		
Door to door collector	7	1	1
Street collector	3		

From the **Charity Household Survey** comes this picture of the voluntary activities of households.

5.2.2 Committees

Invariably, voluntary organisations set up committees to monitor, control and develop their activities. These can and should be filled with volunteers.

New organisations often stick with the people who founded them originally, together with a few friends. As the organisation grows, new skills and contacts will be needed, and fresh vigour and ideas brought to the organisation. These can be provided by well chosen voluntary help working in committees. Particularly useful are people with accounting or financial skills, people who can chair meetings effectively, people with good local contacts, and people with special skills or experience that will be useful to your organisation. Such people need to be carefully vetted and specially invited. Keeping the loyalty and commitment of your volunteers will depend on the conduct of the meetings and the way they are seen by the rest of your organisation.

5.2.3 Peripatetic volunteers

Another sort of volunteer is the person who has time to give but may want to give it at times more suitable to themselves. A number of charities have panels of speakers giving talks to local Women's Institutes and Round Tables. Others employ volunteers to visit donors to offer thanks. Still others use them to make management audits on outlying offices. These are essentially people who are highly motivated and articulate and require a high degree of autonomy and responsibility. They are invaluable, but do need to be monitored closely. If volunteers go off the rails in this role, this creates a problem which needs to be sorted out quickly.

5.2.4 Administrators

You should certainly be considering whether volunteers could be helping you in the office. The fundraiser's time is inevitably limited, and the work often comes in peaks and troughs. Volunteers with less ability or ambition can be vital in carrying out some of the routine but essential fundraising tasks. Who is going to address the 1,000 letters you want to send out for your appeal? How are you going to cope with the response that will come in? And who will answer the phone when you are out? All these tasks and many more are suitable volunteer jobs and can make a significant impact on the effectiveness of your fundraising.

5.2.5 Volunteer organisers

More directly connected with fundraising, are those volunteers who either singly or in groups organise the myriad of local activities that are the lifeblood of many voluntary organisations. The extrovert and confident get a kick out of organising coffee mornings, bring and buy sales, and so on. All they need is the say so from you, and they will go ahead. Their operation can often be improved by giving them feedback about others working in similar situations and by keeping them in touch with the organisation. One problem with this type of enthusiast is that they may not always get the story about your organisation quite right, or they may need to be encouraged to tell people about the work your organisation is doing.

5.2.6 Volunteer selection

Since volunteers can be taken on to do anything from the most menial task to the most important, it follows that you have to take their recruitment and selection very seriously. Exactly as for the recruitment of a new member of staff, volunteers should be given a proper job description and selected according to their ability to do the job. Additionally there will be important issues regarding their terms and conditions that will be important, especially to those on low income, so the hours expected, the expenses to be paid, grievance procedures, and so on, all need to be discussed and agreed.

Recruiting volunteers can be done in one of two ways. The first is where you need a number of volunteers in one place – perhaps to help in the office or help out in a crisis. The other is where you have a particular need for a person with particular skills. For the former, a range of techniques can be used. Many people might turn up at your office or telephone you for information. If they seem interested, then you could ask them directly if they would like to help. Your publicity leaflets which ask for support, may offer the option of giving support in time as well as in cash. Charities which organise large house-to-house collections, invariably use the telephone extensively to recruit, often using the tree approach asking each person to recommend others. Alternatively, speaking tours, an article in the local newspaper, slots on local radio and of course the Public Service Announcement on TV (see Section 4.11). Your local Volunteer Bureau may keep a register of volunteer opportunities for those with some time to give. Your local Council for Voluntary Service may also be in touch with potential volunteers.

Recruiting people with specific skills requires a rather more directed approach. To find an accountant you might well seek the help of the local bank manager; a solicitor, or the local Law Society. In fact professional bodies are a good hunting ground for recently retired people with time on their hands. For more specific skills you will need to go to your own friends to seek personal recommendations.

The next step is selecting from the people you have identified. Unsuitable as well as suitable people volunteer to help. When these people are expected to relate to the public representing your organisation or where they will be involved in handling money, there is a particular need for caution. You should ensure that all volunteers have an interview and that you take up references.

5.2.7 Management of volunteers

Volunteers work for charities for a wide range of reasons. Some are essentially altruistic, while others do it because they want to get something out of it. You will meet volunteers who simply have nothing better to do or those who desperately crave human company after the death of a partner or the loss of or retirement from a job. Still others want to help your cause because of a profound belief in what you are doing. All can be useful members of your team and can enhance your fundraising. Just like the paid members of your team, they will need managing.

Not only should a volunteer have a clear job description, but you should set them objectives. You should train them in what they have to do, give them feedback on how well they are doing, and congratulate them when they have made a positive contribution. They are just like any other human striving to do a good job. They need to know what the job is, how to do it and whether they are doing it right. Ensure that your volunteers are well integrated with the staff and are able to get relevant information and contribute to discussions. Generally volunteers will want to attend fewer meetings than paid staff, unless the meetings are clearly of direct relevance. This should be taken as signifying greater commitment rather than less. Not doing any of this will make the volunteer feel marginal and exploited, and will waste this valuable resource rather than make the most of it.

5.2.8 References

From this book:
  2.1   Principles of fundraising
  4.1   Local fundraising
  5.9   Recruitment, training and secondment
And from elsewhere:
  Volunteer Centre publications from the Volunteer Centre UK

5.3 Writing a proposal

Writing a proposal is probably the most useful skill in the fundraiser's repertoire. For many smaller organisations, the difference between a good and a bad proposal will be the difference between success and failure. The fundraising proposal communicates the needs of the organisation to its potential supporters. And it is largely on the basis of the written proposal that many funders will decide whether or not to make a grant.

What follows should not be regarded as a blueprint which will guarantee success. What it aims to do is to identify the key points to enable you to produce a proposal which matches the requirements of a potential funder. The same basic approach applies when approaching any grant-making body, whether central government, a local authority, a trust or a company. Where key differences exist, these are identified in the text.

5.3.1 Planning

In thinking about how to structure a proposal, you will need to consider who you plan to approach, how you are going to make the approach, what you need to say about yourself and what you propose to do, and when you will be submitting the application.

5.3.2 Targeting your proposal

Whom to send your proposal to will depend on a number of factors:

Urgency: If you need the money really urgently, then there is little point in approaching a government department. The best bet may be to approach those who have already supported you. You have already convinced them of the worth of your work, and they may be willing to support you again.

Scale of need: If you require large sums of money, then you have a choice. You can either apply for a few large grants from the larger trusts or companies or from some statutory source. Or you can mount a wider appeal seeking large and small donations from a larger number of donors. Remember though, if you want a large donation, then you are unlikely to be successful if you approach a small grant-maker.

Type of project: New projects and new initiatives are more likely to be of interest to trusts than other donors. Certain trusts have specific policies to support certain types of activity (and the same is true for the larger companies). You need to go through the grant guides carefully to select a target list of donors who you think might be interested in supporting you.

You should try to personalise the approach as much as you can. Refer to previous contacts and any previous support. Match your proposal to their interests as evidenced by their stated interests and policies or other grants they have made. Try to make them feel that you are writing to them personally. This is obviously much easier to do if you are writing individual letters to just a few donors.

Donors are often interested to know how many other people have been asked and whether others have already agreed to give. The general rule is that only a careful selection should be made, based on an assessment of who is likely to be interested. If this is made clear in the proposal, those receiving it are more likely to take it seriously than a proposal mailed out widely. It also saves a great deal of time for both you and the grant bodies if you can cut down the numbers of applications you make.

5.3.3 Content

What to ask for demands a good deal of thought, and there are many points that you will need to consider.

You should decide whether you are seeking support for the organisation itself or for a specific piece of expenditure or project; and whether you are expecting to get funds from many sources or are hoping for support from just one or a few. Once you have done this, you should try to answer the following questions:

- What is the problem or the need that is to be met?
- What are the aims and objectives of this project?
- What methods will be used to meet the aims?
- What are the short and long-term operational plans?
- Do you have a clear budget?

- What sources of funds have you identified?
- When must money start flowing in?

In defining your approach to companies, an additional factor to consider is the degree to which you can offer something in return to the company. Though for some types of corporate support this is not important, for sponsorship and often for donations it will be a factor. Areas to consider are ways in which you can publicise the company's support (in your annual reports, newsletters etc), the numbers of people that are likely to become aware of the company's support, the interest of the company's own employees in your organisation as fundraisers or volunteers, and the proximity of your organisation to any major plant or branch location of the company.

5.3.4 Timing

Time issues are important in preparing a proposal in a number of different ways. First, it always takes much longer than you think to prepare a proposal; you should allow up to a month if you have not yet fully formulated your thoughts or if you need to consult others. There is a good deal of information to be collected and editing to be done, and finally the perfect reproduction of it all!

Secondly, there are the time requirements of the funders themselves. This may mean that some sources are just not useful to you. For example, applications for European funding may have to be submitted up to 18 months in advance, local authorities each have their own rigid application timetables on an annual cycle, trusts may take up to six months, while companies tend to be quicker.

Thirdly, there is the question of how long you want the money for, whether you require a single sum or continuing support for a number of years. It is frequently said that you get what you ask for; from this it follows that if you need three-year funding, you must remember to make this clear in your proposal, though that is no guarantee that you will get it. Most grant bodies are not prepared to consider funding periods beyond three years, at least initially.

Fourthly, there is the question of what happens afterwards. If your project is to continue, how will it be funded after the initial grant period? If you are applying for money to purchase a piece of equipment or a building, how will the running costs be met? You may not have all the answers now, but you should at least be thinking about the problem.

5.3.5 Writing the proposal

The first thing to do is to find out whether there is an application form which you must use. If there is, ask for a form to be sent to you. For most official sources and for a few grant-making trusts there will be. For most other sources, there will not, and you will have to write the proposal in your own words.

CHECKLIST OF THINGS TO INCLUDE IN YOUR PROPOSAL

1. Have you got a strategy?
2. Have you planned ahead?
3. Have you selected a good project (if you have a choice)?
4. Do you believe in what you are doing?
5. Have you selected a money target?
6. Can you tailor your application to the recipient?
7. Have you used personal contact?
8. Have you prepared a realistic budget?
9. Is your proposal concise?
10. Have you been specific (and asked for what you want)?
11. Do you need to establish your credibility?
12. Have you assumed people know what you are talking about?
13. Check for jargon.

Source: **Hugh Frazer**, DSC.

When writing the proposal there are a range of factors to consider. First the length. There is a lot of information you could put in. If you put it all in, your application would be too long for most funders. For a substantial proposal, this may well be appropriate. For less complicated projects, keep the length to a minimum. Normally a page, or at most two pages, are all that is required; and you can append more detailed information or a photograph or technical information to the proposal, if you feel that it will be of interest to the donor.

At the heart of your proposal you will describe the needs you are trying to address, the aims of your project, and how you will achieve them. You should include as much detail as is necessary for a person who is not knowledgeable in your area. You should also give an indication as to how you would expect to measure the successful outcome of the project.

If the project is new or if you are a new group, funders may well want to ask who you are and why they should entrust their money to you: you have a credibility problem. This can be overcome in a number of ways. CVs of the key organisers can help here. If you have a well-connected committee, why not list them? Or if you have already received support from other bodies such as the local authority, then that will help provide reassurance. If you have obtained press coverage, you can include the

---

SIXTEEN DO'S AND DON'TS FOR YOUR PROPOSAL

DO:

1. Address your appeal to the right person.
2. Tailor your appeal to the recipient.
3. Include a clear statement of your charity's functions/objectives.
4. State clearly the purpose for which the funds are needed and the amount required.
5. Break a large appeal down into manageable, realistic amounts for particular elements/items.
6. Include your latest set of accounts.
7. Offer to go and see the prospective donor and follow up the letter within a week.
8. Make full use of VIP contacts.
9. Keep it brief.

DON'T:

1. Write to the company chair if there is a designated person responsible for charity donations (unless you have a personal contact).
2. Make your appeal letter look mass-produced.
3. Include irrelevant information or large quantities of printed material.
4. Dispute a refusal (companies cannot support every request, even those which meet their criteria).
5. Be put off by a refusal. Try again next year.
6. Feel obliged to offer expensive hospitality to a prospective donor.
7. Make your appeal late in the company's year.

This checklist is the one used by Tina Pecksen who manages a large portion of British Telecom's corporate giving programme.

clippings. Or if the problem itself is not widely recognised, references to other respected reports or endorsements by prominent people will help.

The budget will always be carefully scrutinised by potential funders, so needs to be clear, complete and accurate. Most donors will not be interested in your stationery or postage bill. What they will be interested in are the major areas of expenditure and income. You should identify capital or other one-off costs, salaries, overheads and any other major operational costs. Similarly, income estimates will show the money you expect to generate from the project itself or through fundraising. Beyond this, you may need to show the way in which the money you need in the medium term is going to be raised, say over a period of three years. This may require a summary income and expenditure statement and a capital expenditure statement, both spread over a three-year period. Additionally, you will need to supply your organisation's audited accounts for the latest year for which they are available.

It is useful to include the formal and legal information about the organisation on the letterhead. This includes the charity and company registration details, names of trustees, board members and patrons, which can help create the impression that you are well established, and this will answer points of detail which may come up later. Sometimes people put in the number of the bank account to be credited – optimistically assuming a grant!

You can write the application as a letter, or you can attach a short covering letter. The covering letter should attempt to summarise the application in a concise and punchy style; it should mention any previous contact with its donor, whether or not it was successful; and it could give reasons why the proposal might be of particular interest to the donor. It should have the benefit of brevity, be free of jargon, be concise and to the point – as indeed the application itself should be.

5.3.6 Presentation

How you present your proposal is luckily not the most important aspect, but it can make a great deal of difference. Different standards and expectations apply to different potential donors. A proposal directed at the marketing director of a major company will have to have a different feel to that being sent to a small trust which is receiving 50 others each day. Remember that you will have to meet their own standard of communication, whoever it is you are talking to.

The application can be a letter typed on your best headed paper, or it can be a short letter attached to a formal proposal. The proposal itself could range from two typed pages to a glossy printed brochure. A middle position is the production of some sort of folder containing a number of loose sheets. Be careful here that you do not go over the top in the quality of production. If you appear to be wasting money through over-lavish presentation, people will feel that you don't need the money.

When sending in applications to smaller trusts, you may wish to enclose sufficient copies for all the trustees who will be considering your proposal. You may want to check if more than one copy is needed. Most large trusts, for example, only require a single copy. The trust secretary will usually summarise the proposal and circulate the information, accompanied by a recommendation, to the trustees.

5.3.7 Getting in touch

Skilled fundraisers would not consider sending a proposal out of the blue to anyone but the smallest and most remote charitable trust or company. To ensure a greater chance of success, applicants need to know as much as possible about the target. For example: what constraints are imposed by policy; what sort of things have been supported in the past; who makes the decisions; who they are advised by; whether they expect to get any sort of recognition or benefit in return for their support; and what they already know about your cause and what they need to know. Equally the more the donor knows about your organisation and the quality of its work, the more likely they will be to support you. One approach, given time, is as follows:

- Select a preliminary list of targets;

- Research the targets;

- Adjust and amend target list;

- Phone the potential donor organisation to determine contact person and their application procedure;

- Seek a meeting, if this seems appropriate, or think of other ways in which you can bring your work to the attention of the donor;

- Invite the donor to visit you;

- Find out as much as you can about the detailed decision-making process;

- Contact any key advisers or trustees, if you can get access;

- Write a draft proposal, seek comments from key people and then redraft;

- Produce and send off the final proposal document.

Finally, you might ask (tactfully) whether they know of other bodies that they would recommend you apply to. Care needs to be taken here, as this may present an easy way to say no.

5.3.8 References

Books that give good background information and useful suggestions about writing proposals include:

A Guide to the Major Trusts, DSC
Major Companies Guide, DSC
Raising Money from Industry, DSC
Raising Money from Trusts, DSC
Government Grants, A Guide for Voluntary Organisations, NCVO
Grants from Europe, NCVO

5.4 Producing effective materials

5.4.1 Overview

The creation and production of effective fundraising and publicity literature is one of the fundraiser's most important tasks. Good fundraising ideas can be destroyed by poorly prepared or presented material. An understanding of the design and production processes is vital.

The process of creating any printed material usually follows a similar path. The stages include conception or visualisation, copywriting, design, print and finishing. Many of these stages will be carried out by outside personnel, and each stage might be produced by someone different. This creates considerable opportunities for getting things wrong – deadlines, in particular – and also for losing or watering down the original idea.

A further complication is deciding who does what. There may be many people, within even a small organisation, who feel they can write effectively. Anyone, after all, can write a letter! You need specific writing skills to present a good, clear logical case and to express your ideas forcefully. Then there is the preparation and production of back up material. Here you may be dealing with promotional consultants and designers. They may have the skills you need, but you have to brief them properly and be happy with their approach.

5.4.2 Principles of effective communication

You must have a clear idea of what you are trying to do. It is worth writing down the objective of any particular piece, and including this in the brief to the writer and designer (if you are not doing it all yourself). This is especially important when it comes to annual reports which may have to serve a number of purposes.

If the objective is to raise money, then there must be a clear understanding as to how this is to be done. Is the piece to be sent through the post and a postal response sought from the addressee? And if so, will that response be a cash donation, a covenant, a legacy pledge, or what? Or is the objective to play another part in the fundraising process? It may be a motivator or information tool, like the many newsletters that organisations produce; or an advertisement or support leaflet. Whatever the objective, it is important to be clear and consistent in what you are trying to do.

The next stage of the process must be to identify who you expect to read the material. Clearly what you say to past donors who might be expected to be fairly knowledgeable, will differ from what you say to new donors who will know little or nothing about the organisation. For your existing donors, you should have some picture of who they actually are. Research will tell you something about their age, sex, interests and preferences; and also something about their degree of commitment to the organisation. But you will have to think quite carefully when you are writing to new supporters. You must be clear in your own mind who it is you expect to

TEN SUGGESTIONS FOR WRITERS

1. Get to know your audience.
2. Use simple, direct and everyday language.
3. State your proposition boldly and clearly.
4. Feature real, identifiable cases and people.
5. Communicate the need.
6. State clearly what the reader's support will enable you to achieve.
7. Remember that cleverness rarely pays.
8. Avoid seeming too professional.
9. Remove any unnecessary detail.
10. Give a clear course of action.

Ken Burnett's advice to his staff and clients.

be interested, whether it is for a sponsored walk or a local event which you are producing a poster for.

The next stage is to set a clear deadline for when you need the materials. This is especially important if the material is going to be mailed or presented at an AGM. Give yourself room for slippage, and make sure that everyone involved sticks to their deadlines. You are now in a position to seek quotes from any outside printers or designers if you are using them. With printers, try to obtain three quotes in order to get the best price possible. It is surprising how much the prices vary, even on the most tightly defined jobs: this is a lot to do with how much the printer wants the job and whether it fits their capacity and machinery. Do not be embarrassed about asking printers you are dealing with regularly to quote on new jobs. It does not demonstrate mistrust, rather it shows good business practice and a keenness to get the best price. When asking someone to quote, you should have a clear understanding of:

- **For dealing with printers:**
  Date to printer
  Paper size
  Print quantity
  Paper quality and colour
  Number of print colours
  Illustrations and halftones
  Folding
  Packing
  Delivery
  Date required for receipt of completed job
- **For designers**
  Date to designer
  Visuals needed
  Format, size and price guidelines for completed job
  Copywriting, and who does what
  Photographs needed
  Illustrations needed
  Date of receipt of completed job

Every decision you make about the design and print quality of a book, leaflet or letter says something about your organisation and its ethos. A most obvious current issue is whether to print on recycled materials. It is hard for an organisation that claims to be concerned with the environment not to be doing this, whatever the economics (and it is usually more expensive). There will be a perception of inconsistency if you don't.

A similar problem surrounds the use of expensive or glossy materials. Donors expect that when charities communicate with them, they should not waste money unnecessarily. Though they say this, donors will respond better if what you send them looks nice. The important thing is to make a judgement about the audience and the message. Remember too, that for effective communication with new groups of people, you will need to have something much more substantial and well laid out than you would for your existing donors.

Keep everything simple and understandable. One problem is that organisations tend to develop shorthand ways of describing their work. These are useful when talking to colleagues, but can create a deadening flow of verbiage that is quite meaningless to outsiders. Jargon should be avoided at all costs. Find someone to read your copy who does not have anything to do with your organisation. Ask them to feed back what they have understood! And what they have not understood. Another problem arises when you have to agree the copy with others. Most people's reaction to checking someone else's text is to check for typographic errors and false statements. The result can often be an accurate but heavily qualified text that loses all its punch and impact. Accept their comments, but don't let your text become a committee document. Their skills are in providing the service or in running the organisation, yours are in doing the fundraising.

5.4.3 Conception

The concept stage of any fundraising material is important, especially where its form is not already predetermined by other factors. This stage is sometimes referred to as visualisation. What you end up with at the end of this stage is something that will identify a creative approach, a visual theme, a style and a headline or slogan. Advertising agencies have got this process down to a fine art; this consists of putting a good copywriter and designer together with a good brief, until they come up with the answer.

You can come up with the answer in a number of ways. Themes, headlines and ideas are susceptible to a brain-storming approach. This involves putting a number of interested people together in a room; identifying the object of the exercise and the rules of the brain-storming process; then asking those present to contribute as many ideas as possible. Some may be zany, others can be done at speed, but all must be written up, so that new ideas build on old. Then a process of refinement should be started to develop the approach out of the ideas people have come up with. This can at best only produce ideas and approaches. It will not help you actually write the leaflet or annual report.

At this stage, you will need a designer to produce roughs or scamps. This is an important stage, as it is the last major point at which you can turn back. If you don't like the rough design, you should ask for a new approach before too much time has been spent. If you pass this stage and then decide a new approach is needed, it will cost you money, time and the motivation of the designer. The visualisation need be no more than the front cover of a leaflet with a sample page – enough to give you an idea of how it will feel and look. It is likely to be in sketch form; sometimes these are so good that they are actually preferred to the finished article!

5.4.4 Writing

Not everybody has the skills to write copy, though unfortunately almost everybody does have to communicate on paper. A good copywriter can really make your work live. However, small organisations do not always have the means to hire copywriters and fundraisers are often called upon to do the job themselves.

Getting the best out of a copywriter requires an understanding of how they work and how much they know about your cause. Always look at their portfolio to see what they have done for similar organisations. Some may have an instinctive understanding of your work, while others are better at selling baked beans. Though good copywriters are expensive, you may be able to find one as a volunteer.

If you are writing it yourself, there are a number of things you will have to remember. The first is about structure. An acronym is useful here: A.I.D.A. This describes the process of persuasion and communication.

Attention:	The reader's attention has to be attracted;
Interest:	If you don't identify a reason for the reader to be personally interested, you will lose them;
Desire:	To support your cause is the next stage, and finally;
Action:	Headlines, pictures or strong ideas can all create the attention that you will need to claim the reader's attention in the first place. Their interest can be gained by showing them why you exist and the needs you are serving. Don't imagine that your supporters will continue to support you without a continuing reminder of the importance of what you are doing, or the human cost of ignoring the problem. Desire to support your cause is likely to be generated by an understanding that things can be changed if they give their support. Tigers can be saved, classrooms built and people in need helped and your organisation has the wherewithal to do this. Action demands that you tell them what you want them to do and what sort and size of gift they are expected to make – a covenant, a legacy, cash, their time or whatever.

5.4.5 Design

The design gives the printed piece its character. Good designers can lift the central idea from a piece of text and make it something infinitely more compelling. The elements of this include the copy, the headlining, the photographs and illustrations used, as well as the design style.

You may already have a house design style, including the use of logos. If you do – and consistency is important – then ensure that designers are clearly briefed about it. It will help build up a feeling of continuity and reassurance, and will convey the message of dynamism, safety or whatever is implicit in your house style.

The important elements of the design include the format, colour, layout, type faces, the heading and signposting of the various parts of the text; the use of space and how the various sorts of illustration are used.

Illustrations can take many forms and can bring a design to life. Photographs are the easiest to use; but don't use them if they do not make a point or are not of good quality. You can use a photo library (at some cost), but are more likely to have to find them or take them yourself. You may find the local newspaper a useful source. Photos should always be captioned, as these are among the best read parts of any publication. Illustrations and plans are a good alternative, and can be useful for illustrating things that cannot yet be photographed (such as the building you are planning to put up). Depending on cost, these can be produced in any style you require by choosing an appropriate illustrator.

A good designer will integrate all these elements for you and, having taken your brief, should be able to satisfy your needs. Do ensure you get a clear quote before you proceed.

An alternative to using a professional is to use a desk top publishing system. These are simply computer aids to the design process (see Section 5.16). For creating newsletters and things that are produced regularly in a similar format, they are excellent. However, they do need a skilled operator, and will never be any better than their operator in creating a good design.

5.4.6 Printing

The printing process can certainly improve the quality of a printed piece, but everything you do will have cost implications. The importance of good printing lies as much in the need to get a quality product on time as anything else. If you use a designer, they will ensure that the quality is as required. If you don't, you will have to satisfy yourself that the paper and colours you have specified will create the right impression. If you are not sure, ask to see samples of other items printed on the same paper in the same colours.

Price will depend on a number of factors. These include the paper quality, the number of colours, the number of photographs, the complexity of the artwork (it makes a difference to the plate making process), the quantity, and how soon you need it.

Paper prices can be reduced by buying cheaper or lighter paper or by using the stock papers that the printer holds. If you economise too much, you may create a poor impression. Lighter papers tend to show some of the printing on the back. Another factor which can determine the weight of paper used is postage cost, if you intend to send the piece through the post. If you are near the 60 gram postage limit, it may be worth making up a dummy of what is being mailed using the same materials. Most printing can now be done on recycled paper at some extra cost. If you go to this effort, don't forget to print the fact somewhere. A reduction in cost can be achieved by cutting down the numbers of colours used. Each extra colour requires an extra run through the printing press, which is obviously expensive. You may be able to produce a similar effect by judicious use of screening or tinting, which gives you shades of the same colour and can be achieved without any extra print runs.

5.4.7 Finishing

Finishing usually consists of cutting, binding and folding. Binding can be done in a number of ways. Reports can be heat bound or comb bound; small publications can be stitched or stapled. The more complex the job, the more it will cost. Folding is important, especially when it comes to direct marketing. Be sure to specify what you need, and check with your mailing house if necessary.

5.4.8 Appeal letters

Appeal letters are one of the most important types of literature you have to produce. These present your organisation to a large number of people and create some sort of impression whether or not the recipient responds. Perhaps right at the top of the fundraiser's mind will be the fact that direct mail appeals should be raising money at a cost ratio of 10:1 and can be one of the best sources of income available. Thus the value of getting it right is great. There are several parts of a letter that you should attend to. They are the envelope, the salutation, the entry, the appeal, the call to action, the postscript and the supporting literature. Though only a few of these are actually part of the letter, they all play their part in making the appeal effective.

The envelope can say a number of different things to recipients. Research suggests that 70% never get beyond opening the envelope. Hence you may want to try a teaser line on the envelope intriguing the recipient into opening it to find out what is inside. Alternatively, you may feel that since no personal letter has advertising copy on the outside, plain envelopes may be more compelling to open. Only a knowledge of your audience and careful testing will determine the best approach. However, the more personal the letter seems, the more likely it is to get immediate attention.

The salutation should be as personal as possible. This is possible by writing personal letters (only possible for small numbers), by topping and tailing letters personally with the salutation and signature (only possible for a few hundred), by getting volunteers with good writing to do the topping and tailing for you (this can be very effective), or by using a laser printer fed by computer data to do the job. If none of these is possible, then fall back on "Dear friend" or "Dear supporter". Both of these are an admission a circular letter is being sent, and that you can't do more than treat the recipient as a statistic. Most word processor systems have mail merge software that enables you to link a list of names and addresses with a given letter.

You need to grab the reader's attention. A letter from a respected celebrity or an amazing statement may do this. Or an intensely emotional opening to the letter can do the trick. Once attention has been gained it must be held. The appeal must be simply written; it must be well laid out with short words, short sentences and a variety of paragraph sizes. Key ideas should be underlined, indented or highlighted. In terms of content:

- State the problem;
- Show how you can help resolve the problem;
- Demonstrate your credibility by showing what you have achieved in the past and others who have helped you;
- Indicate how much you expect the donor to give and what this will achieve;
- Make the call to action clearly.

The call to action is crucial and is so often left to chance in the hands of the unpractised. Perhaps it is do with the reluctance of the British to be direct. Yet that is exactly what is required. Start flagging up the call early on in the letter; repeat it throughout the letter and make it absolutely plain near the end. It should consist of what (money, time, goods, etc), how (cash, covenant, credit card), when (how soon must it arrive) and who (send it to me personally).

Save an important idea for the postscript or PS. The PS is well read by donors. So use it for your final argument or clinching statement.

Supporting literature should be used to reinforce the message of the appeal. Don't be drawn into the temptation to squeeze in thousands of words of text that you couldn't find space for in the letter. Use all the same considerations. It is often a good idea to have photographic material with little text. Don't forget to repeat the call to action. Additionally, there will need to be some way of donors getting their donations back to you. This could be a simple reply envelope or a credit card hot-line.

5.4.9 Annual reports

THIRTEEN CRITERIA FOR THE IDEAL ANNUAL REPORT

1. A well planned structure.
2. A clear statement of objectives.
3. A clear understandable financial picture.
4. Visible economy, demonstrating sensible use of resources.
5. Instant appeal.
6. Legibility.
7. Good design.
8. Well written copy.
9. Good use of photos and illustrations.
10. Overall appropriateness of style and feel to the organisation.
11. Empathy with principal audience.
12. Completeness: all components working well together.
13. A sense of excitement.

One of the excellent checklists from **Charity Annual Reports**.

Every organisation has to produce some sort of annual report. This can be an extremely useful publication for your fundraising. The annual report is an opportunity for the organisation to demonstrate its effectiveness and also to raise money both directly and indirectly.

Almost all statutory funders will require a copy of your annual report and accounts. You must produce accounts annually and the report can simply be a paragraph contained within the accounts. Most people would expect you to take the opportunity to do a lot more than this.

Since many organisations produce annual reports out of habit or somewhat grudgingly, if you are to make the most of the opportunity, it is really important to identify what you are trying to do and how you can justify the expenditure. Note the 1992 Charities Act changes.

5.4.10 Control

There are three things to control carefully in any publication. These are the cost, the timing and the message.

- **Costs**

  Costs can be controlled by working out a clear budget in the first place to include all the important elements. This must be adhered to throughout. Each stage of the process needs to have a quote from more than one supplier (remember that internal designers and printers may also be charging). Quotes should be stuck to in terms of specification and cost.

- **Time**

  Time should be controlled by producing a schedule which will include time for the quotation process, and there is likely to be little leeway for delay. The schedule should be constructed on the basis of receiving materials at a given point and passing them on to the next person in the chain at the appointed time. This chain of events requires the good performance of a number of unrelated groups of people. This is the most critical part of the process. Do not assume that even though you have given everybody a schedule, they will understand the importance of sticking to it and the need to tell you when the job is done. You as a fundraiser will have to assume the role of chaser, constantly checking and harrying printers, contributors, illustrators and designers, reminding them of the importance of their part in the process and of their original commitment. Although you can always claim damages or costs in the event of serious breach, your only sanction against sloppy service is to give your custom to someone else next time. In that case it is important for you to keep on top of important jobs yourself.

- **Controlling the message**

  This is important and challenging in a different way. Your original brief will have defined what you are trying to say and to whom. At each stage, go through the text, rough designs and galley proofs to see whether you are achieving what you set out to. If you are not, don't be afraid to admit having made a mistake and go back a step. It will be expensive, but it is better than sending out something ineffectual. If the message is inaccurate or sensitive, you may find press, trustees or volunteers taking an unusual interest. Make sure you have a clear approval procedure so that the organisation is committed to what is being produced.

5.4.11 References

In this book refer to:
    4.2   Direct mail
    5.3   Writing a proposal
And from elsewhere:
    Advertising by Charities, DSC
    Getting into Print, NCVO
    Charity Annual Reports, DSC

5.5 Working with patrons, celebrities and trustees

5.5.1 Overview

Associating your organisation with a well-known personality, could lift it from obscurity into the limelight.

Many causes attract the names of the well-known to the ranks of their supporters for precisely the same reasons that anyone else supports the organisation. However, the way fundraisers decide to use existing celebrity supporters and encourage new associations can have a major impact on the organisation.

Well-known people can be used in a wide variety of ways – from joining your board of trustees to appearing in photo calls. Their association can bring benefits that are worth recognising from the outset. But there are also responsibilities. Celebrities have their own reputations to consider, so they do not want to become associated with bad publicity or controversy. And they may be used to a level of personal support and attention that is difficult for small organisations to sustain. This is particularly the case for having an association with a member of the Royal Family.

5.5.2 Celebrities

Heading the list of celebrities that can be associated with you are members of the Royal Family. This may be as a patron of your organisation, or it could be through a visit as part of a planned tour to your area. It must be emphasised that with any royal activity, the lead time required for organising and planning is very considerable, as is the degree of preparation and liaison with the Palace.

Other celebrities who can become associated with your cause include:
• Sports personalities

- News readers and TV and radio broadcasters
- Pop stars
- Business leaders
- Former politicians
- Peers
- Journalists
- Film stars

The list can include anyone who has a high public profile and is well liked by those parts of the public you hope to draw support from. They can contribute in several ways. Their contacts and links can be important. They may have access to people in a different income bracket or social network, and they may know other people looking for some voluntary involvement. Their presence at any function will draw others. For example, the fundraising dinner, which supporters are paying premium prices to attend, will become very much more attractive if there is a smattering of film stars and media people in attendance. Probably most important though, is the advantages they confer in attracting media coverage. If, for example, a well-known broadcaster is prepared to lead a press conference announcing a new campaign, the press is going to be much more interested than when an unknown charity executive says the same thing. Similarly photo-editors of national newspapers are more likely to publish a photo of a well-known and attractive actress opening some new facility, than when a local councillor is doing the same thing.

You should try wherever possible to find a relevant celebrity. People who have had some direct experience of your cause (someone who has had a friend or child affected, for example) will be a much more powerful advocate for it. Celebrities should be matched to your target donor audience. Footballers, for example, are less likely to be relevant for a middle class southern women's audience, where a newsreader on News at Ten will be extremely acceptable.

When starting to look for suitable celebrities, as a first step you might consult Buckingham Palace about possible royal involvement. It is unlikely that a small or very local organisation will be able to attract royal patronage – and getting an answer can take a long time. For local organisations, go first to the Lord Lieutenant of the County, who can give sound advice. To identify people who will have some direct personal involvement in your cause, you need to scrutinise your list of supporters very carefully. It would be surprising if, over the years, your cause has not attracted some support from well-known individuals. Also consult your board of trustees and advisers, as they may have far reaching networks of contacts. Failing all this, then consider using one of the many directories of personalities. Some of these are for people who want to sell their services in one way or another. If contact has to be made through agents, they may not welcome involvement with a charity for a zero fee!

5.5.3 Trustees

Most well-known people will not be prepared to make any substantial commitment of time to your organisation. But you will certainly need the skills and ideas of outsiders to provide fresh energy. The obvious place for such people is on the board of the charity, or serving on one its advisory committees. Trustee boards are often self-selecting oligarchies, which have more to do with the history of the organisation than with current needs. However, properly structured, well briefed and motivated, they can play a hugely important role in the life of the organisation. Applying proper business disciplines is now more relevant than ever for a voluntary organisation. Well-meaning amateurs may not be able to do this adequately. Thus for a fundraiser, it is imperative to be able to get people on to the board or committee who will ask the right questions, think long-term, advise on crucial issues, and bring real clout to the fundraising.

Trustees and advisers are almost always recruited from within the existing group of advisers and their contacts. If that group is wide enough, then that is fine and will ensure that the organisation does not become too inward looking. If not, then there are consultants who can advise on the types of people who might be useful on a board. There is also a specialist agency, the Trustee Register, which deals in matching prospective trustees to charities who need their particular skills.

5.5.4 Managing celebrities

It is often said that celebrities are the most difficult of people to work with and that their presence can result in major culture clashes. This is undoubtedly true for some organisations, but couldn't be less true for others. Some well-known people demand to be treated as celebrities in all aspects of their lives; others can be deeply appreciative of the opportunity to be involved at all. It is important to build your relationship with such people carefully, as indeed you should do with anyone who contributes to your organisation in any significant way.

Because celebrities can bring you great benefits, you should treat them professionally and politely and try to make sure that their contribution is meaningful for you and satisfying for them. In an organisation of any size,

WHO TO PUT ON THE BOARD

Composition:
1. Professionals: accountant, solicitor, clergy, teacher etc.
2. Experts: in the service you provide.
3. Clients: who have benefited from your work.
4. Residents: and workers in your local community.

Qualifications:
1. A genuine interest in your organisation.
2. Experience in your operations or fundraising.
3. Time to devote to your work.

it is important to control access to your celebrities tightly. This is to help prevent them being asked to do too many things too frequently, or indeed being asked to do things that they have specifically declined to do.

For performers, the question of whether to pay them for appearing at an event may arise. If you want to avoid having to pay large fees in future, then it is wise not to start doing so now. Most performers do not expect or want to take fees from charity events, and certainly should not be encouraged to do so. In general you should be prepared to pay reasonable expenses and only consider paying the most nominal amounts or a fee, and then only in exceptional circumstances. The possible exception to this rule is in the use of musicians.

Working with an agent can be both a help and a hindrance. Attempt to get a direct line to your celebrity supporter as soon as you can. But the agent can be helpful in identifying long-range opportunities and availability (diaries are quickly filled up); they can also help you get an idea of what the person concerned is looking for, as well as their likes and dislikes.

If you are recruiting someone for an event, they will need to have a very clear idea of what is going to happen and what is expected of them. Is a speech going to be necessary? Will a car be provided? At what time can they discreetly slip away? And so on. In exactly the same way, any professional will want to know how they can really help you and how you can get the most out of their presence.

5.5.5 Fundraising committees

There are a number of other ways in which you can bring outsiders into your organisation. One is through the fundraising committee. There are a number of different models for such committees:

- **The Oversight Committee** is a formally constituted group, integral to the structure of the organisation, which may report to the Executive Committee. Its role is to monitor regularly and improve the fundraising across the whole of the organisation. Its role is purely supervisory. This group will not raise money for you.

- **The Advisory Committee** is a looser grouping which may meet less frequently. It consists of 'ideas people' drawn from different walks of life, chosen because of their occupations or talents. It can be a useful source of ideas for the fundraiser and can sometimes be a means of getting new ideas taken up by the organisation. Again it is unlikely that the committee will feel closely identified with the success or failure of the actual fundraising work.

- **The Event Committee** is an essential group where any sort of event is being organised. It is likely to be an ad hoc group specifically created for the purpose of running a ball or any other activity. It has room for both the great and good (useful for the sale of tickets) and the unknown but committed (useful for doing all the work!).

- **The Appeal Committee** can be most effective where individuals are recruited specifically to help raise a given appeal target. Members of this group are chosen because of their ability to give at a certain level and for their willingness to ask others to give. Meetings are likely to be rare, and the role of the chairperson is crucial.

- **The Local Committee** is the group that acts as the local representatives of your organisation. They will consist of the activists in a given area and will usually be prepared to get involved in any activity that is needed.

Sometimes the role of the committee has not been clearly thought through. Getting the right brief for the committee is as vital as recruiting the right people. It is much better to start with the right concept of what the committee is going to do, than to try to change the approach or brief once members of the committee are in place.

5.5.6 References

From this book:
- 5.15 Public relations
- 4.1 Local fundraising
- 5.2 Working with volunteers

And from elsewhere:
- Royal Patrons, CAF
- Trustees Register, Reed Charity Trust
- White Book of Celebrities

5.6 Saying thanks

5.6.1 Overview

Saying thank you to your supporters is both an essential courtesy and a piece of enlightened self-interest that fundraisers omit at their peril. And this applies as much to grants from trusts and other institutions as it does to individual donations.

There are many ways of saying thanks. All of them can have important benefits for your cause. Saying thank you makes donors feel good about their giving; it tells them that their donation has actually arrived; it gives an opportunity to find out about the depth of their interest; it enables you to tell them more about your work; and it enables you to raise more money. Your best prospects for a donation are

A DONOR RESPONSE MATRIX

	letters	other items
Membership leaflet	new subs	NSP
Flagship leaflet	new hi sub	NSP, JP
Kickback leaflet	new life sub	NSP, JP
Trading catalogue	new donor	GH
Old adverts	new hi don	GH, JP
	new mso sub	NSP
	new hi mso	NSP, JP

This is a very small part of the 'fulfilment matrix' used by **Friends of the Earth**, illustrating how each promotion may need a different response which will include a personalised letter, special inserts and, for high donors, the signature of the director.

those people who have given you a donation. So the thank you process becomes crucial.

5.6.2 By letter

Some charities reply to all donations, while others reply only to certain classes or levels of donation. The cost of replying may make it too expensive to reply to smaller donations, and some donors may indicate that they do not want a reply (to save administrative costs). There are important advantages in responding to **all** donations in some way if you can, as a small donation now may mean a large donation later, or for the donor it may be a major commitment of money and concern.

Make your reply swift – say within three days of receipt. Make the letter personal to the donor, and recognise their giving history (the length of time they have been supporting you and their level of giving). Some organisations wait to get the chairperson to sign the letter. This is not necessary – small and regular donors are probably much more interested in building up a personal link with your donations secretary.

At some point you will get sufficient numbers of responses that you need to define exactly who gets what in writing. A response matrix is useful here to help clarify who should get what.

You will need to distinguish first time donors, as they need more of a welcome and more information; regular donors, who may need an invitation to enter into a covenant or make a bequest; and large donors, who may need a more personal form of thanks. You will also need different thank you letters for different appeals if you have several going at once, so as to relate to the particular interest of the donor.

The quality of your response is dictated not only by your reply but also by the speed with which it comes back to your supporter. Larger organisations often have greater difficulty in being efficient than small ones. Set your standards high and try to keep to them. Aim to get a reply back to them within a week, and this probably requires that the letter be sent off within three working days of receipt of the donation.

5.6.3 By phone

To give a really fast and personal response, little can beat the telephone. This is not recommended for small donations, but is an important medium for thanking large donors. As soon as you receive an exceptional gift, ring the donor. Thank them personally. Reassure them that their cheque has arrived safely – donors often feel concerned about committing their generosity to the vagaries of the post. Find out what prompted the gift. Find out what they think of your organisation.

Fundraisers will need to use the evenings to do this, as donors will often be out during the day. One experienced charity director used to take a list of donors home each evening to phone, and make play of the fact that he was ringing from his fireside using his own phone bill. For telephone work you should make sure you are talking to the person who sent the donation. Not all partners are privy to each others bank accounts and giving. Record the fact that you have spoken on the phone together with any useful information you have gleaned from your donor records. You may well want to phone them or visit them again.

5.6.4 Cross selling

Supporters are prime candidates for supporting your organisation in other ways. Other support can range from inviting the donor in Barnsley to help you set up a local group there, to encouraging the regular donor to make a covenant. Cross selling is now common practice for the banks and utilities in their regular customer mailings. Charities of all sizes can use the techniques successfully.

The first step is to ensure that all donations are checked against the donor history file. In this way you can see whether the donor has been giving regularly. If they are regular givers, ask them to sign a covenant. If they indicate that they are working in a factory or significant sized office, ask them to give through payroll deduction or get others to do this. If their writing or their address suggests that they are elderly, you can remind them about the opportunity to leave a legacy.

5.6.5 By visit

Personally visiting donors who are likely to be of importance to the organisation can be a very time consuming business. But research shows that it can be extremely worthwhile. You need to be able to identify those worth visiting and those whom it is possible to visit geographically. The visit can be made by the fundraiser, a trustee or committee member, or a trained volunteer. A preliminary phone call can be made to announce when they are going to be in the area, and an appointment can be set up. Donors may be wary about the object of such visits until they have actually received one. A simple chat to tell the donor more about your work and to thank them for their gift will often naturally lead on to discussion about covenants and wills, without you having to introduce the subject yourself.

5.6.6 By meeting

Where personal visits are not possible, some charities set up meetings, receptions or open days for much the same purpose. Supporters in a particular area are invited and some refreshment is laid on. A senior person from the organisation will give a short talk. It is important then to have staff, committee members or other volunteers present to chat to those invited to the event. One possibility is to hold the event at your office, where all your staff and committees are available. People are always interested in seeing your offices and your facilities. Such events are usually very well received, even when all they see are desks and filing cabinets. It is the people that donors and volunteers enjoy meeting.

5.6.7 By gift

Some fundraisers offer some inducement or token in return for gifts of a certain size. There are two distinct circumstances: one which is heavily promoted by the charity to encourage a particular type of response; whilst the other is a thank you token used to build commitment, help spread the message to others and say thank you. Paper items of low cost and high perceived value are most frequently used for this purpose. A special Christmas card from the president; a certificate for a pledged legacy; or a wildlife print in return for a donation. Though giving is often a private matter, some supporters welcome opportunities to discuss their favourite cause with their friends. A thank you token can help them do this.

5.6.8 By public acknowledgement

A further way in which thanks can be given is through a public announcement or an advertisement in a newspaper, or a mention in your annual report.

The use of the annual report is sensible. Not only does it thank your donors, it sends signals to others too. If you indicate the level of their gifts, this will create a certain peer group pressure for others to give at similar levels. Perhaps more important is the credibility factor – "If *they* have given, then it must be a good organisation". After a certain point this becomes no longer feasible, as the number of donors gets too large. Even then the major donors can be listed or mentioned.

Taking paid advertising to thank donors can be expensive but can be worthwhile if there are other messages to communicate (for example that the cause has widespread or prestigious support). Remember always to get the donor's permission before you do this, as most do not expect to see their names publicly in print.

5.7 Use of the phone

5.7.1 Overview

If direct mail was the medium of the 1980s, the telephone is the medium of the 1990s. It can be used in a variety of different ways, either on its own or in conjunction with other media.

In thinking about the phone, you have to distinguish between outgoing phone calls and incoming ones. The difference is between that of being proactive and reactive. Both approaches are important. Incoming lines are the ones which will handle your response and lines with recorded messages can generate revenue for you. Outward telephoning requires more skill (and sometimes courage) and can be used for a whole range of promotional and fundraising activities.

5.7.2 Donation lines

When charities first began to install response lines for donors it was very much a minority interest. However over the years and with the increasing use of credit cards, donors have appreciated the opportunity to phone-in a donation in the evening. Most response lines are answered by telephone answering machines. These need to have good clear messages and long answer tapes to record a number of calls. Donors need to be told exactly what information to leave.

Not all responses should be by machine. Some donors want to speak to a real person. Not many people would leave a donation of £1,000 on a telephone recording device. So it is important that there is an effective procedure for taking calls at your switchboard or reception. Especially if you spend a good deal of time out of the office, you will want information quickly from people phoning to enquire about giving. Although you might want to use a special number for appeals, it is sensible to list your main telephone number too.

5.7.3 Premium telephone lines

An 0898 telephone line is one where the revenue is shared between British Telecom and the line user. The caller pays at a premium rate of 48p per minute. This can be used in conjunction with either radio, TV or a mailshot as a convenient answering system. The system can be used to receive donations or to give out information. Every caller clocks up a contribution for the campaign. 0839 is the same system operated by Mercury.

5.7.4 Answering services

For some campaigns, you will want to have a real person answering the phone. This can be done by using volunteers. Two things make this problematic. The first is that you may get very little warning of a media appeal which is going to generate a lot of response. Secondly there is the problem of getting the people and lines installed in time to do anything about it. Those charities which rely on media coverage should certainly develop a system for responding to calls at short notice. For others, a telephone agency may be the answer. Some agencies have memorable numbers (such as 081-200 0200). All have large amounts of equipment and numbers of trained operators. Not only will they answer the phone, but they will deal with any mailings necessary and do a detailed analysis of responses. This can be quite an expensive service, so be sure you get a quote first. One agency, which is itself a charity and which provides a specialist service for the voluntary sector, is Broadcast Support Services.

West Sussex telephonist Pauline Lishman has raised £1/2 million for the Spastics Society. Over the last 12 years Pauline has persuaded at least 50,000 volunteers to pound the streets, knocking on doors, collecting for the Society.

From: **Spastics Society Newsletter**.

5.7.5 Recruitment

Outgoing telephoning can be used for a range of things, but perhaps most frequently for the recruitment of people. Teams of professional callers are

WHAT CAN BE DONE OVER THE PHONE

donors phoned	response rate	average pledge
£20+ donors	61%	£51.42
£35+ donors	67%	£65.36
£50+ donors	83%	£102.83

These results were achieved by **Friends of the Earth** in a recent test. They tested 1,250 donors and raised £64,000 in pledges. Two problems confront telephone fundraisers: how do you convert the pledges into reality; and how do you carry the operation out without offending supporters? Complaints are a common occurrence.

now used by a number of charities for purposes ranging from the sale of raffle tickets to the recruitment of house to house collectors.

In the US this technique can be embellished by the use of a taped message from some well-known person which is played before returning to the original caller. This is good for getting the information across in a uniform way, but is not yet culturally acceptable in Britain.

5.7.6 Renewals

For existing supporters of the organisation, the telephone can be a much more acceptable medium. Examples of its use include the renewal of a covenant or membership. Here supporters may have forgotten to renew and so may welcome the reminder. Additionally, this is an excellent way for any charity to find out why members are not renewing. Quite quickly major blockages can be identified and hopefully rectified.

5.7.7 Phonathons

One major technique that is used extensively in the US and has yet to catch on here is the Phonathon, or telephone fundraising campaign. There are two ways that this can be done. One is to assemble a team of volunteers and get them busy phoning supporters. Another uses the same technique but employs professionals who may be selling double glazing in the morning and your cause in the afternoon. Telephone fundraising works best if the cause is really urgent, or if it can be made to seem so. For example, if a disaster has just received extensive media coverage, or if an extremely cold snap has sparked a hypothermia campaign. If the need is obvious then it becomes simpler to recruit volunteers to do the telephoning.

The phone is quite an expensive way of contacting people and so it needs to be used with care. It is unlikely to be of value in soliciting £5 donations. The response rates can be over 50% when calling past donors, which is well in excess of normal mailing response rates. However, the pledge rate may not turn into cash in the bank unless donors are giving credit card donations. For the rest you will need to send a letter to pledgers to clinch the donation. You might expect 60% of pledged donations to be converted into actual support at the end of the day.

5.7.8 The tools for successful telephone solicitation

Essential tools for successfully using the telephone are the script and the list. Creating scripts is a technical task. Until you have experienced the huge range of responses possible, it is difficult to create a good script. A script should contain some information about who you are and about the organisation you represent. (It is not important to distinguish between staff and agency personnel, as the difference is quite irrelevant to the recipient.) Anyone who has received calls at 6pm in the evening just as the children are sitting down to a meal, will vouch for the potential hostility that can be generated by a caller presuming that now is the most convenient time to talk; so callers should attempt to ascertain whether this is a good moment to talk. Failure to do this can diminish the results of the call. When calling people who have supported the organisation before, it is important to refer to their past help and thank them again. This can usefully lead into a short preparatory introduction about the current needs of the organisation or something else about the development of the work, and this should help set the scene for a further request for help. As with any communication, you should not expect that supporters will necessarily know why you want to talk to them unless you state it explicitly. The call to action must be very direct and clear, and should state precisely what you want them to do. Getting a pledge or a verbal agreement is usually the best you can hope to do over the phone, unless you are seeking credit card donations (in which case you can complete the transaction there and then). The call can be followed up by a letter or form to sign. The follow up should be done immediately to achieve maximum response.

Producing the list is not always easy, since most databases do not include phone numbers. This is something that is changing. If you plan to use the telephone, then perhaps you should include space on the reply coupon in your promotional literature for the supporter to put a phone number. There is then the implication that if they do so they will not mind being called. The same considerations about lists apply as for mailings (see Section 4.2).

5.7.9 Management of the telephone

The main management decision is whether to do it in-house or to subcontract to an agency. Clearly, while setting up an operation and testing whether it is viable or not, the use of an agency is very helpful. This is quite a complicated issue. Early experimentation can easily be carried out in-house when the volume of calls is small. But when it gets to be substantial, then a number of management issues come up that fundraisers may want to pay someone else to deal with. For example, there needs to be a ready supply of phone numbers; a team needs to be dedicated to looking these up, if you do not have a ready source. You will also need to recruit and train callers; this is definitely not something just anybody can do. Successful callers have an easy outgoing confidence that is communicated over the phone. Though many people are used to the phone, put them in a situation where they have to ask a supporter to give and they become quite reluctant. You will need to be able to produce the scripts and change and modify them as soon as the need arises. And there must be close supervision of the process to ensure that the most fragile and valuable asset of all – your charity's reputation – is maintained. For all these reasons, if you are planning a major campaign, it makes a lot of sense to carry out volume trials with an agency. This will incur set-up costs but will lift much of the day-to-day management responsibility from you. When you have found it to be a successful venture, you can then look at the logistics of doing it in-house, or as some have done, recruiting a team of home-based part-time callers.

Which ever way you set about it, you need to engage in at least two levels of testing. First you need to test the concept of telephoning. It is not guaranteed that your prospective supporters are going to be readily available on the phone (or more importantly, cheaply available). So you should test telephoning against other media, such as advertising or direct mail. Having satisfied yourself that using the telephone is viable, then a variety of approaches will need to be tested. These should include the use of in-house callers as against an agency, a range of scripts and any use of recorded segments of an outgoing message.

5.7.10 Telephone use by professional fundraisers

Where a professional fundraiser uses the telephone to solicit money or to sell goods to raise money for the charity, and people respond with payments by any means (credit cards, sending a cheque or cash, etc) then the professional fundraiser must within seven days of receipt of the payment write to people who have given or paid more than £50 giving them the right to cancel. The donor then has seven days to cancel the agreement to give or purchase. This only applies to **telephone solicitation** by a **professional fundraiser** or **commercial participator**. The definition of a professional fundraiser and a commercial participator is given in Section 5.1.7.

5.7.11 References

In this book see:
    4.2   Direct mail
    4.8   Membership
And from elsewhere:
    Advertising by Charities, DSC
    The Telephone Book, McGraw Hill

5.8 Involvement

Fundraising effectiveness can be enhanced by using a number of devices which give the donor an appearance of fuller involvement. It is also a fundamental truth that for maximum impact, supporters should be involved in all aspects of a charity's work, from service delivery to campaigning and fundraising.

5.8.1 Overview

Donors and supporters are likely to give more generously the more they understand about your cause. Though it is sometimes tempting to conceal the intricacies of policy issues and discussion that goes on in any well-run organisation, this is not always the best thing to do. For if supporters are aware of the genuine difficulties in reaching your target group and the steps being taken to ensure that the best service is given, they are much more likely to become firmly committed to your work. Obviously, not every supporter can work from the inside of an organisation, but there are a number of ways of giving them a fuller picture that will build their commitment and their support.

5.8.2 Mailings

Sending mailings to supporters is a necessary and vital form of communication. However, in itself, it is the antithesis of being involved in the organisation, requiring as it does relatively little thought or action on the part of the recipient. You can improve the mailing process in several ways. Where you have a large number of supporters, you have an opportunity to use the strength of their numbers, both to inform yourselves better on what they think (and who they are), and to use their views to make important campaigning points. Sending a questionnaire to supporters in regular appeal mailing can increase response rates. Some people will be motivated by the appeal and some will be motivated by the request to provide information. The result can often be a wealth of information about your supporters **plus** increased response rates. Asking supporters to return cards to a government minister or to a planning authority can, if directed through the organisation's offices, do the same.

A further and quite different type of involvement is through a contest. Competitions where the skill is knowledge of what your organisation stands for can often develop greater understanding of what you are trying

---

Dear Mrs Thatcher,
Today is South
Africa Freedom Day.
But there can be no freedom while
apartheid lasts. I want to see
Britain doing more to end apartheid.
Sanctions by other countries
are already working. Britain must join
with them now.

P.S.

Signed

Involving Your Supporters in the Campaign:
The **Anti Apartheid Movement** needed both to raise money from its members and to make a political point about sanctions against South Africa. They invited supporters both to send a donation and to send in a cardboard orange with their name on. The thousands of oranges, each one addressed (via AAM offices) to the Prime Minister, were then hung on a huge model tree and taken to Downing Street. Using this method they both persuaded more members to give a donation and got more of them active than they would otherwise have done.

Mailing to:	Cash response	Oranges sent
To AA members	7.5%	20%
To CND members	3%	7.8%

This questionnaire will take just two or three minutes to complete. Your answers will be helpful in guiding our environmental campaigning.

1 Various environmental issues have been in the news recently. Could you tell us which issues concern you and rank them in order of importance (1-9, 1 being most important).

Tick where necessary	ISSUES CAUSING CONCERN	ISSUES IN ORDER OF IMPORTANCE (1-9)
RIVER AND SEA POLLUTION	☐	☐
ANTARCTICA	☐	☐
DESTRUCTION OF THE OZONE LAYER	☐	☐
WHALING	☐	☐
POLLUTION FROM CARS	☐	☐
NUCLEAR POWER	☐	☐
NUCLEAR WASTE	☐	☐
ACID RAIN	☐	☐
THE GREENHOUSE EFFECT	☐	☐

2 Would you prefer to see money spent on more road building or on public transport?

☐ ROAD BUILDING   ☐ PUBLIC TRANSPORT   ☐ DON'T KNOW

3 Are you satisfied with the government's performance on environmental matters?

☐ YES   ☐ NO   ☐ DON'T KNOW

4 Do you think Britain should continue to import hazardous waste?

☐ YES   ☐ NO   ☐ DON'T KNOW

5 Have you noticed a deterioration in your local environment in the last ten years?

☐ YES, A LOT   ☐ YES, A LITTLE   ☐ NO CHANGE
☐ THERE HAS BEEN AN IMPROVEMENT

6 Please use this space to tell us about other environmental anxieties which may be concerning you

_____
_____

Finding out what your supporters think: As well as providing a useful source of information on what the attitudes of your supporters are and what their priorities appear to be, this sort of device reminds supporters of the range and importance of your work; and if they are persuaded to return the survey form to you then they may well send you a donation. Most organisations find that a survey increases donation response.

Source: **Greenpeace**.

to do. But use this with care. Attractive as it may be to get supporters looking at every line of your copy for the answer to a clue, some tests have indicated that large and regular donors do not respond well when given this sort of encouragement.

Most supporters never get to see the work you are doing. You can build commitment by inviting them to visit you. This can be done in a number of ways. Open days at your office will yield a surprisingly high level of interest, even if your office is remote from the projects you are organising. If possible, project visits are even better. Overseas development charities have for years organised project visits for staff, donors and volunteers. Not because the much visited projects want it, nor because they enjoy the administration involved; but simply because the excitement and understanding that is generated by such a visit could never be replicated through indirect means.

5.8.3 Campaigning

Many voluntary organisations have as part of their brief a message to communicate to both public and government alike. The campaigning is usually spearheaded by the paid staff, but can often be reinforced by volunteers. This can also build commitment. Those who become involved in advocating a cause, will develop a much deeper commitment to it. You can imagine that for a small group to have to confront their local Member of Parliament about your work, they must be very confident. It is exactly these people that are likely to become your best supporters.

Fundraisers should never allow fundraising to become divorced from the advocacy of the cause. It is important to ensure that there are a number of different ways for people to support an organisation: giving money, volunteering, fundraising, **and** campaigning. Some people will only be able to do one of these things. However where an overlap can be generated, for example by donors getting involved in the campaigns or helping with the administration or being involved with the direction of the charity at trustee level, both overlapping activities will gain.

5.8.4 Local activities

It is sometimes assumed that volunteers should not be approached to give money. This again assumes that people will compartmentalise their concern and their response. This is plainly not true. People can get drawn into many aspects of an organisation's work. From the fundraiser's point of view, two things need to be borne in mind. The first is that donors could be invited to become involved at a local level. Most will not wish to. Some will, and will continue as donors too. Even if they don't, their support may be reinforced by being told that local people are also working for the organisation. The second is that all those who are giving their time should also be given the opportunity to support with money. Though this seems obvious, it is often the case that volunteers are never asked for financial support. There may be a feeling that they should be protected from other requests so as not to disturb their pattern of support for the organisation. If this is felt to be the right approach, perhaps some market research might be done.

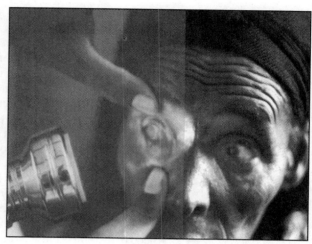

Inside there is a square of plastic that will open your eyes: This highly effective mailing to previous non-supporters invites recipients to see what it is like to have a cataract by putting a small square of plastic (sent in the envelope) in front of their eyes.

Source: **Help the Aged**.

5.8.5 The service

The ultimate involvement that any supporter can give, and the most attractive, is being involved in the work of the organisation directly. For example, the Samaritans depend entirely on highly trained volunteers; visitors to the National Trust properties are guided around by volunteers who like the surroundings and the contact with the public. This involvement can be highly motivating for supporters, though it is not always possible for every organisation.

5.8.6 References

From this book:

- 3.4   Giving by individuals
- 4.2   Direct mail
- 4.1   Local fundraising
- 5.9   Recruitment, training and secondment

From elsewhere:

Lobbying: an insider's guide to the parliamentary process, Pluto Press
The A-Z of Campaigning, Wilson

5.9 Recruitment, training and secondment

5.9.1 Overview

Staffing your charity with good fundraisers will make the difference between success and failure. After its reputation, your organisation's most important asset is its people.

Finding the right staff to undertake fundraising functions is a painstaking and difficult process which you may only get right 50% of the time. Getting it right begins with the concept of a job, goes through the recruitment and selection process, and continues with the training. Obviously continuous good management is required to capitalise on these assets, though this is not covered here.

The trend of the 1990s is towards independent work and flexible work arrangements. Increasingly people are wanting to work from their homes, to work part-time and not to have to sacrifice other important elements of their lives. In the recruitment of fundraisers therefore, managers may need to recognise these trends and to accommodate them wherever possible.

Beyond this, there is a dearth of experienced fundraisers available to resource the many new voluntary organisations that are now emerging (including many schools and hospitals who are meeting a part of their budget from fundraised income), and the increased fundraising needs of those who have been around for a time. This is creating both an upward push in salaries and a need both to find others with comparable skills from outside the voluntary sector and to improve skills through training.

5.9.2 Recruitment

The very first stage of obtaining staff is recruitment. Important preliminary activities include the following.

Budgetary provision needs to be made for any staff appointment. Not only will there be the salary to pay, you also have to allow for National Insurance and pensions which can add 10% or more to the basic salary. Many organisations will also have an overhead allowance to cover the cost of heating, lighting, etc, calculated on a per person employed basis. Sometimes an appointment is made on the basis that the fundraiser will raise their own salary. This is not always wise. There are four reasons for this. First, they may be ineffectual and have absorbed a good few months worth of salary before you can do anything about it. Secondly, most fundraising takes some time to develop, thus the income will always lag behind the costs. Thirdly, it is not the best motivation for any fundraiser. And fourthly it is the responsibility of the Management Committee to ensure that the organisation has adequate resources to carry out its work.

More important than this though is the question of what the person will do and what sort of person is needed. The best discipline is to write a job description and a person specification. The job description should cover as much detail about the job as is possible. It should include job title, internal structure of the department or organisation, any staff reporting, main objects and details of tasks or responsibilities. The person specification will very often be attached to the job description and covers the main areas of personality, attitude, skills and experience that are necessary. Dangers here lie in setting ridiculously high standards that are neither strictly necessary nor attainable. Age, sex and background should not be barriers or even a part of this specification, except in very special circumstances.

Additional information that candidates will ask for at some point include full details of the terms and conditions under which they will be employed. They will also want to know as much as possible about the organisation, especially if they are going to be asked to raise money for it.

Preliminaries over, the recruiting itself can now begin. There are a number of routes that can be tried, depending on the sort of person you are looking for and whether they must come from within the voluntary sector. Sources to be considered include:

- Word of mouth
- Networking
- Selective mailing
- Advertising in trade journals
- Advertising in the national press
- Advertising in the local press
- Use of recruitment agencies
- Use of headhunters.

Networking involves advertising in journals or otherwise making the vacancy known through the various fundraising bodies such as the WIFD, ICFM and Charity Forum, or just using your friends or existing employees.

Using recruitment agencies and headhunters can appear an expensive course of action. However, a number of agencies have large lists of people registered with them who are looking for jobs within the sector. The arrangement is often that they give you access to appropriate people and you only pay a fee (usually based on the first year's salary) when someone is successfully chosen. This process is a fairly reactive one in that there may be very good people who have not registered. Headhunters take a brief and then search for possible candidates, and are possibly the most expensive route to take. For fundraising directors or other senior executives this may make sense, but certainly not for more junior staff.

5.9.3 Selection

Once you have a choice of recruits, the most difficult and sensitive of tasks takes place – the selection process. It usually has several stages which are: the initial screening or short-listing; the interviewing; and the evaluation or choice.

Initial screening should be carried out on the basis of the original job description and person specification. Though this is not a science, you have to go through this process since it is not feasible to interview dozens of candidates. It is also unfair to ask wholly unsuitable people to attend when you can predict this with a high degree of certainty from a CV. All candidates should have been asked to submit a CV and to fill in your own application form, which can make the process of screening a good deal simpler. At this stage you should have some idea as to how many people will be involved in the interview process. Having several interviewees improves the accuracy of selection considerably, but adds to the cost and time taken. Depending on circumstances, you might want to call in short-listed applicants for an initial interview. This can serve the purpose of confirming their interest in the organisation and assessing their suitability to be on the short list.

The interview itself should be carried out with at least one person who has interview skills or training. If several people are involved, make a plan at the beginning so that each person covers one area and the interviews are consistent. The art of interviewing is both to have a clear idea of what it is you are looking for and to give applicants plenty of opportunity to talk. If you the interviewers talk for more than about 30% of the time, you are not giving your applicants a chance.

The disciplines brought in by equal opportunities can be extremely helpful in choosing the right candidates. Ruling people out because they have young children or have a disability may be very short-sighted; by the same token, ensuring that all candidates have the same opportunity to demonstrate their skills – by asking them all the same questions, for example – makes comparison much easier.

A useful part of any selection process is the assessment exercises you devise as a part of the interview process. These must be relevant to the job, but could include writing a letter to supporters, devising a fundraising strategy, or giving a 5 minute presentation as if to a sponsoring company. These can be announced on the day or in advance. Applicants are usually already under great pressure and will not necessarily perform typically if they get no warning at all. There are also a range of aptitude and preference tests – called psychometric tests – that could help you in the process of selection and interviewing.

To evaluate all you have heard you should get together all the people who have seen the candidates to collate everyone's views. This is where your decision making can be improved considerably, especially if interviews were done separately by different interviewers. It may sometimes be appropriate to invite people from other parts of the organisation or from external partners. Give this stage plenty of time and, if in doubt, make no decision rather than accept the best of a group of inadequate applicants. This is where referees can come in useful. Local government often take up references before interviewing. For the best use, wait until you have specific questions and phone up referees who have worked with the candidate before. This can often confirm a nagging doubt about a candidate.

5.9.4 Secondment

An alternative route to the recruitment of professional staff is to try to get a secondment. Great care needs to be taken to get the right person. Essentially secondment is a gift in kind from a commercial organisation. The secondee may therefore not be the high-flying thrusting executive, but may be someone who is approaching retirement or who no longer has a role in the seconding organisation. One agency exists to promote staff secondment, the Action Resource Centre. Either through them or when you approach a company directly, you should be quite clear what you want. However, if a friendly company makes an offer of a person, then you may want to consider whether there is a role that the person could usefully fill even though they are not the person you were actually looking for. It is quite unusual for secondees to be good fundraisers.

In secondment all sorts of different forces are at play and so it is really essential to get the relationship right both with the employer and the secondee. You should expect that secondees will come with their salaries and expenses paid, (often these will be considerably higher than your own). During their term, they will be under your management and supervision and should therefore be expected to perform as well as other comparable staff.

Before getting over-enthusiastic about the prospects of getting a secondment you should note that secondment is an extremely expensive way for companies to give support, and that the chances of getting a full-time secondee are very slim. Most go to industry sponsored projects rather than charities.

An alternative is a part-time secondment to undertake a specific task. This could be to draw up a marketing plan or undertake market research. The idea of the 100 hour secondment, either during office hours or in someone's spare time, is gaining ground.

A retired volunteer is another option. They have their pension and are often looking for occupation rather than remuneration. They may have talent, experience and enthusiasm, and can offer a great deal to the fundraising process. There are a number of agencies promoting voluntary work by retired people, including REACH and RSVP.

Somewhere in between are those people who have retired early and are looking for another job. They may have a pension of sorts or a redundancy pay off, but still require additional remuneration. Retired service personnel and early retired civil servants fall into this category. Remember though that their aptitude for the job, rather than their previous job title, is what is going to be important.

5.9.5 Training

Once staff have been recruited, some training is likely to be necessary. There are several approaches to this. The sink or swim approach, which is a rather crude method of on the job training, is not recommended despite being frequently practised. The first step is to plan some induction programme for a new recruit which will help them orientate themselves into what may be a new organisation and consequently a quite different culture. Some decisions about ongoing training are then needed. Training can be delivered through reading of literature, through attending conferences and charity events, through personalised training, or through attending courses. Suitable bibliographies are listed below, as they are at the end of each section of this book. A number of regular conferences are appropriate to fundraisers, all of which cost money and time. Worth mentioning are the ICFM's National Fundraising Convention, the International Fund-raising Workshop, the Charities Forum organised by the Directory of Social Change (DSC), the Charities Aid Foundation's annual conferences, as well as other ad hoc conferences, all of which are well advertised. A growing range of charity and specifically fundraising courses are now available. Basic or foundation courses are available from the Institute of Charity Fundraising Managers (ICFM) and the Directory of Social Change (DSC). Other courses are laid on by local Councils of Voluntary Service and commercial organisations from time to time. If these are not specific enough, then it is possible to find companies or consultants who will bring training into your offices for a fee. For larger charities, this can be cost-effective.

5.9.6 Salaries

Salaries have always been a stumbling block in the public relations of charities, and are now equally so in the recruitment of fundraisers. It used to be deemed proper that all charity employees be paid at very low levels in order to make the most of donors' money. In recent years this has been recognised as a short-sighted view which has led to a significant gap between salaries inside the voluntary sector and those in the real world. It is now recognised that the need to protect and maximise the public's contribution demands the highest levels of professional skills. To get these skills, charities may have to be prepared to pay something much closer to market rates.

The surveys that have been carried out suggest that for smaller charities, salaries of managers can be as little as half that of their opposite numbers in industry. This can pose great difficulties in recruiting people of the right quality. Ways around this could include:

- Increasing your salary levels
- Adding flexible benefits (pension, car, etc)
- Offering rapid increments
- Offering performance based pay or incentives for achievement.

THE SALARY GAP

Total income (£ million)	Salary in charities (£)	Salary in industry (£)
1 – 3	12,816–16,640	12,000
3 – 10	14,417–16,500	17,137–24,785
10 – 20	16,091–20,765	18,000–25,000
20 – 70	17,816–23,427	21,400–27,520

This data, taken from the **Charity Recruitment** survey, shows the substantial gap between the salaries offered in industry and those offered by charities for a fundraising manager (or a single fundraiser in a smaller organisation).

5.9.7 References

From this book:
2.2   The fundraiser
3.3   Companies
And from elsewhere:
Charity Recruitment
Charity Appointments
Directory of Social Change (DSC)
Institute of Charity Fundraising Managers (ICFM)
National Council for Voluntary Organisations (NCVO)
Charities Aid Foundation (CAF)
Action Resource Centre (ARC)
Women in Fundraising and Development (WIFD)
Charity Forum
REACH: the Retired Executives Action Clearing House
RSVP: Retirement and Senior Volunteering Programme (Community Service Volunteers).

5.10 Targeting and profiling

5.10.1 Overview

For those large charities undertaking fundraising campaigns through the mail, the question of how to find new supporters can be aided by targeting.

The development of large databases with massive computer power has brought a whole range of new tools to the aid of fundraising. These started with the advent of geographic analyses such as ACORN, which set out as a classification of residential neighbourhoods. This was later supplemented by financial systems that focused on the wealth of people and most recently have developed into what is called lifestyle information.

The general application of these tools is to build up a profile of a charity's supporters by comparing their characteristics with the known characteristics of a larger database. Using this profile of your typical supporter, other names matching this profile are then selected from the original list and used for mailing. The purpose is to find a more effective way of choosing mailing lists than is currently available. Thus the extra cost that is involved in this profiling and matching process, should be offset by the higher returns that would be expected from the mailing.

5.10.2 Pinpoint systems

The first system of interest to mailers was the ACORN system which works from the electoral register. The system maps information about the type of housing in which people are living onto the information already contained on the register. Comparing housing type with incidence of your existing donors will suggest where you should be prospecting in future. This is a useful system for house to house collections and mailing work. However it works only at the postcode level and assumes that everyone in the same postcode behaves the same. Also, the classification is based on census data and thus relates heavily to the number of rooms in a house and similar information and can also become quickly out of date. Pinpoint is a development of this system using more up-to-date methods.

5.10.3 Financial systems

The next types of targeting system are those built around shareholders of British companies. Since the onset of privatisation, the shareholder lists of the large privatised companies are of a size and contain the type of person of particular interest to the direct mail fundraiser. A number of products map the wealth and social preference of the names on these share owner lists in the same ways as for the electoral register. The current names of available systems include MOSAIC, Super Profiles and FINPIN.

5.10.4 Lifestyle systems

Probably the most interesting method of large-scale list building uses a massive and continuous system of questionnaires. This invites buyers of products to fill out a long survey about all aspects of their life, including their charitable giving. From this information the same process of matching and extrapolation to the remainder of the list, can take place. Fundraisers report good results from using these lists, though the high costs of doing so needs to be carefully weighed up before proceeding.

5.10.5 References

From this book:
    4.2   Direct mail
    4.1   Local fundraising
From elsewhere:
        ACORN
        MOSAIC
        Super Profiles
        FinPin
        The Lifestyle Selector, NDL

5.11 Testing, evaluation and control

Keeping control of your fundraising is essential. Donors, supporters and trustees will scrutinise your results periodically and want to know why your results were what they were. High fundraising costs can be the worst advertisement for new donors. Fundraisers must know exactly what is going on and how they can improve their performance.

5.11.1 Overview

Control of fundraising centres around the need to generate the maximum funds whilst consuming the minimum of resources. Ideally your fundraising strategy should consist only of those elements which are going to be most cost-effective. The first issue then is to identify which fundraising methods are actually going to prove most cost-effective for you. This is where testing comes in. Demonstrating what is cost-effective requires some measure which relates the effectiveness of one form of fundraising against another. Finally you have to keep track of what you are doing and compare your performance with what you achieved in the past and how others are doing.

Fund Ratios: keeping control of your efficiency: The ICFM has launched a system of inter-charity comparison which has been used successfully in industry in the past. The illustration shows just one part of the output showing a range of measures of fundraising effectiveness across a number of anonymous charities. As a subscriber to this system you are told which other charities are contributing and which is your own performance. This can be extremely useful in identifying where you may be falling behind the leaders.

5.11.2 Measuring fundraising effectiveness

There are a number of measures of effectiveness that you can use. The most important measure is the **fundraising ratio**. This is simply the income raised by a particular fundraising idea or method divided by the cost of doing it. This gives the best indication of the costs needed to raise a given amount of money. The higher the ratio, the better the method. Many organisations use a guide ratio of 5:1. This indicates that if all income is raised at this rate, 80% of income will be available for the organisation, and 20% to meet the cost of fundraising. It is a useful measure since it relates directly to what appears in your accounts. The actual percentage will very much depend on your organisation and cause. If you are new to fundraising or developing your fundraising programme, the ratio you achieve may well be lower than 5:1. If you have a large endowment generating an income, a well-established legacy income flow or large government grants, then you would expect a much higher ratio. A guide ratio of 5:1 may be what charities aim at, and a 10:1 ratio would be ideal.

An alternative approach is to use the **net income** measure. This is the amount you actually receive of the fundraising costs. The argument here is that your trustees can only spend the difference between income and expenditure. Concentrating on achieving a high ratio, as suggested above, may produce only very little income, although it has been raised very efficiently. What is as important is to measure the available net income. Such a device is often used for trading in shops and for local activities, where it is deemed that local expenses are not really within the control of the charity anyhow. It also conveniently overlooks the very considerable amount of resources that can be absorbed by volunteer-based fundraising activity. Organisations which use both measures for different parts of their fundraising however will have the problem of comparison.

For mass fundraising campaigns, you are likely to need two other measurements. The first is the **response rate**. For mailings, house to house calls, collections and other fundraising methods where you are asking a large number of people to help, it is important to know how many of those people respond positively. The response rate is simply the numbers responding divided by the numbers approached.

This will help you decide whether your approach is better than last time, and if you can improve this, you will also improve the amount of funds you receive. But your success also depends upon the amount each respondent gives. This measure is the **average donation**. The two figures together can be satisfactorily combined into the **yield**, which is simply the money raised divided by the number approached.

For situations where you are more interested in building up your support in order that you can later go back to those same people, you should consider the **cost per new donor**. For cold mailings, for example, the ratios you will get are usually very low. This does not mean that the fundraising method has no value; far from it, it means that you are measuring the present value of something that is expected to have a future benefit. Ideally here you should also have a measure of the **lifetime value of a supporter**. This can then be compared with the investment needed to find such a person. Even if you cannot accurately estimate their lifetime value, you should attempt to measure the effectiveness of this sort of activity on a cost per new donor basis.

5.11.3 Controlling effectiveness

Controlling the effectiveness of your fundraising requires two pieces of information. The first is a **realistic plan**. Control then centres on ensuring that you stick to your plan, and that the sums which appear in your bank account are what you predicted they should be. Clearly the first essential ingredient in this is to have a budget for both your costs and the income you plan to generate. Fundraising budgets should be based on past experience as much as possible. If you do not have the experience, you should ask the advice of other fundraisers rather than expose your organisation to the risk of getting it completely wrong. You should also be cautious in estimating the yield from new fundraising methods not tried by your organisation before.

Annual budgets should be broken down into periodic budgets taking account of inflation, and the growth and development of your plans, and any seasonable elements such as the Christmas period. Income and expenditure should be shown separately over each period. A quarterly basis is the one most frequently used. Results should be produced for each quarter and compared against the original budget. If there is a problem, action can be taken accordingly.

New fundraising areas should be tested wherever possible. If the organisation has fixed a ratio for acceptable fundraising, say 5:1, then it is not sensible to expect that new schemes or new fundraisers will raise this immediately. Often their results are 'ramped' in such a way that they are expected to produce 2:1 in the first year, 4:1 in the second and so on. How quickly you can be expected to reach full profit potential depends on the situation. Three years would be a normal minimum.

If you are running any large-scale operation, you will want to know whether perhaps there is some other charity that is doing it much better than yourself. This is where Interfirm Comparison Fundratios come in. This is a relatively new idea to charities but an immensely useful one. The idea is that the efficiency of major charities (those subscribing to the scheme) are compared anonymously. Thus it is possible to identify your own results, but not put a name to anyone else's. Potentially this is a very powerful tool in fundraising management. Registration is through the Institute of Charity Fundraising Managers.

5.11.4 Testing

In order to improve fundraising performance, most fundraisers will want to test what they are doing against some known control. There are a very large number of things you can test and many opportunities for testing. First you need to decide what to test. The important thing is to test only one thing at a time, since if this is not done you can never be quite sure about what is causing the different result. Thus in many test programmes, there is one well-known and tried control group and large numbers of test groups in which just one element has been changed in each.

The first things to test are those things that will make the most difference. So, if you are to launch an appeal to supporters for cash, then here are some of the important things you could test:

• Using the mail or the phone;
• Which supporters to appeal to;
• The message you use;
• Whether you ask for cash or a covenant;
• How often to ask and at what intervals.

Unless you are organising a very major fundraising programme you should not seek to test things like the letter heading, the colour of paper or other things less likely to have an impact on the results.

In some areas of fundraising, testing will have a quite limited role. A single campaign to raise a capital sum will not be easy to test (though feasibility studies can be carried out). However a continuous mailing programme to supporters lends itself to testing and improvement.

5.11.5 Statistics of testing

Typically when you are testing, you will find that you have different sets of results drawn from entirely different groups of people. Some differences are to be expected to occur randomly across the sample. Others will indicate that one group genuinely did do better. Your job is to structure your tests so that you get reliable readings and can tell beyond reasonable doubt which activity is performing better. Statistical theory will tell you whether the different results are significant or just due to chance. This will be affected by sample size and the response rates achieved.

Sample size determination

To determine the numbers of any group that should be included to make a test valid you should use the formula:

Sample size = 3.84 x c x (100 – c)/ b x b where: **3.84** gives a confidence level of 95%
c is the expected response rate in %
b is the tolerance in %.

There are two useful formulae for testing. The first indicates the size of a test sample required to give a reliable result. The second indicates what the margin of error is once you have the results. Using this, you can determine which group performed best. For example, if you want to test donor mailings where your response rate is expected to be around 15%, then you can be 95% confident that your results will lie between 14% and 16% if you use a sample size of 4896.

Test against control

The final use of this formula is to compare (say) your last mailing with the latest version that you are testing. If you can be confident that your test mailing is better than the original version, then you should move to the improved version for all your mailings.

For example, the test group got a 6.4% response, but using the formula we can calculate a tolerance or margin of 0.73%. The control group that has been running for a number of years got a 6.1% response rate, but there is a tolerance of 0.25%. The possible responses are:

Test	5.67% – 7.13%
Control	5.85% – 6.35%

This means that the difference between the test and the control could have occurred quite by chance. The results are quite inconclusive, and further testing could be needed before the approach would be changed with any confidence. What this example illustrates more than anything else is that the design of a test and the calculation of the result is a highly sophisticated and technical business – one where you may need to take professional advice.

5.11.6 References

From this book:
    4.2   Direct mail
    5.13 Market research
From elsewhere:
    Marketing, a guide for charities, DSC
    Direct Mail Handbook, Royal Mail

5.12 Tax-effective giving

Though saving tax is rarely a motive for giving by itself, it can combine powerfully with other types of motivation to encourage giving and to raise the level of gifts. Fundraisers need to have a clear and full understanding of how tax-effective giving works and how to use tax incentives to encourage giving, and be able to convey this to potential donors.

5.12.1 Overview

The Inland Revenue returns around £750 million each year to charities through a wide range of tax concessions. This high level of tax relief is achieved less through the knowledge of donors and more by the persistence and skill of fundraisers. Almost every aspect of fundraising is affected, making this an important subject. The scene is changing quite rapidly. Through the 1980s, tax concessions have been one plank of Conservative government policy to shift responsibility for the welfare state onto the public. The major tax-effective methods of giving include the Gift Aid scheme, giving by covenant, legacies, payroll giving and company gifts. Fundraisers need to review their approach to tax-effective giving each year in the light of the Chancellor's Budget, where new tax concessions or changes may be introduced. The figures given in this book are those for the 1992/93 tax year.

5.12.2 The covenant

The cornerstone of all tax-effective giving remains the deed of covenant. It provides a vital source of income for many charities. A covenant involves a commitment by a donor to make regular payments to a charity. These payments must be annual (although they can be paid in more frequent instalments) and the period of commitment should be capable of exceeding 3 years. Thus the simplest covenant is for 4 years. The amount is usually fixed at the same sum each year, but can vary according to some pre-set formula (such as an annual membership subscription level) so long as calculating the amount to be paid each year is completely outside the donor's control. Appendix 6.5 gives the Inland Revenue's preferred form of words for a Deed of Covenant.

A covenant is a legal document and must be drawn up and signed correctly if it is to be effective. When this is done, the charity can reclaim tax at the basic rate which the donor has already paid on his or her income. It also reduces the tax bill for a donor paying income tax at the higher rate.

A covenant at a 25% basic rate of income tax will increase the value of a gift by 33%. At the same time, it will reduce the cost to the donor paying higher rate tax (at 40%) by 20%. There is no limit to the amount that may be given under deeds of covenant, so long as the donor has enough taxed income to cover the annual amount of the covenant. Donors who do not pay income tax in the UK should not be asked to enter into a Deed of Covenant.

5.12.3 Gift aid by individuals

The scheme for making single donations tax-effectively which was introduced in 1990 is called Gift Aid. It now applies to gifts of £400 or over. The charity can claim back the basic rate income tax – just like an ordinary covenant. The donor benefits from any higher rate tax relief. Rather like the covenant system, the charity needs to get each donor to sign a form (R190 SD) to prove that the gift complies with the rules and has been paid out of taxed income. This form can be signed after the payment has been received. The donor needs to do nothing at the outset other than send the money (but it cannot be used for donations paid in instalments of less than £400). Appendix 6.5 gives a sample of the form required. This system also applies to companies with some variations. Booklet IR112 from the Inland Revenue explains the scheme in more detail.

5.12.4 Payroll giving

Payroll giving is both a new idea and an old one. For years some of our best known charities have been collecting money in the workplace through the use of payroll deductions. What is new about it is that it can be done tax-efficiently. Before a donor can give, the employer has to be operating a payroll giving scheme. These schemes are approved by the Inland Revenue and operated by a payroll agency. The major agencies offering schemes are the Charities Aid Foundation (Give As You Earn), Littlewoods (Work Aid) and Barnardo's. The job of the agency is to receive the donation from the employee and to pass it to the charity of his or her choice. If a donor decides to give through a payroll scheme, let us say £100 per annum, then the donor signs a payroll coupon authorising the deduction and this instruction is passed to the wages section who then makes the deduction from his or her salary each pay day until the instruction is cancelled. Rather than the deduction being made from take-home (after tax) pay, it is deducted from pre-tax pay. This means that the donor does not have to pay tax on the amount of the gift. Thus a £100 gift costs in effect just £75. The value to the charity is £100 less any small charge made by the Payroll Agency for operating the scheme. The maximum any individual can give under the scheme is currently £600 per annum.

5.12.5 Deposit covenants

Deposit covenants are a complicated method of getting the value of a covenant applied to a single donation. The donor enters into a covenant, but pays the four years' annual instalments all at once. The charity holds the future payments on deposit or as a loan, gradually reducing the loan to meet the covenant payments as they fall due. This scheme requires the donor to sign a properly executed Deed of Covenant and a formal Letter of Loan at the time the donation is made. There is no limit to the size of such a gift except that the donor must have paid sufficient tax to meet the charity's claim from the Inland Revenue. For sums of £400 or more, the Gift Aid scheme introduced in 1990 is much simpler and does not require the donor to sign any paperwork at the time of making the gift (see Section 5.12.9).

5.12.6 Loans

Interest-free loans are yet another way of helping a charity. There is no tax to be reclaimed on any loan. However there is an advantage to both sides. The charity has access to capital hopefully at low or no interest for quite long periods. Alternatively it can invest the loan and benefit from the interest. It is very common, after this step has been taken, for donors to realise that they can survive very well without the capital; consequently many loans are converted into gifts after a time. It is one way of the donor testing out your charity, to see if they are comfortable with the idea of giving a substantial amount. From the donor's point of view there are advantages in lending. The interest on the money that is loaned does not form a part of their taxable income and thus you are saving them a certain amount of tax which they may appreciate. Always conduct any borrowing in a scrupulously businesslike manner and treat your lenders extremely carefully during the life of any loan.

5.12.7 Legacy giving

Giving at death is a big source of income for charities. The increase in house values in the 1980s (although they have obviously been recently affected by the recession) should maintain this form of giving. There are good fiscal reasons why people should give this way. Beyond £150,000 (for 1992/93) most of an estate will be subject to inheritance tax at 40%. This can amount to a substantial sum. Gifts to charity are completely free of tax and are thus highly attractive. For example, Miss Kind has just died and left an estate of £400,000. Out of this she left your charity a legacy of some £10,000. Since the estate will be paying inheritance tax at 40%, the gift will have cost a mere £6,000, a useful extra for her favourite charity.

5.12.8 Gifts in kind

Sometimes gifts other than money are offered or sought by charities. A painting, piece of furniture or block of shares, for example. If these are of some value, then there is a chance that the owner will be charged Capital Gains Tax which can be levied up to a maximum of 40%. At a time when the value of sought after items has been rising, it is quite likely that such items will incur some CGT. The tax-effective way to deal with this is for the owner to donate the article outright. The alternative, which is usually the one that donors adopt, is to sell the object and give the charity the proceeds. This will always be more attractive tax-wise if the donation is made via a Deed of Covenant.

5.12.9 Company giving

Company giving is an increasingly important area for fundraisers who need to know the main rules. Unlike individuals, companies are invariably well provided with qualified accountants who can put schemes into effect. The senior people with whom you initially negotiate however, may not be so familiar with the tax position.

Contributions made for advertising or sponsorship can usually be claimed to be a legitimate business expense. Thus the payment is made before any charge to corporation tax. This means that depending on the rate of corporation tax, the actual cost to the company will be substantially less than the contribution. The current rate of 33% for larger companies means that the cost of giving £100 is only £67.

Most payments you receive from companies will be in the form of charitable contributions. Increasingly these will be made via the company's own charitable trust or through an arrangement with the Charities Aid Foundation, so that the company has organised its giving tax-effectively already. Where the company is making the payment direct to the charity, it either has to make a Gift Aid payment or enter into a Deed of Covenant. Covenants can be for any amount, but must run for at least four years. There is a £400 minimum for a Gift Aid payment by a Close Company; there is no minimum size for a Gift Aid payment by an Open Company. This payment is net of income tax at 25%, which has to be paid to the Inland Revenue, and is subsequently reclaimed by the charity. The tax for a £400 payment amounts to £133. The cost to the company is £533, as is the value to the charity. But the company also saves Corporation Tax (as for sponsorship payment) and the after tax cost for a large company is only £385 in this example.

5.12.10 Sponsorship and VAT

If you are receiving money from sponsorship or fundraising events, VAT rears its head; the issue needs to be understood by fundraisers planning activities of this type. There are quite strict rules as to when VAT will apply and certain concessions available to charities.

If a charity is under the current VAT threshold (£35,000 per annum for 1992/93), then it will not be subject to VAT on its sales. Unless the event brings it above the limit, the charity need not worry about VAT at all. Most charities however will find that when they are in receipt of ticket sales or sponsorship, VAT will have to be charged.

Sponsorship is a business transaction with the sponsoring organisation. It is not a charitable donation. Most sponsors will be able to offset the VAT charged on the sponsorship against the VAT collected on their own sales. So it will not in fact cost them anything. However it is important that you agree with the company at the outset whether VAT will be charged on the agreed sponsorship sum.

For ticket sales to an event, a return is being given to the purchaser, so the sale is not a charitable donation. If you are registered for VAT, then VAT has to be charged. In this case, there is a concession. The ticket price should be split into two parts, as much as possible being considered as a genuinely optional donation which is not subject to VAT. The donation part must be optional and the entry charge part must reasonably reflect the cost of attending the event. If a £20 ticket price includes a £15 optional donation, very few ticket buyers are likely to take the theoretical option of paying only the £5 part.

5.12.11 References

Elsewhere in this book:

6.5	Standard form of covenant
3.3	Giving by companies
3.4	Giving by individuals
4.7	Committed giving
4.5	Legacies

And externally from:

Gift Aid, A Guide for Donors and Charities, IR113, Inland Revenue

Enquiry Point, Inland Revenue, Claims Branch (Charity Division)

A Guide to Gift Aid, DSC

Tax-Effective Giving, DSC

5.13 Market research

5.13.1 Overview

Market research is a vital element in the life of a charity if it is to depend on funding and support from the public. At a certain point you will need to find out about your donors in order to be able to modify your approach accordingly. Research is the essential tool for doing this.

There are many different types of market research that you can carry out, and for a wide variety of purposes. In this section we look at researching your own donor base, finding out what the public thinks of you, and using research to seek out new supporters. All research involves collecting data gleaned from small groups of people and making extrapolations from that to derive views about the attitudes of the public at large.

Demography refers to the vital statistics of age, sex, and location of individuals in the general population. Psychographics denotes their attitudes and preferences, as shown by newspaper readership, church going, voting patterns, and so on. Opinion research usually refers to the attitudes of the public to given questions. This might be put in a question such as *"Do you think stray dogs should be shot?"* : *agree, disagree, don't know. . .*

5.13.2 Donor research

There will often be a group of supporters upon whom the organisation's well-being depends. These may be volunteers, donors, sponsors or others. When an organisation is very small, it is quite often just a small group of enthusiasts and well-wishers who are involved. At this stage, it is possible for the organisers to keep in touch personally. But as the numbers grow, this is no longer possible. It is at this point that the organisation will need to find out more about its supporters. You will want to know who they are and what they think of you. Who your supporters are will help you identify other sorts of people you might aim to recruit as new members – or

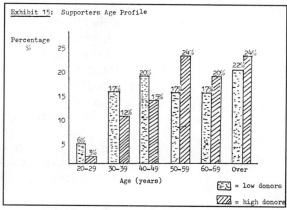

indicate people that have not yet been influenced by your message. What your supporters think is also important, as you will no doubt be dependant on their time or money to finance the organisation's work. If they are becoming disenchanted with what you are doing or can no longer meet your expectations, you have a problem to address.

A postal survey is the most usual form of supporter survey. If you have a mailing list or can enclose the questionnaire with a newsletter, then this

This chart was compiled by **Freeze** after a survey of their supporters. It provides with little cost a clear picture of where they should focus their attention.

is relatively easy to do. There is an important issue behind interpreting results: to what degree are the results of the sample of people who responded representative of the whole? These are people who are keenly interested rather than an average sample. The question of the statistical significance is covered in Section 5.11.5. Another issue is also important. If you have achieved a response rate of less than 10%, then only a minority have responded. They have one thing in common – that they have responded. Do they also have other things in common? For example, if it was a long questionnaire, then only those people who had the time might have responded, and thus your results could be biased in favour of older people. Poor survey techniques can lead to a false result.

Examples of questions you might want to ask are:

Age
Sex
Marital status
Children
Income band
Working status
Job
Newspaper readership
Voting habits
Church membership
Union membership
Other membership
Giving methods
Frequency of giving
Preferred areas of support
Other charities supported
Voluntary support
Legacy support

Because of the nature of the exercise, surveying your own supporters is a great deal cheaper than doing the same job for the public at large. It can be relatively easy to carry out yourselves, especially if you pay attention to the question composition and to the methods of getting the responses back to you with a minimum of effort (by making the survey seem important and easy to respond to, by enclosing a reply paid envelope, or by offering some incentive to those responding, such as a free entry into a prize draw, etc).

5.13.3 Public opinion research

Finding out what the public at large feels is more difficult and expensive. But for some organisations it can be essential. There are a number of ways this can be achieved. Postal surveys are not usually effective here, and so are not frequently used. Omnibus research is one useful technique: this is where a research company puts together the questions from several organisations and sends interviewers out to ask them all at once. If you want to know just a few things, then this can be cost-effective and can be done quickly. If you want to know how the public are likely to react to a given appeal or style, then focus groups will be better. This is what is called qualitative research which ends up with different sorts of answers, and is particularly useful for situations where yes/no answers will not do.

Omnibus research

A general interview is conducted. This takes time, involves professionals and is expensive. However, the findings can be invaluable. Using this type of record, a charity can learn how it is perceived, how it is compared to others in the same field, who are its prospective supporters, and their attitudes. The interviews are invariably conducted by professionals, as is the construction of the questionnaire to which they work. You should get responses which are well-balanced and results that are reliable. Important results derived from this sort of survey are the differences between supporters and non-supporters. Have you saturated one group with information – unlikely – or do your supporters define themselves by certain attitudes? If you are a charity whose lifeblood depends upon the current public awareness of your cause, then this type of research will tell you how well you are doing. Prompted and spontaneous awareness are two useful measures of how well your publicity is working.

Omnibus research is valuable too, because of the speed with which it can be done. The Anti-Apartheid Movement frequently put in questions about the public's approval of sanctions as an issue. Within a short period, it could see who agreed and who did not and whether there was any fall off in support among various groups.

USING OPINION RESEARCH

Question: Do you think we should or should not apply economic sanctions against South Africa, such as boycotting their goods or withholding finance?

	Total	Cons	Lab	S/D	SDP	Other	Don't know
Should	45	37	54	48	56	59	40
Should not	35	46	27	33	29	26	28
Don't know	19	17	19	20	15	15	32

This is an example of information gleaned through an omnibus survey carried out by **Gallup**. This simple device can provide important campaigning information and can in itself be newsworthy.

Focus groups

Focus groups are useful when you have a new strategy that you want to explore prior to launching it. It works by gathering a number of people in one place for a period of discussion. There should always be an experienced facilitator to help steer the conversation and record the results. A new name for the charity, new advertising strategies, and important issues can also be explored in depth this way. The groups themselves are formed in different locations to give balance and compare different types of supporter and public. Reports and transcripts are made available to the client. The results can prove extremely interesting, especially if you are testing the response to proposed or actual materials.

Surveys carried out just before or after a major initiative, are especially useful in determining how best to proceed.

5.13.4 Prospect research

A completely different sort of research is important for finding large numbers of people to support your organisation. This was covered in Targeting, Section 5.10. To find small numbers of rich potential donors you will need to carry out your own research to identify the preferences, habits and wealth of particular individuals. This mainly comes from the press. A number of agencies have made it their business to collect this information over the years and can provide valuable leads to organisations needing to recruit a few key individuals.

5.13.5 Sources of data

Regular information is available to the keen observer from a number of places. Your local library is always a good starting point. Reports from the Office of Population Census and Survey contains a wide range of research at a national level. Much of this appears annually in the publication, Social Trends. For other information about people's behaviour and buying habits, most business libraries will provide access to the Mintel surveys. Your local reference library should be able to tell you about any local research that has been carried out and help you find out about relevant academic research that has been published. This information can be particularly important in highlighting the importance of issues and social problems.

5.13.6 Statistics

Not all research data is worth having. Proper samples are needed to give meaningful results. Samples can suffer from several forms of bias. One is associated with the nature of the sampling process. For example, does it cover all the areas of the country? Does it cover all age and income groups? And is the sample self-selecting, or have you only selected those who answer?

Equally important is sample size. For example, if you were to ask two people about their views and hope that they were representative of a group of four people, then you might be in for a shock. The question may be a simple yes/no attitude question, such as, "Do you agree with hanging in this country?" Suppose that two of the group said yes, and two no. Researchers using a sample of two might get two yeses, or two noes, or one of each. In all cases they would have got the answer completely wrong if the actual split in the population as a whole was 70:30. To determine the sample size required to get it right 95% of the time, you should use the formulae in Section 5.11.5.

5.13.7 Managing your research

If you are seriously in the business of making people aware of your cause and your organisation, then you will need to take market research seriously. Some larger charities now organise regular research on a planned basis – sometimes as often as quarterly. To do this you need to establish baseline data and questions, so that you can track information and changing attitudes over a period of time.

Basic research on your own donors can be done internally. The phrasing of questions is a skill which is not difficult to learn. However, more detailed research will require someone professionally qualified to carry it out. This can be done through an advertising, PR, or direct mail agency, if you see and approve one. Equally you can go to one of the many independent firms in operation and get a quote for the job. However you do it, make sure that you see and approve all the questions that will be asked.

5.13.8 References

In this book:
    3.4   Giving by individuals
    5.10 Targeting prospective donors
    5.11 Testing, evaluation and control
    5.14 Marketing
Also worth reading:
    Marketing, A Handbook for Charities, DSC
    Charity Household Survey, CAF
    Any standard text on statistics

5.14 Marketing

Marketing is not the exclusive concern of aggressive companies, nor is it just about selling. Fundraising demands marketing skills and a full understanding of the principles of marketing will help the fundraiser a great deal.

5.14.1 Overview

Marketing is often described in terms of the five P's. These are:

> **PLANNING**
> **PRODUCT**
> **PRICE**
> **PLACE**
> **PROMOTION**

Though the terms may not be familiar, they are all strictly relevant to fundraising. The whole of this book is in fact about marketing; about marketing a cause to someone who can contribute money and time to supporting it. This section simply sets out the link between classical marketing theory and fundraising. Most of the points covered here are dealt with in more detail elsewhere in this book.

5.14.2 Planning and market analysis

A key part of the marketing process is the planning that precedes it. This should start with a clear understanding of the charity, the market in which it is operating, the other (possibly competitive) charities, and the attitudes of potential supporters (see Chapter 2).

Useful tools for this include:

- S.W.O.T. analysis which gives a picture of the strengths, weaknesses, opportunities and threats to your charity;
- A positioning map, which plots where you are in relation to other charities and significant variables such as reliability, urgency, and so on;
- Market share analysis, which measures what proportion of a given sector of voluntary income you receive; and
- Market research, which identifies the attitudes of your potential or actual supporters to giving, to the cause in general, and your particular charity.

The outcome of all this analysis should be a picture of those groups in the population which are the best for you to target – in jargon, your target audiences.

5.14.3 Product

The service provided by your organisation will be the product. It consists of the following ingredients:

- The actual 'tangible' product or need which your charity exists to meet.
- What the donor gets from the association with you – perhaps the satisfaction of knowing that one more child will walk, or of being publicly seen to be generous.
- The frills: the invitation to meet the child you have helped; the attendance at a special function each year; and so on.

All these can be added together, so that the concept as a whole appeals to your target audience. The point is, you are competing for a share of the disposable income of your supporters. You have to tempt them to purchase your product rather than someone else's. You need to make your product as attractive as you can to your supporters.

Each product you launch will have a *life cycle*. According to marketing theory, from time to time you will need to re-promote your product to keep it attractive and in people's minds. Equally, theory teaches that every product will eventually run out of steam and have to be replaced by another. What, for example, happened to all the 10p a week collection schemes that were so common in the 1960s and 1970s? They have faded away to be replaced by direct mail and charity shops. The same has happened to the original workplace giving schemes, which have now been replaced by Give As You Earn.

Just as each company will produce a range of products, so any charity is likely to have a range of its own fundraising products. These might include a covenant scheme for major donors, membership subscriptions for the mass support, and a schools fundraising scheme for the young. These can all happily co-exist, so long as they are not in competition with one another.

5.14.4 Price

Donors do not automatically know what they are expected to do, nor how much they are expected to give. Your role as fundraiser is to steer them towards what is likely to be achievable and affordable to them, and at the same time ensure you meet your own needs. This is a vital part of the process.

The most obvious way of doing this is to ask for a precise amount. "We are asking each person to give £10", for example. However this is not always satisfactory as it begs the question of "why £10?" The response to that is to offer a specific example of what the money will do – £10 can buy a new walking frame for a child. The donation may not actually be spent on that, so the wording has to be carefully constructed if you are not to create a binding obligation to spend the money that way or commit a breach of trust. There are two useful approaches:

One is to provide a shopping list which illustrates a range of things that their money might be spent on.

The other is to take the membership route and have a range of levels of support from which the donor can choose. Each will be set in such a way as to confer a greater status to those who give more.

Not only does the price you ask determine the type of supporter you get, it also determines the amount of benefit you generate for your organisation. For example, a £5 covenant will cost as much to service as a £25 covenant, and a £5 donation would be immediately swallowed up by administration costs. When setting the price, you must take into account the cost of administration involved. There is often a tendency to ask for too little. Generally people are far more generous than you think. Then there is the opportunity cost. For major potential donors, you will do yourself a disservice asking for only £5. Not because it is expensive to administer, but because they might have given £5,000!

5.14.5 Place, type of gift

The place of giving refers to the channel through which money and other support is given. It will usually be closely linked to promotion. For example, a personal request to help provides an opportunity to write a cheque and hand it over. A request made in a speech or over the radio, should also contain easy ways of giving support. The place – the way the donor makes a commitment and gets their help to you – is always important. Whether it is providing pledge forms on each table, a bucket at the door, a credit card hot line or a well placed advertisement, this needs to be thought about when the promotion is being devised.

The place will determine not just what you can ask for, but will also affect how they see the charity. For example, a charity that decides to raise money from running a series of balls, will only interact with a certain range of people in a particular atmosphere. Equally the same charity could appeal to a wider audience by running a series of village fetes. The two approaches might ultimately achieve the same result in terms of money raised. However, they would have done this by using completely different techniques, from quite different sources, using different resources and helpers, and in the process creating a completely different organisation.

5.14.6 Promotion

A classic example of good marketing is **Comic Relief**. The whole thing is geared to people who are young at heart (who else would wear a plastic red nose?) who are invited to organise events.

Promotion of your cause is about how you project yourselves to the public. It is not only the medium but the message too. The message is conveyed by a whole range of things within your control. Your name – or at least the name of your appeal – sends an important message, particularly if you have made this name well-known. People recognise Comic Relief or Save the Children, and these names evoke images of what the charity is doing.

How you present yourself creates an impression of credibility, urgency, dynamism, and so on.

Most important is how you express your needs in your written and visual material. Is it a rational or emotional appeal? Is it supported by human content that makes it personal? Good designers and copywriters can create the image and feel you require for your organisation, if they are well briefed.

The medium of your promotion is another important ingredient. Are you going to rely on personal recommendation to get your message across? Or are you going to use other means of communication? Possible media include TV, radio, newspaper advertising, public relations, direct mail, posters, house to house calling, exhibitions, company promotions, books, leaflets, events, speaking at meetings and many others.

The 5 P's of the marketing mix are in fact all interdependent; if one factor is changed then it will affect all the others.

5.14.7 References

In this book see also:

Also worth reading:

Marketing, a Handbook for Charities, DSC

5.15 Public relations

Good public relations can create a positive climate of opinion and counter any negative feelings or images that people may have about your organisation and its work. It is an essential ingredient of successful fundraising.

5.15.1 Overview

For a fundraiser the value of PR lies in two things. First, it can draw the public's attention to a cause or a need, whether this is national or local. Without this attention and understanding, the task of the fundraiser becomes much more difficult. If when you get to see the head of the local company there have recently been articles about your charity in the press, you will already be starting from the point where that person accepts your cause as being serious. PR can also help position the organisation in relation to others in the same field. "Why do we need so many charities, all apparently researching the same diseases? Shouldn't they all combine?" will be a natural response of the public. Good PR can help identify the special importance of your work against all the other organisations and get this recognised by the public. This can help eliminate an important barrier to public generosity.

5.15.2 Disasters

While the media relish a good story which blackens the name of a charity, charities need to ensure that they are capable of countering the bad press and media coverage they occasionally receive. There are a number of possible situations all of which need proper handling.

A newspaper might publish an article claiming that you are badly administering your money. The readership and reputation of the newspaper will be enough to do you a great deal of damage, even if the author is a freelance with a known chip on their shoulder. In such cases, action needs to be taken quickly.

The first people to contact are your donors. They need to be reassured that what they have read is not true; and they need to be given the facts. Next you should reply to the offending article as quickly as possible. Though the damage at this point has already been done, it can be mitigated by an article or letter in reply. Then you should issue a statement to other papers and to your own staff and trustees setting out the facts of the matter. Finally, and if the circumstances warrant this, you should consider a formal complaint to the Press Council or the Broadcasting Standards Commission.

On some occasions you will get advance warning of media interest. On these occasions you should: establish the exact facts; identify a spokesperson to put your case to the media, making sure you keep the message consistent; or consider inviting the senior management of the paper or the television station to withdraw the offending article.

If in fact the coverage has some element of truth in it, you are in a less defensible position. In such circumstances, a different approach is required. You should accept responsibility for the situation; identify the immediate action that has been taken to remedy it; and invite the paper to do a follow up in a more positive vein to help rehabilitate the organisation.

In all these situations there are a number of useful guidelines:

1. Ensure that the staff of your organisation do not speak to the media unless they are specifically authorised to. There is nothing so damaging as the leaked report or the inept interview from a well-meaning staff member.

2. Make sure that the facts are established at an early stage and are accurate. Then make them well-known.

3. Make sure that your internal communication systems are working well, that you can get any new twists of the story across to colleagues speedily, and that trustees and supporters are kept informed.

4. If you haven't already got one, draft an emergency plan in which you anticipate the possible disasters that could happen and allocate responsibilities accordingly.

5.15.3 Campaigning

A number of voluntary organisations are in part campaigning organisations. However for a charity, campaigning can only be an ancillary activity to help it meet its objectives, and it cannot involve itself in any overtly political activity. Guidelines on what is permissible and how far you can go are available from the Charity Commission. For organisations that do campaign, PR is clearly a major tool to help them achieve their aims. This also has important implications for fundraising. Sometimes campaigning and fundraising are seen as two separate activities that require different people and skills. The truth is that if the campaign is seen to be an intrinsic part of the organisation's reason for existing, then when the campaign gets good coverage, good fundraising results will follow. For example, the fundraising of an organisation like the Child Poverty Action Group will be greatly enhanced by a well publicised and effective campaign to save Child Benefit.

5.15.4 Fundraising and public relations

Most organisations do not see campaigning as a primary part of their work, but many have successfully set themselves up as experts in a particular area.

This is an interesting approach since then the media will naturally turn to the organisation when there is a story and they need informed comment. However if the story is sensitive and the organisation cannot be publicly identified with this information, then this strategy will not help.

You can also try to get the name of your organisation mentioned in the media, as many times as possible, hopefully in a good context but almost irrespective of whether there is any informed comment on the cause. This can be done by issuing press releases, setting up stunts or events, holding press conferences, or writing letters. Better still is to use these same skills to set up interesting fundraising events that the media will want to cover.

Timing is all important in media work. Not only because of the natural deadlines of the different media, but also because of the need to use the coverage to enhance your own fundraising. Thus the media exposure should ideally be timed to happen **just before** the fundraising, in whatever form you can obtain it.

5.15.5 Letters

One of the most helpful ways of creating the positive climate of opinion about your cause is to write letters to the papers. This can be done by staff, or often better by volunteer supporters. The best papers for a local organisation or a local branch of a national organisation to target are the local papers and free sheets in the area. In this way you can spread the word about your charity quite widely for little cost. The theme of any letter should ideally be topical. If it is linked to a local event or signed by a well-known local personality, your letter is more likely to be published. But letters just alerting readers to new needs or services you provide may also be published. Answering letters that others have written to the press is another opportunity. A letter of thanks for local help after a flag day or other event can give you the opportunity to show how successful the event was, how efficiently the money was raised, and how well it is going to be spent.

5.15.6 News releases and press conferences

When you have something new to report, sending a press release to a selected list of media is one of the most effective ways of publicising it.

An effective press release answers the questions who, what, when, where, and why. To be effective at a local level, it should have a clear local angle – a link to a local person or a local event, or a local organisation. Ideally, you should write it in the form of a short article, so that editors can use it verbatim, if they wish. Some might be really interested in the story and want more background information, which you can include separately. Picture editors will appreciate good photos.

If the event is of real interest, then you might consider holding a press conference. You invite the press to come in person to hear your story, and you can expect to be closely questioned on the project and on your organisation.

The timing of the press conference is critical. Its proximity to other stories can make or break yours, though you may have relatively little control over this. If you hold the conference on a Saturday, do not expect to get into the Sunday papers which (apart from the hard news) will already have been printed by then.

Location is extremely important. An interesting venue can add to the feel of the story – launching a campaign from the roof of the Met Office in London would be ideal for a story connected with the weather, for example. The venue should also be easily accessible to journalists. If you hold a press conference in London you are more likely to get reporters or photographers from the national media turning up; similarly you might want to hold a press conference at an event which is guaranteed to get good coverage itself – such as a political party conference.

One way of making the press conference go with a swing is to announce that it will be given by some well-known people, renowned either for their entertainment value or for their serious interest. An actress or celebrity will often use pithy words for journalists or be well rehearsed in the photo call for photographers. Similarly, reporters will know that senior figures at press conferences can usually be drawn on the issues. If you are using a celebrity, having the conference chaired by a senior person from your organisation will help control the questions and steer them away from the celebrity who might not know the answer.

To get your message across with no deviation or hesitation, there is nothing quite like a dry run first. If you can't manage this, you will have to give the spokesperson a full briefing.

For those who don't get to the conference, you should compile a briefing pack. It often transpires that some of the fullest coverage from a press conference comes from people who have not even attended! But you might never have got this coverage without having the conference first.

5.15.7 Photocalls and events

The media are always attracted to the unusual, the famous and the picturesque. Sometimes it is necessary to express your needs in this way, rather than expect that your campaign or fundraising message alone are in any way newsworthy.

If your main way of raising funds locally is to run coffee mornings, how might you use the media to help boost those events? Apart from a one-line mention in the local paper, no-one in the media is going to take much interest. One answer is to use a celebrity. Celebrities do not have to be major national names to be of interest to the local media, though it does help if they are. You could find out which celebrities live in your area and who will be visiting the area at the time you plan to hold the press conference (the theatre, the ballet, or a sporting event often bring well-known people). Just by getting them to pose for an appropriate picture you can raise the chances of getting coverage for your coffee morning. Another possibility is to get photographers to come to a staged coffee tasting. Another is to hold a coffee morning with supporters drinking from a huge coffee cup. It is the extra dimension that makes the event newsworthy, and the visual aspect will attract the photographers.

A development of this is to organise a stunt of some sort. This need not depend on a well-known person, but can use the stunt's zaniness to attract attention, and its visual excitement to attract TV or radio coverage. A stunt built around your coffee morning campaign might have the boy scouts having a coffee morning in the back of a Hercules transport plane in flight, or someone leaping off a bridge (with the usual strong elastic attached!) sipping their coffee as they go. The challenge with these sort of activities is not just having to set them up, but also selecting an activity that is relevant to your work. Needless to say, dangerous stunts should not be encouraged. There is the additional risk that if anything goes wrong your organisation will receive the blame, whether it was deserved or not.

Presenting the cheque is perhaps the simplest ways to get some positive coverage for your cause. In this case the donor appears to be getting better coverage than the recipient. Many corporate donors will automatically suggest that a photo call is arranged as they hand over their gift.

5.15.8 Managing public relations

Ideally, the control of PR should be integrated with the fundraising work. Some organisations see this role as quite separate, with the result that the PR person does not maximise the fundraising potential of the organisation; nor does the fundraiser maximise the PR potential. If there is someone who has a specific PR role, they should be asked to produce plans to show how they can best support the fundraising needs, as well as meet the PR objectives of the organisation.

In small organisations, PR will not be a separate function, and will probably be carried out by a senior member of staff or even a committee member. This is as it should be, but everyone should be encouraged to give PR the importance it deserves.

One option is to appoint a PR agency to handle your public relations. There are many around the country, and some which work mainly with the non-profit sector. They need to be briefed well, and can then help you with all aspects of the work. You can monitor the results of your PR through the use of a press cutting agency. This will show you whether you are getting your money's worth.

However you handle the PR, there should be proper co-ordination. Links with the press should be handled only by designated people, and preferably be channelled through one individual. The risks of any well-wisher discussing confidential issues, getting information wrong or just appearing ill informed are just too great to allow.

5.15.9 References

Useful source:
A Basic PR Guide for Charities, DSC

5.16 Using computers

5.16.1 The uses of computers

The uses of computers can be as diverse as their types. The most important uses for fundraising purposes are:
• Databases for appeals and big gift fundraising,
• Word processing,
• Spread sheets for figure work and for general use,
• Desktop publishing (DTP).
Computers come in a wide range of sizes and with a dazzling array of names and types. Most organisations use personal computers or PCs.

5.16.2 Databases

The main purpose of having a database is to conduct appeals more effectively. In its most simple form, the database holds a list of donors or supporters, with information on their past giving, trading purchases, standing orders and covenants, personal information, their address and telephone number, and so on. This information will be used at different times for differing reasons. Your database should be able to do the following things:
• Add donors;
• Amend donor information;
• Add new types of information;
• Delete donors when they have lost interest;
• Provide fast access to any donor.
All of this is necessary just to keep a list of names up to date. To be truly useful the database needs to do a number of other things as well:
• Select particular combinations of donors;
• Output information in various formats, for example as address labels;
• Produce letters of thanks and receipts;
• Print out donation statistics;
• Print an analysis of response rates;
• Print out analyses of donor characteristics;
• Print out a tracking analysis of donor history.
Only in the last five years or so has it been realistic to consider having a sophisticated database on a PC. This is now possible and there are a number of specialist software packages for fundraising work now available.
    A key issue to consider is whether to use a relational database. This will allow you to choose all those donors who have covenants, for example,

by going to each covenant record directly without having to look up every donor. Systems which are built in this way offer much greater flexibility and speed when it comes to making complicated selections for an appeal.

For big gift fundraising programmes, a database is essential. While the basic usage is the same, you are able to make links between the many people who have given you support, who have expressed interest, and those who you want to attract. Your supporters may be members or trustees of an organisation like Rotary or a charitable trust. If you can discover any such links, this can help you make contact at the right level. The ability to record background detail on your supporters can be helpful when you make approaches to them. Your computer system should be able to help you by regurgitating background information, personal contacts or anecdotes about the people you are approaching at the touch of a button.

5.16.3 Word processing

Word processing packages are a great boon to an efficient fundraising office. They can be used to produce a well presented formal letter, and also vary and personalise a standard form of wording for different recipients.

To make a word processor work well for you, you need to develop keyboard skills (two finger work is fine but extremely slow for anything more than a few pages) and have a good printer. The software package can come in many forms. Three of the top word processing packages are WordPerfect, WordStar and MSWord. Each is tried and tested. However, there are a wide range of other programmes, some at a considerably lower cost. You should do three things before purchasing a software package. Try it out for yourself (on your own computer or someone else's); check that it has got all the facilities you need; and see that there is someone to give you support when you need it. Facilities you might need are:

• Mail merging for form letters;

• The ability to take and send files to other machines;

• On-screen help when needed;

• Spell checks;

• The ability to move large blocks of text around;

• Windows to see several bits of text simultaneously;

• Replacing and searching text.

Types of printers available include: dot matrix; inkjet; and laser. These are in order of increasing cost. Cheap matrix printers cost around £200 and cheap laser printers around £800. The matrix is fast, but low quality. The image is produced by a number of little pins making up the letter; the more pins, the better the quality will be.

The newer inkjet (also known as bubblejet) printers are slow, but produce crisp characters.

Laser printers can be very quick and quiet and the quality is excellent. But they are more expensive to buy and run. Most come equipped with a standard set of typefaces. If you need special fonts, then the cost will be even more.

5.16.4 Spreadsheets

Spreadsheets are an electronic means of manipulating figures.

An example serves to illustrate their use in fundraising. Let us say that you are building up some income estimates for a fundraising campaign. This involves estimating the number of names on your mailing list, new recruits and deletions, what the response rate will be, and how frequently you plan to mail. If, having produced your estimate, you need to know what would happen in a worst case situation, you would normally have to do a good deal of recalculation to come up with the answer. A spreadsheet can do this almost instantly, and with no fear of error. They will be useful for a variety of jobs including:

- Budgets
- Appeal results
- 'What if' calculations
- Inflation adjustments
- Graphs
- Charts

The main functions that you may want to specify when buying spreadsheet software are:

- Graphical functions for drawing charts and graphs
- Database functions
- Size of spreadsheet (numbers of columns and rows)
- Whether it can it talk to other computers

COMPUTER FUNDRAISING SYSTEMS

Company	Package name	User run
CMG	Infobase	yes
Root Softcare	CMACs	yes
The Computing Group	Fundraiser	no
Wilkins	—	yes
Donorbase	Donorbase	yes
Dolphin	—	yes
Minerva	Charisma	yes
GFI Solutions	Raisers Edge	yes
Southwark	—	no

Some of the main fundraising packages that are available and which machines they are designed for.

5.16.5 Desktop publishing

Another benefit of the PC is its ability to design and print to a very high quality. To be effective, you will need a mouse attached to your computer, a proprietary DTP programme, and a laser printer. The programme will enable you to use headlines, text and simple designs in an attractive form suitable for publishing. If printed out on a laser printer the quality of the finished artwork is surprisingly good.

DTP is useful for producing newsletters, leaflets, posters and other display material. Using a laser printer you can provide good quality artwork to send to the printer or run off on the photocopier. You can add photographs or small line drawings to the artwork subsequently. There are a range of proprietary DTP programmes. Before buying, test them out on a computer similar to your own.

5.16.6 Implications

However enthusiastic you may be, you will have to share that enthusiasm with everybody else in the office too. Your staff and volunteers will need to be properly trained to use the equipment. Security is the other major issue to take note of. You will need to undertake a series of procedures to ensure that your information remains safe and secure. These will include everything from resisting balancing coffee mugs on the machine, to regularly backing up all your files. Finally you must make sure that the machinery is physically secure. Small modern computers are very attractive to thieves.

5.16.7 Buying computers

There are several ways of buying computers. PCs are now commodity products which can be bought off the shelf. So if you know what you want, it will certainly be cheaper to order a PC in this way.

If you do not have that confidence, you can go to a small local supplier and specify your requirements. This way, you will have a name and a phone number to ring if it breaks down. The value of this is in the training and back-up support they should be able to supply.

If you are looking for something altogether more sophisticated or custom-built, you will need to go a different route. This will involve getting a full systems specification (setting out what you want to do), and then putting it out to tender. You will then have the surprisingly difficult task of choosing who to get to do the work and of paying the very substantial bill for it.

5.16.8 References

Outside sources:

Use friendly charities to recommend a system for you
Read all the charity magazines for suppliers
See A&A Magazine issue 16 (March 1990) for a useful survey of membership systems.

6 SOURCES

6.1 Useful addresses

1959 Group of Charities, Beacons, Northbrook Avenue, Winchester, Hants, 0962-862272, (Christmas card sales consortium).

Action Match, Canning Town Public Hall, 105 Barking Road, London E16 4HQ, 071-473 2270 (encourages sponsorship of good cause projects).

Action Resource Centre, 102 Park Village East, London, NW1 3SP, 071-383 2200 and regional offices: Avon 0275-394040; Bradford 0274-484030; Derby 0332-364784; Gtr London 071-383 2200; Gtr Manchester 061-236 3391; Leeds 0532-370777; Leicestershire 0533-543398; Merseyside 051-708 9929; Nottinghamshire 0602-470749; Tower Hamlets 071-375 0259; West Midlands 021-643 9998; Scotland 031-334 9876, (encourages secondment and in-kind gifts by companies).

Angal Products, 68 First Avenue, Mortlake, London SW14 8SR, 081-788 5464, (fundraising and collecting devices).

Arts Council, 14 Great Peter Street, London SW1 3NQ, 071-333 0100, (statutory arts funding body).

Association for Business Sponsorship of the Arts, Nutmeg House, 60 Gainsford Street, London, SE1 2NY, 071-378 8143, (promotes arts sponsorship by business).

Association of Charitable Foundations, High Holborn House, 52-54 High Holborn, London WC1V 6RL, 071-404 1338, (promotes dialogue between different sectors; encourages good grant-making practice; plays an educational/informative role).

Association of Community Trusts and Foundations, High Holborn House, 52-54 High Holborn, London WC1V 6RL, 071-831 0033, (umbrella body for community trusts).

Barnardo Publications Ltd, Barnardo Trading Estate, Paycocke Road, Basildon, Essex SS14 3DR, 0268-520224, (provides fulfilment service for charity gifts and cards).

BBC Appeals Office, Broadcasting House, Portland Place, London W1A 1AA, 071-580 4468, (for information on The Week's Good Cause broadcast, radio and TV appeals on BBC).

BBC Radio, Broadcasting House, Portland Place, London W1A 1AA, 071-580 4468.

BBC Television, Television Centre, Wood Lane, London W12 7RJ, 071-743 8000.

British Direct Marketing Association Ltd, Grosvenor House Gardens, 35 Grosvenor Gardens, London SW1, 071-630 7322, (for guidelines on telephone marketing practices).

British Institute of Management, Management House, Cottingham Road, Corby, Northants NN17 1TT, 0536-204222, (promotes better management).

Broadcasting Support Services, PO Box 7, Room 27, 252 Western Avenue, London W3 6XJ, 081-992 5522.

Business in the Community, 227a City Road, London EC1V 1JU, 071-253 3716, (promotes the involvement of companies in the community, organises the Per Cent Club of top givers).

Business to Business, 148-150 Curtain Road, London EC2A 3AR, 071-729 5944 (occasional newsletter for associations: 'Associations, Management and Marketing').

Charities Advisory Trust, Radius Works, Back Lane, London NW3 1HL, 071-794 9835, (promotes effective trading by charities, provides a complete Christmas card service to charities).

Charities Aid Foundation, 48 Pembury Road, Tonbridge, Kent TN9 2JD, 0732-771333, (promotes charitable giving, operates Give As You Earn payroll giving, administers covenants for charities).

Charity Appointments, 3 Spital Yard, Bishopsgate, London E1 6AQ, 071-247 4502, (operates recruitment service).

Charity Christmas Card Council, 49 Lambs Conduit Street, London WC1N 3NG, 071-242 0546, (runs Christmas card shops).

Charity Commission, St Albans House, 57-60 Haymarket, London SW1Y 4QX, 071-210 3000, (official regulatory body for charities).

Charity Forum, 60 Laurel Avenue, Potters Bar, Hertfordshire EN6 2AB, 0707-662448, (organises occasional meetings and seminars on fundraising and public relations).

Charity Magazine, The Old Court House, New Road Avenue, Chatham, Kent ME4 6BA, 0634-409127, (monthly magazine of the Charities Aid Foundation).

Charity Projects, 1st Floor, 74 New Oxford Street, London WC1A 1EF, 071-436 1122, (grant-making trust raising money mainly through Comic Relief).

Charity Recruitment, 40 Rosebery Avenue, London EC1R 4RN, 071-833 0770, (operates recruitment service).

Children in Need, offices:

England and National, Admin Unit, PO Box 7, London W3 6XJ, 081-752 4694;

Wales, Broadcasting House, Llandaff, Cardiff CF5 2YQ, 0222-572383;

Scotland, Appeals Office, Broadcasting House, Queen Margaret Drive, Glasgow G12 8DG, 041-330 2345;

Northern Ireland, Broadcasting House, Ormeau Avenue, Belfast BT2 8HQ, 0232-338000; (Children in Need is an annual appeal for projects for children).

Commission for European Communities, London Information Office, 8 Storey's Gate, London SW1P 3AT, 071-973 1992, (information on the EC).

Community Computing, 11-13 Spear Street, Manchester M1 1JY, 061-237 1474.

Community Service Volunteers, 237 Pentonville Road, London, N1 9NJ, 071-278 6601, (operates a volunteer placement programme and the Retirement and Senior Volunteer Programme).

Countryside Commission, John Dower House, Crescent Place, Cheltenham, Glos. GL50 3RA, 0242-521381, (grants for countryside purposes).

Craigmyle and Co Ltd, The Grove, Harpenden, Herts. AL5 1AH, 0582-762441, (fundraising consultants, publishers of Charitable Giving and Taxation).

Dale Promotions, Westward House, King Street West, Wigan WN1 1YZ, (fundraising and lotteries material).

Department of Education & Science, Sanctuary Buildings, Great Smith Street, London SW1P 3BT, 071-925 5000, (government department).

Department of Employment, Caxton House, Tothill Street SW1, 071-273 3000, (government department, information on European Social Fund).

Department of Environment, 2 Marsham Street, London SW1P 3EB, 071-276 3000, (government department).

Department of Health, Alexander Fleming House, Elephant and Castle, London SE1 6BY, 071-407 5522, (government department).

Department of Social Security, Richmond House, 79 Whitehall, London SW1A 2NS, 071-210 3000, (government department).

Direct Marketing Association, Haymarket House, 1 Oxendon Street, London SW1Y 4EE, 071-321 2525, (for information on mailing lists).

Directory of Social Change, Radius Works, Back Lane, London NW3 1HL, 071-435 8171, (publishers of books and grant guides for charities, organises conferences and training courses).

European Foundation Centre, 51 Rue de la Concorde, 1050 Brussels, 010-3-22-5128938 (membership organisation with information on foundations and associations).

Friends of the Earth, 26-28 Underwood St, London N1 7JQ, 071-490 1555, (information on recycling).

Gaming Board for Great Britain, Berkshire House, 168/173 High Holborn, London WC1V 7AA, 071-240 0821, (information on lotteries etc).

Independent Television Commission, 70 Brompton Road, London SW3 1EY, 071-584 7011, (regulates Channels 3 and 4).

ITC Appeals Office, 70 Brompton Road, London SW3 1EY, 071-584 7011, (for information on TV appeals on Channel 4).

Inland Revenue, Charity Division, St John's House, Merton Road, Bootle, Merseyside L69 9BB, 051-922 6363; or Charity Division for Scotland, Trinity Park House, South Trinity Road, Edinburgh, EH5 3SD, 031-552 6255, (information on tax-effective giving and claims for repayment of tax).

Institute of Charity Fundraising Managers, 208 Market Towers, 1 Nine Elms Lane, London SW8 5NQ, 071-627 3436, (professional body for charity fundraisers, runs training courses).

Institute of Public Relations, 15 Northburgh Street, London EC1V 1JU, 071-253 5151, (professional body for public relations).

Institute of Sales Promotion, Arena House, 66/68 Pentonville Road, London N1 9HS, 071-837 5340, (for the British Code of Sales Promotion).

Lotteries Council, 81 Mansel Street, Swansea SA1 5TT, 0792-462845, (information on lotteries).

National Council for Voluntary Organisations, Regent's Wharf, 8 All Saints Street, Kings Cross, London N1 9RL, 071-713 6161, (national body for the voluntary sector in England).

Northern Ireland Council for Voluntary Action, 127 Ormeau Road, Belfast BT7 1SH, 0232-321224, (national body for the voluntary sector in Northern Ireland).

Norton and Wright, 66-77 Kirkstall Road, Leeds LS3 1LP, (printers of lottery material).

Payroll Giving Association, 231 Kennington Lane, London SE11 5QU, 071-820 1699, (promotes payroll giving, co-ordinates activities of the payroll giving agencies).

The Per Cent Club, c/o Business in the Community, 227a Curtain Road, London EC1V 1JU, 071-253 3716, (top corporate givers club).

REACH, 89 Southwark Street, London SE1 0HD, 071-928 0452, (promotes retirement volunteering).

Retirement and Senior Volunteering Programme, c/o Community Service Volunteers, 071-278 6601, (promotes retirement volunteering).

Scottish Community Education Council, West Coates House, 90 Haymarket Terrace, Edinburgh EH12 5LQ, 031-313 2488, (promotes community education in Scotland).

Scottish Council for Voluntary Organisations, 19 Claremont Crescent, Edinburgh EH7 4QD, 031-556 3882, (national body for the voluntary sector in Scotland).

Smee and Ford, 82 The Cut, Waterloo, London SE1 8LW, 071-928 4050, (legal agents providing will notification service for charitable bequests).

Telethon, 3rd Floor, Maple House, 149 Tottenham Court Road, London W1P 9LL, 071-387 9494, (Channel 3 biennial fundraiser).

Trustees Register, Reed Charity Trust, 114 Peascod Street, Windsor, SL4 1AY, 0753-850441, (keeps list of senior people prepared to serve as trustees).

Voluntary Services Unit, Home Office, Queen Anne's Gate, London SW1H 9AT, 071-213 4376, (Home Office department with responsibility for the voluntary sector).

The Volunteer Centre UK, 29 Lower King's Road, Berkhamsted, Herts. HP4 2AB, 0442-873311, (national body promoting volunteering).

Wales Council for Voluntary Action, Llys Ifor, Crescent Rd, Caerphilly, CF8 1XL, 0222-869224, (national body for the voluntary sector in Wales).

Webb Ivory Ltd, 224 Walworth Road, London SE17, 071-701 4261, (Christmas cards and gifts service).

Women in Fundraising and Development, Maggie Taylor, 42 Middleton Drive, Pinner, Middlesex HA2 2PG, 081-868 0207, (network for women fundraisers).

6.2 Bibliography

The following is a selected reading list on fundraising and related matters. Each section of the book has a short list of relevant publications at the end, (all of which are listed here). Details given here are title, publisher, author or editor and date of publication. Addresses for availability are as per the address list, unless otherwise given.

The A-Z of Campaigning, Wilson.

AIDS Funding Manual, DSC, Prabhudas, 1992.

All in a Good Cause, a creative handbook for fundraising, Westland, 1986.

The Arts Funding Guide, DSC, Doulton, 1992.

Advertising by Charities, DSC, Burnett, 1986.

A Basic PR Guide for Charities, DSC, McIntosh, 1985.

British Code of Sales Promotion, Institute of Sales Promotion.

Broadcast Charitable Appeals, DSC, Leat, 1990.

Building for Life: the Wishing Well Appeal, from 49 Great Ormond Street, London WC1N 3HZ.

But is it Legal? NCVO, Capper, 1988.

CAF Guide to Charity Sponsorship, CAF, Clay, 1990.

The Central Government Grants Guide, DSC, Doulton, 1993.

Changing Europe, NCVO, Benington, 1992.

Charity Annual Reports, DSC, Burnett, 1987.

Charities and Broadcasting: a guide to radio and TV appeals and grants, DSC, Parker, 1988.

Charity Christmas Cards: how to produce them, how to sell them, how to make money from them, Charities Advisory Trust, Blume, 1984.

Charity Household Survey, CAF, 1991.

Charity Shops, NCVO, 1986, 6pp.

The Charity Trading Handbook, Charities Advisory Trust, Blume, 1981 (out of print).

Charity Trends, CAF, annually.

Commonsense Direct Marketing, the Printed Shop, Bird.

The Complete Guide to Fundraising, Mercury, Sterrett, 1988, (from bookshops).

Corporate Donations and Sponsorship as Sources of Income for the Arts, CAF, Barratt Fates & Meek, 1980.

Conservation Grants for Local Authorities, Public Bodies and Voluntary Organisations, Countryside Commission, 1984.

Conservation and Business Sponsorship, World Wide Fund for Nature, 1990.

Corporate Citizen, DSC/Irvine, (quarterly journal).

The Craigmyle Guide to Charitable Giving and Taxation, Craigmyle and Co Ltd, annually.

Direct Mail Handbook, Exley, Andrews, 1988, (from bookshops).

Directory of Grant making Trusts and Organisations for Scotland, SCVO, 1986.

Directory of Grant Making Trusts, CAF, Villemur, 1993.

The Educational Grants Directory, DSC, Fitzherbert and Eastwood, 1992.

Environmental Grants, DSC, Woollett, 1993.

European Social Fund: note by the DOE, annually from the Department of the Environment.

Finance from Europe: a guide to the grants and loans from the European Community, EC, 1982.

Finding Sponsors for Community Projects, DSC, Gillies, 1990.

Funding Strategies Information Pack, Greater London Popular Planning Unit, 1986.

Fundraising A-Z: a manual for charitable and voluntary organisations, Kirkfield Publications, Robinson, 1982, (from bookshops).

Fundraising and Grant Aid: a guide to the literature, NCVO, Bates, 1986.

Fundraising and Grant-Making, CAF, 1989.

Fundraising for Expeditions, Royal Geographical Society, 1986.

Fundraising for your School: what you need to know, DSC, Mountfield, 1993

The Fundraising Handbook, Mullin, 1981 (from bookshops).

Fundraising Notes, DSC, 12 leaflets on: developing a strategy; doing research; drawing up a budget; fundraising sources; planning an appeal; planning a capital project; raising money locally; setting up; writing an application; earning money; organising an event (£7.50 for the set).

Fundraising for Schools, Kogan Page, Gorman, 1988 (from bookshops).

Fundraising for Sport: a guide for sports clubs, the Sports Council, Griffiths, 1985.

Fundraising through Trusts, NICVA, Courtney, 1985.

Funds for your Project, SCEC, 1984.

Getting into Print, NCVO, Vaughn, 1988.

Getting the Best from Secondment, ARC.

Gift Aid: a guide for donors and charities, Inland Revenue, 1990.

The Giving Business, Business Matters, BBC Education, London, W12 7RZ.

Good Franchise Guide, NCVO, 1992

Government Grants, NCVO, Jones, 1989.

Grants from Europe: how to get money and influence policy, NCVO/ERICA, Davison, 1989.

Group Fundraising: a handbook for local organisers, Printforce, Saint, 1985.

A Guide to Company Giving, DSC, Eastwood, 1993.

A Guide to Gift Aid, DSC, Norton, 1992.

A Guide to Government Grants for Voluntary Organisations in Scotland, SCVO, 1982.

A Guide to Grants for Individuals in Need, DSC, Casson & Brown, 1992.

A Guide to the Major Trusts, DSC, Farrow & Fitzherbert, 1993.

High Street Giving, DSC, Humble, 1990.

HIV & AIDS: A Funding Guide for England and Wales, DSC, Prabhudas, 1993.

The International Foundation Directory, Europa Publications, Hodson, 1983.

Investment of Charity Funds, DSC, Norton, 1993.

Leaving Money to Charity, DSC, Norton, 1983.

Legacies: a practical guide for charities, DSC, Norton, 1983.

Lobbying: an insider's guide to the parliamentary process, Pluto Press, Dubs, 1989 (from bookshops).

The London Grants Guide, DSC, Stubbs, 1992.

Lotteries and Raffles, NCVO (out of print).

The Major Companies Guide, DSC, 1991.

Malpractice in Fundraising, NCVO.

Management of Voluntary Organisations, Croner Publications, 1990.

Marketing, a Guide for Charities, DSC, McIntosh, 1984.

Museum Trading Handbook, CAT.

Money and Influence in Europe, DSC and VMG, Dawson and Norton, 1983, (out of print).

Networking in Europe, NCVO, Harvey, 1992.

The Northern Ireland Fundraising Handbook, Belfast Simon Community, 1983.

Organising Local Fundraising Events, DSC, Passingham, 1993

Organising Things, Pluto Press, Ward (from bookshops).

Peace and Security: a guide to independent groups and grant sources, DSC, Forrester, 1989, (out of print).

Please Give Generously, a guide to fundraising, Swainson Zeff, 1987.

Present Alms: on the corruption of philanthropy, Phlogiston Publishing, Mullin, 1980.

Professional Fundraising Magazine, Greenhouse Publishing.

Raising Money from Industry, DSC, Norton, 1989.

Raising Money from Trusts, DSC, Norton, 1989.

Raising Money for Women: a survivors guide, NCVO, Bowman & Norton, 1986.

Researching Local Charities, DSC, Eaglesham, 1988.

Royal Mail Guide to Mailsort, Royal Mail, 1990.

Royal Patrons, CAF, 1987.

Sell Space to Make Money, DSC, Semple, 1987.

Six Steps to Signing: a fundraiser's guide to GAYE, NICVA.

The Sponsorship Manual, ABSA.

Starting and Running a Voluntary Group, NCVO.

Tax-Effective Giving, DSC, Norton, 1992.

The Telephone Book, McGraw Hill.

Trust Monitor, DSC, (journal published three times a year).

The Urban Programme Explained, NCVO, Hodson and Marsh, 1986, (7pp).

Urban Aid Explained, SCEC, 1985.

US Foundation Grants in Europe, DSC, Robinson, 1991.

VAT: a practical guide, DSC, Sayer, 1992.

West Midlands Grant Guide , DSC, Eastwood & Felgate, 1991.

Woman's Own Book of Fundraising, Collins, Nicholl, 1986.

ABBREVIATIONS USED

ARC **Action Resource Centre**, 102 Park Village East, London NW1 3SP, 071-399 2200, (see Section 6.1 for regional offices).

CAF **Charities Aid Foundation**, 48 Pembury Road, Tonbridge, Kent TN9 2JD, 0732-771333.

CRE **Commission for Racial Equality**, Elliot House, Allington Street, London SW1, 071-828 7022.

DSC **Directory of Social Change**, Radius Works, Back Lane, London NW3 1HL, 071-435 8171.

NICVA **Northern Ireland Council for Voluntary Action**, 127 Ormeau Road, Belfast BT7 1SH, 0232-321224.

NCVO **National Council for Voluntary Organisations** (publishing as Bedford Square Press), Regent's Wharf, 8 All Saints Street, London N1 9RL, 071-713 6161.

SCEC **Scottish Council for Education**, West Coates House, 90 Haymarket Terrace, Edinburgh EH12 5LW, 031-313 2488.

VMG originally **Voluntary Movement Group**, now known as the **Charity Forum**, 60 Laurel Avenue, Potters Bar, Hertfordshire EN6 2AB, 0707-662448.

6.3 Community trusts

Community trusts are a relatively new phenomenon in this country, with their origins largely in America where there is a greater tradition in the value of local citizen action. Community trusts are independent charities acting as both grant-seekers and grant-makers within a clearly defined area. They serve two main roles:

To stimulate the establishment of endowment funds, the income from which can be used for grant distribution to serve local needs.

To address the needs of the community by applying the resources and the knowledge and experience of one sector in the community to another.

They aim to bridge the gap between the public, private and voluntary sectors by providing a conduit for statutory and private donors to give within their own local community to small locally based voluntary organisations. In addition, they work to stimulate local debate between different sectors of the community, advising other grant-making bodies and providing information to donors and beneficiaries on the local needs of their community.

A list of the name, location and phone number of community trusts active in December 1992.

Barnet Community Trust, London, 081-346 9723
Calderdale, Halifax, 0442-345631
Cleveland, Middlesborough, 0642-245284
Colchester & Tendring, 0206-769892
Dacorum, Hemel Hempstead, 0442-231396
Hertfordshire, St Albans, 0727-867906
Isle of Dogs, London 071-454 1066
Isle of Wight, 0983-524058
Glasgow City, Glasgow, 041-332 2444
Gloucestershire, Gloucester, 0452-528491
Greater Bristol, Bristol, 0272-211311
Greater Manchester, Manchester, 061-829 5542
Highland, Inverness, 0667-55960
Lanarkshire, Motherwell, 0698-75469

Milton Keynes, Milton Keynes, 0908-690276
Northern Ireland, Belfast, 0232-245927
Nottinghamshire, Nottingham, 0602-470749
Redbridge, Ilford, 081-553 9469
Richmond, 081-940 6235
Royal Berkshire, Reading, 0734-882741
South Glamorgan, Cardiff, 0222-462775
South Yorkshire, Sheffield, 0742-731765
St Katherine & Shadwell, 071-782 6962
Stevenage, Stevenage, 0438-736368
Telford & Wrekin 0952-291350
Tyne and Wear, Newcastle, 091-222 0945
Wiltshire, Devizes, 0380-729284

For details on community trusts, contact Kim Maxwell, Association of Community Trusts and Foundations, High Holborn House, 52-54 High Holborn, London WC1V 6RL, 071-831 0033.

6.4 ICFM codes of practice

The following codes of practice are included not only because they relate to important fundraising methods. These particular codes have also been written to include much sound advice representing the best possible practice. For the complete codes of practice, guidance notes, copies of standard contracts and draft terms of reference, contact ICFM.

6.4.1 Code of practice for fundraising in schools

1. **The ICFM'S policy on fundraising in schools is:**
   a. To offer the child a positive opportunity for involvement in helping others by raising funds.
   b. To put trust at the heart of all fundraising with school children. Clear instructions should be given regarding payment of sponsor money. There should be no harassment of children but the child should be on his/her honour to pay in all money raised.
   c. To ensure that the content of talks given is both educational and non-political and at an appropriate level for each age group.
   d. To take into account and to accept the Head Teacher's view of the School's charity commitments and to fit in with it.
   e. To make contact with children in or near school premises only with the prior knowledge and approval of the Head Teacher or a member of the School's staff designated by the Head Teacher.

2. **Safeguards for children**
   a. Children should be told both verbally and on printed material not to approach strangers for money and that to go knocking from door to door is against the law. Every effort should be made by the Charity to ensure that parents are made aware of the need for children to approach only friends and relations for sponsorship (see footnotes). Children should be encouraged to discuss fully with their parents a list of whom they may approach, and examples of 'safe' sponsors should be identified and given in the course of the fundraising talk.
   b. Participation in any fundraising activity should only be via an authorised adult. For children up to the age of 16, it should be for the parents to decide whether or not a child may take part in a fundraising event.

3. **Organisation of an event**
   a. The use of incentives to encourage or reward individual efforts to raise money is seen as a very sensitive issue, and the greatest care needs to be exercised in offering them to children.

   Token gifts, such as badges, may be given provided that they are made available to all participating children, and are given for the purpose of prompting the children and potential donors to think about the work of the charity concerned.

As a general principle, only incentives of purely token value should be given to children. Where gifts of some monetary value have been donated, their distribution should be under the tight control of the charity's representative and only after consultation and agreement with the Head Teacher (see 4a).

b. Particular care should taken with under 7s, who should not be encouraged to compete for badges or any other incentives.

c. Potential supporters should be given the option of sponsoring a child or giving a donation – at a level of their choice.

d. Sponsored events should have maximum limited time/units clearly defined on their printed material in order that the sponsor can determine the maximum level of money promised at the time of sponsoring.

e. Fundraising material should be written in clear, simple language. From time to time special material may need to be prepared for those who do not have English as their mother tongue, subject to the Head Teacher's advice.

4. The fundraiser and the school

Field staff should be instructed:

a. To discuss with the Head Teacher the educational content of the talk to be given and the pattern of the event to be undertaken as well as all other additional arrangements. To go step by step through what is involved for the charity's representative, for the staff, for the children, for the parents. All agreed details, including the financial arrangements, should then be confirmed in writing by the charity's representative.

b. To organise fundraising events to a controlled time limit.

c. To make the organisation of the event and collection of money as trouble free as possible for School staff.

   i. If cash is collected, the charity's representative should return on the date promised and call again (or make adequate arrangements) for any late monies.

   ii. If the School prefers, monies may be paid in by the use of a bank giro system. The charity's representative should then ensure that guidelines are given and extra giro forms left at the school.

   iii. All monies received should be acknowledged promptly by the charity and the onus should be on the charity to ensure that the amount acknowledged is correct.

d. An appropriate message of thanks should be given to the Head Teacher or any staff involved, to the children and their families.

5. General

a. Any letters of criticism received should be dealt with as quickly as possible, and monitored at senior management level in the charity.

b. Head Teacher's comments on events undertaken should be monitored on a regular basis.

c. Field staff should be trained, supervised and monitored on a continuing basis in every aspect of their work.

Footnote: For both street collections and house to house collections, permits or a certificate of authority are required. In both cases, collectors must be a minimum of 16 years of age.

6.4.2 Code of practice for reciprocal charity mailings

1. **Basis of exchange**

   The content and character of the lists to be exchanged should be clearly understood. Precise definition of the lists should include:

   a. Quantities – numbers to be mailed.
   b. Statistical information on giving: how recent; the frequency; the average value of donations; and the frequency of which the list, or parts of it, may be used.
   c. Details of past list exchanges with other charities or other organisations (see footnotes).
   d. Type (i.e. cash, banker's order, covenant, etc) and numbers of supporters on the list.
   e. Notes so as to avoid duplication in any follow up mailing.
   f. An outline agreement reached at the outset about the availability and timing of roll out numbers.
      Each party must be sure at the very least that they are exchanging 'like with like' – lists of equal value.

2. **Methodology of exchange**

   It is mailing materials, rather than the actual names and addresses, which should always be exchanged. Therefore each charity mails the other's material to the agreed part of the list, without losing control over their own list. All label or type formats, sizes and positions should be agreed between the two charities.

3. **Material**

   Each charity should indicate their approval of the other's material by signing each item in a sample prior to the actual mailing. Each charity has the right to insist on changes, if they consider the other's mailing to be unsuitable for them to take on.

4. **List standards**

   Each charity should declare the original standard and quality of their list (whether a computer file or a manual index).

5. **Unique sleepers**

   Each charity should put a minimum of ten unique sleepers onto their file – at least one for each different section of the list. This provides security against any possible misuse and because the sleepers are unique ensures that any future misuse is not wrongly attributed.

6. **Mailing date**

Dates for the mailing should be agreed beforehand and should be evidenced in some way. Any problems in keeping to the agreed dates should be communicated to the other charity immediately.

7. **Informing donors**

The two charities should make it clear at the outset whether their donors are to be informed that they are engaging in reciprocal mailing. Each has the right to refuse or insist that this happens and it can become a condition of the exchange. Methods and times of informing the donors are the list owner's decision, although the other list owner has the right to see, in order to approve, any such communication.

8. **Data Protection Act**

Charities carrying out these mailings must register under the Data Protection Act. Each charity should provide the other with a copy of its registration, prior to the mailing.

9. **Mailing Preference Service**

The ICFM recommend that all participants in reciprocal mailings belong to the Mailing Preference Service to protect their supporters' privacy.

10. **Written terms of agreement**

Charities should exchange written agreements of the mailing's terms and conditions, setting out step by step the agreements reached under each item listed in the Code of Practice. Whether using letters or contracts to do this, ICFM suggest charities might seek legal advice in this area (see footnotes).

11. **Results**

Prior to the mailing, the exchange of results and what requirement there is for detailed analysis after the mailing, should be agreed by both charities and adequate resources should be ensured so they are able to carry this out.

12. **Supporter response fulfilment/complaints**

Both charities should agree procedures and materials for acknowledging response to the mailing. This should also include an agreed standard complaints policy, with discussion taking place between the two charities before non-standard complaints are responded to.

13. **File maintenance**

All non-delivered items and changes to the supporter file should be returned to the list owner as soon as possible for file maintenance.

Footnotes:

1. Charities should be aware of the dangers of entering into reciprocal arrangements with organisations which are not registered charities.

2. In order to avoid any possible illegality under the Data Protection Act 1984, charities should obtain from the Data Protection Register the following notes:

   Guideline 4: the Principles

   Guideline 19: concerns fairly obtaining personal data

   In terms of the fiscal treatment of reciprocal mailings, it is doubtful that the Inland Revenue will be concerned since for their purposes there is unlikely to be any profit directly bearing from the transaction. However, it may be seen as a trading activity, thus potentially making the charity liable for VAT. However, if both charities are VAT registered then there will be no net gain or loss, as both will pay output tax and reclaim an equal amount of input tax.

3. Please see the Draft Terms of Reference for Reciprocal Mailing. However, it is just a guide and any charity entering into a reciprocal mailing is strongly advised to consult their own professional adviser to draw up a written agreement.

6.4.3 Guidance for standard contract between charities and fundraising consultants

These notes both safeguard the interests of and provide a framework for agreement between the two parties – the charity and the fundraising consultant.

Preliminaries

1. Have you considered employing one of your own staff, either full-time or part-time?

2. Are you clear which type of practitioner you wish to employ: a Consultant; a Fundraiser; or a Co-venturer?

3. Get advice from other charities who have recently engaged in a similar practice, and ask them who they engaged; if they were satisfied; what if anything went wrong; and whether they would do the same again.

4. If you are not able to do (3) consult the National Council for Voluntary Organisations and get a list of consultants from the Institute of Charity Fundraising Managers.

5. Get a copy of the ICFM Standard Form Agreement.

Considering the short list

6. Draw up a short list of possibles and ask them to indicate: their experience and qualifications; whether they are willing to work for you; how soon they will be available; when they are available; what their charges will be, how they will charge you and when they wish to be paid; what expenses they will ask for, their estimate of these and how they will be controlled; what their views are of your targets and what they would expect to be able to raise; other charities for whom they have worked and referees at these charities; whether they have

a copy for you of a standard form of contract; and what provision will be made for premature termination of the contract by either party and the discharge of any outstanding obligations.

7. Consider their responses remembering that they should also have read these guidelines. Do not simply look for the most enthusiastic, but instead for the one that fully appreciates the difficulties to be overcome. What questions do they ask? How searching are they? Do they appreciate your strengths and weaknesses?

8. Look carefully at their estimates of the sums they expect to raise, their time and their expenses. Are they realistic?

9. Ask them what methods they would employ, what they would actually do and how. Do you approve of these methods?

10. If they propose to operate a lottery, make sure the arrangements are legal (see Section 6.2.4).

11. Discuss how they will allocate their time to you, amid their other work. Will they be able to do you justice?

12. What other staff will be employed? You must meet them before you commit yourself.

13. Be very careful of anyone who asks to be remunerated by commission on the funds raised. The Charity Commission and others advise against it and it is susceptible to malpractice. A time basis for charging is much more preferable. However, if you do agree to payment by commission, ensure that the consultant is aware that by law, donors must be informed what percentage of their gift is retained by the practitioner. See it is only charged on relevant gifts – i.e. not a legacy or a government grant.

Negotiation with your chosen candidate

14. Ensure you have control over fundraising methods to be used and that they will not bring your charity into disrepute. Make sure that no-one in the practitioner's organisation can claim to be your employee.

15. Ensure all donors are asked to make cheques payable to the charity and not the fundraiser's own organisation and that all cash will be credited to your charity's bank account as soon as possible. Do not agree to any deduction of expenses or remuneration from receipts.

16. Take up a banker's reference.

17. Ask if they have ever been bankrupt, or a director of a company gone into liquidation. Is the contract in the practitioner's or the company's name? If the latter, is the practitioner willing to personally guarantee the company's adherence to its obligations? If necessary, consider making a status enquiry through Dun and Bradstreet Limited or a similar organisation.

18. Ensure the practitioner cannot incur obligations on your behalf without your prior written agreement. Also be sure the money reaches you quickly, so that it cannot be diverted to meet the practitioner's and

not your own obligations. If necessary, ask for a bond or fidelity insurance policy.

19. Make sure that information obtained from you or obtained on behalf of you by the practitioner is your property and is not available for their other clients except with your consent.

20. Insist when you are ready, on a written contract. To prevent any unwitting commitment beforehand, make any earlier letters, 'Subject to Contract'.

21. Make sure that the contract is a correct reflection of preliminary agreements, as this is ultimately a binding agreement, over and above previous correspondence or informal agreements.

6.4.4 Code of practice for lotteries

Introduction: what is a lottery?

1. A lottery is a method of distributing prizes by lots – by chance.

2. If the lottery is completely free, then it is not subject to the restrictions of the Lotteries and Amusements Act 1976.

3. Where a fee is in any way involved, then it is subject to the above Act.

4. The Act states that: 'all lotteries which do not constitute gaming are unlawful, except as provided by this Act'. Several types of lottery are provided for by the Act, although any for private gain are unlawful. The following are allowed:

> Section 3 – Small lotteries incidental to exempt entertainments;
> Section 4 – Private lotteries;
> Section 5 – Societies lotteries.

5. Small lotteries run during an exempt entertainment (i.e. a bazaar, exhibition, etc, where the lottery is not the main attraction) do not need to be registered or to make a return to the regulators, if they are not run for private gain and no more than £50 of the proceeds are used for the prize or its purchase.

6. Small lotteries are ideal if the prizes are all donated. There is no printing restriction on the tickets to be sold at the time and place of the entertainment and the value of prizes is unlimited.

7. Private lotteries do not need registration either, but tickets must be printed in conformity with the Act. Principally, the lottery cannot be publicised outside the premises of wherever the lottery is being promoted. Private lotteries are ideal for groups of people working or living together – large organisations which do not rely on externally publicising the lottery. All proceeds must go towards prizes and/or the society's purposes, but stationery and printing costs may be deducted.

8. In practice, all other society lotteries which are not small or private, must be registered with the Local Authority and if ticket sales are set

to exceed £10,000 then they must be registered with the Gaming Board of Great Britain.

9. Tickets may only be sold to or by people 16 years of age or over.

10. In addition to the 1976 Act, the Lotteries (Amendment) Act 1984 abolished certain restrictions on foreign lotteries, and other regulations and orders have further been added as extensions of the Act.

11. The Lotteries and Amusements Act 1976, the Lotteries Regulations 1977, the Lotteries (Amendment) Regulations 1981, the Lotteries (Amendment) Act 1984, and the Lotteries (Amendment) Regulations 1988, can all be purchased from HMSO.

The ICFM's lottery policy

a. Lotteries offer a positive opportunity for ethical and secure fundraising.
b. Lotteries for charity should be run in accordance with the law.
c. No misrepresentation is permitted in the conduct of a lottery.
d. There should be absolute parity of chance in a lottery.

Legal safeguards

a. All lotteries promoted by ICFM members should be correctly registered with the Gaming Board and/or the Local Authority as required by law. Section 5 Lotteries should register first with their Local Authority and then with the Gaming Board if: total ticket values exceed £10,000; total ticket values exceed £30,000 if a Society is promoting more than one lottery on the same day; or if any one prize exceeds £2,000.

b. Any revised methods during the term of registration must be approved by the Local Authority or the Gaming Board as appropriate.

c. No one under 16 may buy or sell lottery tickets.

d. Lottery accounts registered with a Local Authority must be submitted to that Authority within the statutory period – no later than the end of the 3rd month after the lottery. If registered with the Gaming Board, accounts should be submitted as soon as possible, but not later than the end of the third month after the lottery.

e. All prizes must be awarded to the legal owners of the winning tickets, as indicated on the ticket, except by agreement between the winner and the promoter.

f. It is illegal to sell tickets or chances in a lottery where there is a set of lotteries in which the determination of those lotteries is combined to secure the winning of several prizes by the holder of a group of winning tickets or chances.

The conduct of a lottery

a. Procedural and legal advice on promoting lotteries is available from the Gaming Board, Local Authorities and the ICFM Lotteries Standing Committee.

b. Ticket distribution is subject to strict control and audit procedures.

c. In registered and private lotteries, tickets may only be sold for their face value.

d. If a donation to charity is an element of the ticket purchase, the amount of the donation must be clearly stated.

e. Tickets cannot be sold in any street, or any shops where customers may be accommodated.

f. All unsold tickets, counterfoils and remittances must be returned to the promoter for audit.

g. All purchased ticket counterfoils must be included in the draw.

h. Sub-draw winners must be included in the main draw.

i. The draw must take place on the date stated on the ticket.

j. There must be witnesses to the draw. A full statement of winners signed by the promoter, the witnesses and the person making the draw should be made public. The promoter or a formal representative should be present.

k. If winners are published, it should not be possible to trace them directly.

l. All winners should be notified within 7 days of the draw, with the prize distribution following as soon as possible.

m. Every effort must be made to award the prizes. If unclaimed, prizes should be kept available for six years as required by the statute of limitations.

The promoter's responsibilities

a. If it is registered, the promoter is legally responsible for the conduct and legality of the lottery. Anyone else party to the contravention of the Act is also guilty of an offence.

b. As well as ensuring statutory conditions of prize, expense and turnover levels, the promoter is responsible for ensuring tickets are printed and sold legally.

c. The promoter and the charity are responsible for ensuring ticket sellers (even if they are sub-contractors) are aware of the regulations.

d. The promoter is responsible for completing and submitting the accounts to the Local Authority and the Annual Return and Accounts to the Inland Revenue.

General

a. It is advisable to have a facility to deal with related correspondence swiftly and appropriately.

b. If a handling house is employed, there must be a system to readily identify and separate donations from ticket purchases.

c. Field staff should be conversant with the above code of practice and should regard lotteries as a viable fundraising vehicle.

(See ICFM guidance notes available with this code of practice).

6.4.5 ICFM guidelines for telephone recruitment of collectors

Introduction

This policy recognises: the value of the telephone to encourage the general public who may not otherwise give; and that it can be both positive and effective in recruiting volunteer fundraisers. Charities will need monitoring and training procedures to ensure it is not abused and funds raised are secured.

1. **Training telephone recruiters**

    Training should be by an informed member of staff either with a group or with individuals. An accompanying manual should include the following: general information on your charity; general information on the structure of the collection; content and style of telephone contact; a standard script; precise details of expectations of collectors; precise details for monitoring contacts – you should include a printed example; how to deal with complaints and queries; and if applicable, clear indication of the payment terms.

2. **Monitoring telephone recruitment**

    Monitoring procedures should be understood by everybody, at all times. Charities should: control who is approached by pre-selecting numbers; know who phones whom; maintain standard record forms indicating number of contacts, identification of each call and the results; and develop a clearly understood method of spot checking.

3. **Content and style of telephone calls**

    All calls should be managed within an agreed structure which conforms to any relevant codes of practice (see footnotes). It should include: the caller's name and the charity; the purpose of the call; an unequivocal statement of the non-obligation to participate; no misleading or untruthful statements; an opportunity for the contact to say NO; what is asked of the contact, i.e. dates of collection, areas to be covered and methods of payment; an explanation of what they will receive; an assurance that the contact is over 16; and the name and telephone number of the charity collection organiser.

4. **After the telephone call**

    The results of all calls should be recorded; and the volunteer should have confirmed in writing their responsibilities and duties in regard to the collection.

5. **After the collection**

    All proceeds must be reconciled by the charity with the individual collectors; and charities must identify and investigate collectors who have not banked proceeds within 3 weeks of the collection and be responsible for their security. There must be a procedure for random checks of the witnesses who verify proceeds of collections; and complete collection records must be maintained for at least 3 and preferably 5 years after the collection.

Footnotes: The British Direct Marketing Association publish 'Guidelines for Telephone Marketing Practices'. Copies are available directly from them.

(For the complete codes of practice and guidance notes contact ICFM – these are **not** the complete guidelines.)

6.4.6 Code of practice: outbound telephone support

Introduction

The code's purpose is to enable outbound telephone fundraising to be undertaken both professionally and sensitively, and applies to both internal and external telephone fundraising operations. It is defined here as the use by voluntary organisations, either in-house or via an external agency, of the telephone to request support from individuals.

1. Basis of relationship with external agency or in-house team

i) All external or in-house contractual arrangements should be made on the basis of an agreed fee and not as a commission payment.

ii) A written confirmation should be provided that the fundraisers will abide by this ICFM code of practice.

iii) All parties should abide by any relevant legislation and regulations associated with the use of the telephone and respect and recognise confidentiality to all parties at all times.

2. Information provision

The following should be clearly communicated within the script:

i) The name of the caller.

ii) The name of the charity the call is being made for (if registered this should be clearly stated.)

iii) That the call's purpose is to request support.

3. Prompted information

If requested the following additional information must be provided:

i) Name and address of the agency making the call.

ii) The cost to the charity of the call.

iii) Name and address of the charity for whom the call is being made.

iv) Any information relating to the charity or telephone message on which the agency has been briefed. If a particular question cannot be answered satisfactorily a contact must be given automatically, so more details can be obtained.

4. Targeted audience exclusion

The following potential telephone recipients should be excluded:

i) Those registered with the telephone preference service.

ii) Any individual who has registered any objection to the use of telephone solicitation for that particular charity.

iii) Anyone known to be under 16.

iv) Telephone fundraising should not consist of random digit dialling or sequential dialling, either manually or by computer.

Telephone preference service

All voluntary organisations engaged in telephone support should subscribe to the telephone preference service and exclude all subscribers.

The telephone briefing process

The client and the agency (if involved) should agree a detailed campaign brief before calling begins. There should be agreement on the following:

i) Objective of the call.

ii) Details of the target audience.

iii) The process of how the calls will actually be made.

iv) A specified process for how the calls can be fulfilled: how the money will be collected.

v) The means by which any income will be processed.

vi) The process in which donor details are managed, held and passed back to the client organisation.

Content and communication of requests for support

i) Telephone message

(a) Telephone fundraisers should always recognise the other party's right to terminate the conversation at will, and should accept such termination courteously and promptly.

(b) Both agency and client should agree in writing the content and tone of the telephone message.

(c) Once agreed this script should not be deviated from significantly by any party during the telephone conversation except with written permission from the client and/or the person responsible for the campaign within the charity.

(d) The script should not contain any information known to be dishonest or untrue.

(e) The tone, content and style of call delivery should comply with the Advertising Standards Authority's regulations.

(ii) Telephone fulfilment

(a) All solicited support should be channelled directly through the voluntary organisation rather than the agency.

(b) The charity should acknowledge receipt of support in line with their own internal policies.

(c) Any written material sent by an external agency should be agreed in writing by the client charity beforehand.

Objections and complaints

Response to complaints and objections should be made as follows:

i)   During the phone call

(a) The caller should record all objections. If done by an outside agency, information should be passed on to the client charity.

(b) The caller should voluntarily disclose a contact name and address at the charity to whom complaints can be addressed.

(c) The charity should note all telephone objections/complaints and comply if the recipient does not wish to be contacted again.

(d) The charity should respond to all complaints.

ii) After the phone call

(a) Any complaints received should be passed on to the charity.

(b) The charity should respond to all complaints/objections in line with their internal policies.

6.5 Introduction

The following pages contain some of the forms and documents you will need for your fundraising. You can base your documents on the wording used here, or you can get hold of the forms used by other charities. Note that the wording has to be legally correct for a Deed of Covenant, a Will, or a Codicil to a Will, if the document is to be legally binding and effective.

This is how Oxfam have organised the necessary information to present covenant forms to their supporters. The LS in its circle is now redundant. The approved forms from the Inland Revenue are shown here too. They can be designed to suit your own purposes so long as the information and wording is all there. There are a number of points about dates that covenant administrators and fundraisers should note.

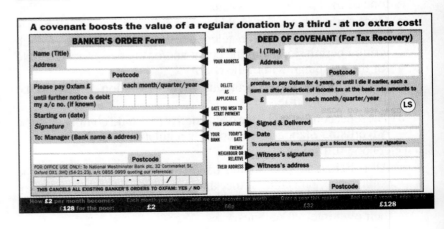

APPROVED FORM OF COVENANT BY AN INDIVIDUAL TO A CHARITY FOR USE IN *ENGLAND AND WALES*

DEED OF COVENANT

TO .... *(name of charity)*

I promise to pay you for .... (A) years, or until I die. If earlier, such a sum as after deduction of income tax at the basic rate amounts to £...... (B) each *(week/month/year)* from .... (C)*(date).*

Signed and Delivered (D) ....

Date ....

Full name..

Address ....

Witnessed by:

Signed (E) ....

Full name..

Address ....

This form can be used by English and Welsh charities. A Northern Ireland charity should use the words "*signed, sealed and delivered*" at (D).

A. State number of years which should be at least four.
B. State amount you wish to give each week, month or year for period of the covenant.
C. This is the date of the first payment which should be on or after the date of the covenant.
D. Donor to sign here.
E. Witness to sign here.

Please note that only an individual who is a UK taxpayer or who is in receipt of income from which tax has been deducted at source should enter into a Deed of Covenant.

APPROVED FORM OF COVENANT BY AN INDIVIDUAL TO A CHARITY FOR USE IN *SCOTLAND*

A. State number of years, which should be at least four.

B. State amount you want to give each week, month or year for period of the covenant.

C. This is the date of the first payment, which should be on or after the date of the covenant.

D. Donor to sign here.

E. Witnesses sign here. (A Scottish covenant requires two witnesses; however, no witness at all is required provided the donor writes the words "*adopted as holograph*" in handwriting above his/her signature.

Please note that only an individual who is a UK taxpayer or who is in receipt of income from which tax has been deducted at source should enter into a Deed of Covenant.

DEED OF COVENANT

TO ....*(name of charity)*

I promise to pay you for ....**(A)** years, or until I die. If earlier, such a sum as after deduction of income tax at the basic rate amounts to £.........**(B)** *(each week/month/year)* from .... **(C)** *(date)*.

Signed **(D)** ....

Date ....

Full name ....

Address ....

Witnessed by:

Signed **(D)** ....

Full name ....

Address ....

and

Signed **(D)** ....

Full name ....

Address ....

A STANDARD FORM FOR A DEPOSITED OR LOAN COVENANT

The deposit covenant consists of a Letter of Deposit and a Deed of Covenant.

---

1. The Letter of Deposit

I hereby deposit the sum of..... with (your charity) free of interest. so that such sums may be deducted by you from this sum and constitute the four annual payments due to you under my Deed of Covenant to which this letter is attached. In the event of my death, I Hereby waive repayment of and give you absolutely any amount of the deposit outstanding at that time.

Signed and delivered as a Deed ....

Date ....

Witness's signature ....

Witness's address ....

---

2. The Deed of Covenant

A standard form of covenant for *one quarter* of the total amount given.

Deposit covenants need to be promoted with caution: the payment should be made on or after the date on which the Deed of Covenant and Letter of Deposit are signed. Where you receive a payment without the necessary documentation, the Inland Revenue now accept that you can send a Deed of Covenant and Letter of Deposit to the donor for signature provided that you hold the cheque and do not pay it into your bank account until the signed documents have been returned to you. It is important to observe this procedure if the tax relief is to be obtained. For gifts of over £400, Gift Aid is an easier way to go.

GIFT AID FORM FOR COMPANIES

This form can be used for any gift of £600 or more received from a Close Company (*most private companies*) or for any amount from an Open Company (*most public companies*). But it cannot be used where the company has made the donation via a charitable trust or via the Charities Aid Foundation. When the company signs the form, it will also have to pay an amount equal to a third of the payment to the Inland Revenue, which amount is then reclaimed by the charity. But by using this procedure, if the company pays Corporation Tax, it will save an amount equal to or greater than the Income Tax it has paid in Corporation Tax. The precise tax saving depends on the company's Corporation Tax rate.

You must use the official form. Supplies are available from Inland Revenue Claims Branch, St John's House, Merton Road, Bootle L69 9BB.

Gift Aid - Certificate of a single payment by a company to a charity

Instructions
1. Please use BLACK ink   2. Please fill in boxes as shown below

ABCDEFGHIJKLMNOPQRSTUVWXYZ 1234567890

I certify that the company
enter company name

has made a single payment to
enter charity name

in the sum of £
enter net amount after deduction of tax

on
Day   Month   Year

and that the conditions overleaf have been satisfied

All these conditions must be satisfied for the payment to qualify for tax relief

Signature
Specimen
Day   Month   Year

As
enter capacity in which signed

Company Address
Building

Number and Street

District and/or town

County

Postcode

Is the company a close company?   Tick box if 'Yes'

Tax District

Tax Reference   /

When you have completed this certificate please return it to the charity

For charity use   Donation record number

For Inland Revenue use   Donor record traced   Tax District notified

Inspector   Other action

R240(SD)   DRS DATA & RESEARCH SERVICES PLC/U33560890/BYTS

GIFT AID FORM FOR INDIVIDUALS

Gift Aid - Certificate of a single payment by an individual to a charity

Instructions
1. Please use BLACK ink 2. Please fill in boxes as shown below

`ABCDEFGHIJKLMNOPQRSTUVWXYZ1234567890`

I certify that I *enter your name*

have made a single payment to *enter charity name*

in the sum of £ *enter sum paid to the charity, not less than £600*

on Day Month Year

and that I am resident in the UK and have paid or will pay basic rate tax on the gross amount of the gift (see note A overleaf)
and that the payment
- was made in money and was not subject to a condition that any part of it can be repaid
- was not due under a deed of covenant nor was it paid under a payroll giving scheme
- was not paid for any benefits beyond the limits described overleaf (see note B overleaf)
- was not linked with the acquisition of property by the charity except by gift (see note C overleaf)
- when added to others I have made under the Gift Aid scheme in the same income tax year does not total more than £5 million

All these conditions must be satisfied for the payment to qualify for tax relief

Signature

Date Day Month Year

Address
Flat No. OR name
House No. OR name
Street Name
District and/or town
County
Postcode

Tax District

Tax Reference / **National Insurance No.**

When you have completed this certificate please return it to the charity

For charity use Donation record number

For Inland Revenue use Donor record traced Tax District notified

Inspector Other action

R190(SD)

DBS DATA & RESEARCH SERVICES PLC/U3550090/8YKG

This form can be used for any gift of £600 or more received from an individual who has sufficient income to pay tax in the UK. The form can be sent to the donor for signing after you have received and banked the donation.

You must use the official form. Supplies are available from Inland Revenue Claims Branch, St John's House, Merton Road, Bootle L69 9BB.

STANDARD FORM FOR PAYROLL GIVING

This is one of the many payroll giving forms that have been recommended by the Payroll Giving Association. Note that you need to use the standard format to ensure that the donation will be processed by the Payroll Agency. Further details from the Payroll Giving Association, c/o Charities Aid Foundation.

PLEASE COMPLETE IN BLOCK CAPITALS
I WOULD LIKE TO GIVE TAX FREE FROM MY PAY TO:

£   per week   per month   (Please tick)
I already give to charity by payroll deduction
     YES   NO   (Please tick)
This will be **ADDED** to existing donations.

DECLARATION: I confirm that my total gifts to charity through payroll giving will not exceed the statutory limit (£480, 1989/90) in any tax year and will not be used in payment of a covenant.

Full Name _ _ _ _ _ _ _ _ _ _ _ _

Address _ _ _ _ _ _ _ _ _ _ _ _ _ _

_ _ _ _ _ _ _ _ _ _ _ _ _ _ _

_ _ _ _ _ _ _ _ Postcode _ _ _ _ _

Signature_ _ _ _ _ _ _ _ Date _ _ _ _

Source Code (for office use)

Employers Name _ _ _ _ _ _ _ _ _
(In full)
Workplace Address _ _ _ _ _ _ _ _

_ _ _ _ _ _ _ _ _ _ _ _ _ _

_ _ _ _ _ _ _ Postcode _ _ _ _

Employee/Staff No._ _ _ _ _ _ _ _ _
from payslip . We can not identify your gifts
without this.

STANDARD FORM OF INTEREST FREE LOAN

I ....(*supporter's name*)

of..(*address*)

agree to lend (*your charity*) the sum of (*amount*) free of all interest for repayment on (*state date or period of notice for repayment*).

In the event of my death prior to repayment, I waive my rights to repayment.

Signed ....

Dated ....

Witness:

Signature ....

Address ....

If you wish to include a waiver on death, to be fully effective, this disposition should either be included in the supporter's will or the Letter of Loan should be signed and delivered as a Deed (with the appropriate wording for this above the lender's signature).

Note: There are two conditions which must be met if an interest-free loan is to be made without there being the possibility of the lender having to pay tax on the notional interest forgone:

1. The loan must be actual money (in whatever currency), and not interest or dividend-bearing assets such as gilt-edged stocks or shares, nor bullion or commodities which can be realised for cash and subsequently repurchased. If a supporter wishes to make over the interest or dividends on particular investments s/he is far better advised to pay these under Deed of Covenant drawn up for the purpose.

2. There must be no identifiable income arising from the investment of the proceeds of the loan for the lender, and this usually means that:

   a. There is a common investment fund for all loans received by charity;

   b. There is no direction by the lender as to how the money should be invested;

   c. There is no power by the lender to determine how any income arising from the loan should be distributed or spent; or the loan is not invested to produce income for the charity to meet its expenditure commitments or to reduce its bank overdraft, or is lent to a third party within the terms of the charity's trust deed.

STANDARD WILL FORMS

1. FOR A SPECIFIC ITEM OR SUM

> I bequeath to *(charity name)* of *(address)* free of all tax the sum of £........ to be applied by *(charity)* for its general charitable purposes, and I further direct that the receipt of the hon treasurer or other proper officer of *(charity)* for the time being shall be a full and sufficient discharge for the said legacy.

2. FOR A RESIDUARY BEQUEST

> I devise and bequeath to *(charity name)* of *(address)* ("all" or fractional share of) the residue of my estate to be applied by *(charity)* for its general charitable purposes, and I further direct that the receipt of the hon treasurer or other proper officer of *(charity)* for the time being shall be a full and sufficient discharge for the said legacy.

3. FOR A CODICIL

> This is a codicil made by me *(name)* of *(address)* dated .... to my will dated.................. I leave to *(charity)* a pecuniary legacy free of all tax of £..... In all other respects I confirm my said will.
>
> Signed ....
>
> In the presence of us both present together at the same time who at his request and in his presence and in the presence of each other have hereunto subscribed our names as witnesses.
>
> **Witness 1**
>
> Name ....
>
> Address ....
>
> Signed ....
>
> **Witness 2**
>
> Name ....
>
> Address ....
>
> Signed

Index of topics